Cracking the Highest
Glass Ceiling

Cracking the Highest Glass Ceiling

A Global Comparison of Women's Campaigns for Executive Office

Rainbow Murray, Editor
Foreword by Pippa Norris

Women and Minorities in Politics
Melody Rose, Series Editor

 PRAEGER

AN IMPRINT OF ABC-CLIO, LLC
Santa Barbara, California • Denver, Colorado • Oxford, England

Library of Congress Cataloging-in-Publication Data

Cracking the highest glass ceiling : a global comparison of women's campaigns for executive office / Rainbow Murray, editor ; foreword by Pippa Norris.
    p. cm. — (Women and minorities in politics)
  Includes bibliographical references and index.
   ISBN 978–0–313–38248–2 (hard copy : alk. paper) — ISBN 978–0–313–38249–9 (ebook)
1. Women executives. 2. Women—Political activity. I. Murray, Rainbow, 1979–
HD6054.3.C73   2010
324.92′2—dc22   2010014652

ISBN: 978–0–313–38248–2
EISBN: 978–0–313–38249–9

14 13 12 11 10   1 2 3 4 5

This book is also available on the World Wide Web as an eBook.
Visit www.abc-clio.com for details.

Praeger
An Imprint of ABC-CLIO, LLC

ABC-CLIO, LLC
130 Cremona Drive, P.O. Box 1911
Santa Barbara, California 93116-1911

This book is printed on acid-free paper ∞

Manufactured in the United States of America

*For all the women candidates
who were the inspiration for this book*

Contents

List of Figures

List of Tables

Series Foreword

Across the globe women are advancing in executive leadership roles at a pace that would be a shock and a pleasure to suffragists from a bygone day. And yet, throughout the successes and failed attempts to grasp executive power are some remarkably enduring challenges for the contemporary female contenders. Rainbow Murray's *Cracking the Highest Glass Ceiling* is a primer for readers interested in the challenges still present in contemporary female campaigns for executive office.

Cracking the Highest Glass Ceiling is the second book in a series on "Minorities and Women in Politics," and the first to tackle the questions of gender in campaigns: How do women compete for the manliest jobs on earth? Under what conditions are they successful? How do cultural norms intertwine with and affect female success? And are the consistencies to be found across cultures and distinct electoral systems? These questions and more are explored in the present book and serve to set the stage for future volumes in this series. The series was designed to highlight both the achievements of minorities and women in politics as well as the complex and seemingly intractable barriers to further inclusion—the present book does both with a refreshingly international flavor and scope.

The questions that frame this book were first raised at a political science conference in 2008, where Dr. Murray presented her research on Ségolène Royal's campaign in France, which had recently concluded. Remarkably, as others of us each presented our findings from studies of women seeking executive office in the United States and Venezuela, remarkable patterns emerged—and perplexing dissimilarities as well. Out of this fortuitous meeting, Professor Murray laid an ambitious course to explore systematically, using the best scholarship available, the consistencies and irregularities across cultures and political systems. The result of that ambition is the book you hold in your hands.

Coming on the heels of the historic 2008 American election—in which both a man of color and a white woman competed for the American presidency, this book sets the stage for many more books on gender and politics, and considers the topic within a global context. Too often the literature on gender and politics is focused exclusively on the U.S. case. This U.S.-focused lens leads to a form of scholarly myopia: knowing what we do about women in politics in this country, we are apt to export our expectations to other countries—where the domestic lessons may or may not apply. We also miss the lessons that are to be learned through study abroad: What can the lessons of Angela Merkel or Ellen Johnson Sirleaf teach us about the campaign performance of Sarah Palin or Hillary Clinton? Only by casting a wider net can we begin to distinguish the conditions of sexism that are unique to a given culture from those that are more deeply embedded in the human experience and therefore are cross-cultural. Murray provides us with such an opportunity here, and along with her skilled authors will inspire others to a new way of looking at gender and politics.

Melody Rose, PhD
Series Editor
Chair, Political Science
Founder & Director—Center for Women, Politics & Policy
Portland State University

Foreword

WOMEN NATIONAL LEADERS WORLDWIDE: BARRIERS AND OPPORTUNITIES

Women have ruled as monarchs for centuries—symbolized by the powerful historical figures of the Egyptian pharaoh Cleopatra, Elizabeth I in Tudor England, and Catherine the Great in Russia. But in the contemporary world, relatively few women have been directly elected to reach the apex of political power. In 1960, Sirimavo Bandaranaike of Sri Lanka became the world's first female elected prime minister, followed by Indira Gandhi of India and Golda Meir of Israel, and in 1974, Isabel Perón of Argentina became the first woman president. Today (2010) among the 192 sovereign states recognized by the United Nations, only half a dozen have a woman prime minister. This includes Sheikh Hasina Wajed in Bangladesh, Johanna Sigurdardottir in Iceland, Jadranka Kosor in Croatia, and Angela Merkel in Germany.[1] Another ten nation-states are governed by elected women presidents, including Mary McAleese in Ireland, Tarja Halonen in Finland, Gloria Macapagal-Arroyo in the Philippines, and Ellen Johnson Sirleaf in Liberia. Many other women have contested election to head of government, as discussed by case-studies in this book, but few have succeeded.

The barriers appear to be formidable.[2] Yet given both the scarcity and diversity of women executives, it remains difficult to pin down the precise reasons. Women executives are clearly not drawn disproportionately from any one cultural region, type of society, or category of regime. This leaves theories of modernization and cultural explanations as somewhat implausible; traditional attitudes towards women and men's roles in countries such as Pakistan, Liberia, and Bangladesh may prevail but this does not prevent women from breaking through into the top leadership roles. Moreover, leaders such as Mrs. Thatcher, Benazir Bhutto, and Mrs. Gandhi are elected from diverse educational backgrounds and political experiences. True, in the past, kinship ties by blood or marriage connections were often emphasized, and the "widow's mandate" was identified as one popular route for women who succeeded their husbands to become national leaders in Latin America and Asia. But, as the Bush dynasty illustrates, the importance of kinship ties is hardly exclusive to women. Institutional explanations are popular, and women are marginally more likely to become leaders in mixed types of executives (which contain both a non-hereditary president as head of state and a prime minister as the formal or constitutional head of government), rather than in pure parliamentary or presidential systems.[3] This may well be a by-product of women leaders breaking through in younger democracies, where mixed systems are common.[4]

If other explanations are largely inconclusive, does the process of political communications play a critical role, particularly by shaping the perception of women and men as political executives in electoral contests? After all, the role of the news media is a common way to approach the challenges and opportunities facing women candidates campaigning for local, regional, and national legislative office. An extensive literature has developed in social psychology exploring the role of gender stereotypes, which can operate through the personal traits commonly associated with women and men, as well as through the ideological perception of women and men candidates, and the typical types of issues where women and men are regarded as most effective. In referring to gender stereotypes, it is worth emphasizing that this is not necessarily negative (or indeed positive) for women or men; rather it emphasizes the role of cognitive shortcuts which function to facilitate judgments where citizens lack extensive information. In contexts where the public is concerned about issues such as educational services, environmental pollution, or welfare spending, or in campaigns focused on the issue of change where the public wants to get rid of corruption by throwing the "old guard" out and bringing in "clean hands," then stereotypes may serve to benefit women candidates. But as this book argues, executive office is most commonly regarded as focused upon perceived masculine traits and issues, where women are thereby disadvantaged by stereotypes. Moreover, women leaders may also find it difficult to strike the appropriate balance between being strong and effective (e.g., Thatcher) while also meeting societal demands for warmth and likeability—although this is also a challenge for men. The use of social stereotypes is expected to be particularly strong where voters lack other cues to evaluate leaders, for example, if presented with a bewilderingly long list of candidates without much information about their policy record, party platform, ideological values, or personal characteristics. But if voters gradually learn more about candidates during campaigns—and about leaders during their period in office—then the role of social stereotypes in shaping their judgments is expected to diminish. The formative period, when candidates first enter the national stage, is likely to prove particularly critical in such judgments.

The question at the heart of this book, therefore, is whether there is systematic evidence that the framing and priming provided by the news coverage of women and men candidates for executive office usually either reinforces or challenges pervasive gender stereotypes. The cases are diverse—including winners and losers. The answers provided here are important—and may well be surprising.

Pippa Norris
Harvard University

NOTES

1. www.guide2womenleaders.com.

2. Andrew Reynolds, "Women in the Legislatures and Executives of the World: Knocking at the Highest Glass Ceiling," *World Politics* 51 (1999): 547; Farida Jalalzai, "Women Political Leaders: Past and Present," *Women & Politics* 26 (2004): 85; Farida Jalalzai, "Women Rule: Shattering the Executive Glass Ceiling," *Politics & Gender* 4, no. 2 (2008): 1–27; Farida Jalalzai and Mona Lena Krook, "Beyond Hillary and Benazir: Women's Political Leadership Worldwide," *International Political Science Review* 31, no. 1 (2010): 5–21.

3. Jalalzai and Krook, "Beyond Hillary and Benazir."

4. Pippa Norris, *Driving Democracy* (New York: Cambridge University Press, 2009), chapter 6.

Preface

In August 2008, several of the contributors to this volume came together at the annual meeting of the American Political Science Association. We were all participants in a panel organized by Magda Hinojosa, comparing the campaigns of women presidential candidates in different countries. I spoke on Ségolène Royal; Magda spoke on Irene Sáez; Dianne Bystrom and Melody Rose both gave papers on Hillary Rodham Clinton. The preceding day, it had been announced that Sarah Palin would be the second name on the Republican ticket for the impending U.S. presidential elections.

On reading the papers by my fellow panelists, I was struck by the fact that we were considering different case studies, with very different individuals, cultures, and political systems. Yet, we were all telling very similar stories. We agreed that it would be fascinating to add further case studies and bring them together into an edited volume to see whether the trends that I had identified between the different cases were a coincidence or a true pattern. By the end of 2008, a full cohort of case studies and authors had been assembled, with each author a specialist in the politics of their featured country. This book is the product of our work together throughout 2009.

Although in some respects this is an edited book, it could also be regarded as a single project with multiple authors. I am indebted to all of the authors for their engagement with the themes of the book, their endless professionalism, and feedback on the opening and closing chapters. It has been a real pleasure to work with them all on this project.

There are a number of people without whom this project would not have been possible. In addition to the fantastic team of authors and the inspiring selection of women candidates, we are much indebted to Melody Rose, who has provided expert guidance and unwavering support throughout the project. Robert Hutchinson at Praeger has been all that anyone could ask of from an editor: professional, prompt, polite, accommodating, and supportive at every turn. Finally, my partner Robin encouraged me to pursue this book even though I already had a busy schedule; without his support, love, and comprehension, I could not have invested the many hours needed to bring this project to fruition. I am forever indebted to him.

PART 1

Introduction and Framework

CHAPTER ONE

Introduction: Gender Stereotypes and Media Coverage of Women Candidates

Rainbow Murray

I n the 2008 U.S. presidential elections, one of the satirical highlights was a "Saturday Night Live" sketch in which Tina Fey and Amy Poehler impersonated Sarah Palin and Hillary Rodham Clinton respectively. The sketch, which is based on the theme of sexism in the media, contains the following interchange:

> Poehler as Clinton: "Sexism can never be allowed to permeate an American election."
> Fey as Palin: "So please, stop photoshopping my head on sexy bikini pictures!"
> Poehler as Clinton: "And stop saying I have cankles!"
> Fey as Palin: "Don't refer to me as a 'MILF.'"
> Poehler as Clinton: "And don't refer to me as a 'flirge.' I googled what it stands for and I do not like it."[1]
> Fey as Palin: "So we ask reporters and commentators, stop using words that diminish us, like 'pretty,' 'attractive,' 'beautiful' . . ."
> Poehler as Clinton: " . . . 'harpy,' 'shrew,' 'boner-shrinker' . . ."[2]

This is a fictional sketch, designed to be humorous. But it succeeds precisely because people recognize the truth within the sketch, and the stereotypes about women in politics that are visible daily in media reporting. Discussions about Clinton's masculine features and Palin's attractiveness prevent voters from perceiving the candidates as legitimate contenders for public office, and distract voters from evaluating the women based on their qualifications. These stereotypes, which have been widely noted in studies of American electoral candidates, are one of the reasons why there has never been a U.S. woman president.[3] Given the low number of women presidential candidates and the rapid changes in women's status over time, it has been hard to draw meaningful conclusions about the role of media stereotyping in presidential elections. The recent worldwide wave of women standing for high executive office provides a new opportunity to place the United States within a broader comparative context. Why have women won executive elections in some countries but not others? Are gender stereotypes a particular problem in some countries or are they universal? How much do voters judge a candidate based on his or her gender, and what is the role of the media in shaping these judgments? These are all questions which this book seeks to answer.

A NEW WAVE OF WOMEN CANDIDATES

Within the past decade, there has been a surge of women who are viable candidates for top executive office. In some countries, such as the United States, France, Chile, Argentina, Liberia, and Venezuela, the highest office is the presidency. In countries where there is no president or where the president is a symbolic figurehead, the highest available office is that of prime minister. The circumstances of electing a president are different from those of electing a prime minister, but in both cases women are beginning to make significant breakthroughs. In Germany, the election of Angela Merkel as Chancellor in 2005 (and again in 2009) propelled her to the top of the Forbes list of most powerful women in the world.[4] Ellen Johnson Sirleaf became the first woman president in Africa when she won Liberia's presidential elections in 2005, while South American women won the presidencies of Chile (Michelle Bachelet, 2006) and Argentina (Cristina Fernández de Kirchner, 2007). Meanwhile, one of the world's longest-serving elected female executives, Prime Minister Helen Clark of New Zealand, was defeated in 2008 after three consecutive terms in office. With a few notable exceptions such as Margaret Thatcher (United Kingdom), Kim Campbell (Canada), Golda Meir (Israel), and Indira Ghandi (India), many of the women leaders elected prior to these recent victories were either symbolic figureheads who shared power with a male leader, or women who had entered executive office without being directly elected.[5]

Despite these recent successes, the picture is not entirely rosy. In several of the countries examined in this book, including two members of the G8,[6] strong women candidates were not able to crack the highest glass ceiling. In Venezuela, Irene Sáez went from being the front-running candidate in the 1998 election to arriving a distant third behind her two male rivals. In France, Ségolène Royal also went from a strong position at the start of the election to defeat. Most recently, when Hillary Rodham Clinton entered the Democratic primaries she appeared almost invincible, only to find herself eclipsed by Barack Obama. Meanwhile, Sarah Palin provided an initial bounce to the Republican ticket before rapidly declining in popularity.

Two initial observations can be drawn from the above examples. First, the unsuccessful candidates all started their campaigns from a position of strength and yet ended in a losing position. We argue that this phenomenon is caused partly by an initial surge of popularity as the idea of a woman president captures the public imagination. As the campaign develops however, gendered stereotypes in the media set in and serve to erode public confidence in a woman candidate, causing a decline in the woman's credibility and popularity. This trend implies a strong and negative role for the media in framing attitudes towards women candidates, a theme explored in greater detail below. But if the media do have such a role, how can we explain those cases where women achieve victory despite negative media attention?

Second, the unsuccessful women studied in this book were all contesting presidential elections, whereas most women who have won executive elections did so within a parliamentary system. This may be due to the increased role of parties within parliamentary elections, compared to the greater emphasis on the individual candidate in a presidential election. While the image of a party leader (who is also the prospective prime minister) is certainly influential in parliamentary elections, it is one factor among many. By contrast, a presidential candidate carries much of the weight of the election upon his or her shoulders, and the individual qualities of the candidate will have a greater bearing upon the electoral outcome. Gender stereotypes may therefore have a greater impact on women candidates in presidential elections. However, this does not in itself provide a sufficient explanation for why some women win and some lose, as many women party leaders have lost parliamentary elections, while some women have succeeded in winning presidential elections.

Clearly, the trajectories and outcomes of women executive candidates vary significantly from country to country. Learning the causes of these differences, as well as identifying similarities between the campaigns, would help us to understand why some glass ceilings have been shattered while others remain firmly in place. However, as explained later in this chapter, there is a real lack of studies comparing women executive candidates in different countries. While single-country case studies give us some clues as to why we are seeing the patterns that we have observed, they are not sufficient to explain differences from one country to another. Additionally, and most importantly, in the absence of a comparative study of women executive candidates, it is easy to draw false conclusions. For example, negative coverage of a woman candidate's viability may falsely be attributed to that candidate's abilities rather than to wider patterns of gender stereotyping. Similarly, institutional and cultural differences may lead us to underestimate the role of gender stereotypes, by implying that negative coverage of female candidates is idiosyncratic to a particular country or to a particular campaign. As will be demonstrated throughout the book, the success of some candidates was not synonymous with the absence of gender stereotyping. Instead, and for various reasons, these women were able to overcome or even benefit from these stereotypes in ways that were not possible for the unsuccessful candidates. Thus, gender stereotyping can pose barriers but also create opportunities, depending on other features of the political context.

Although there is a lack of work looking comparatively at women executive candidates worldwide, there is a considerable amount of work looking at women election candidates more generally. Work in this area is dominated by literature based on the United States, with more limited international examples, reinforcing the need for a comparative study. Within the United States, there are numerous studies of women candidates at the congressional and gubernatorial level.[7] These studies provide many of the foundations upon which our work builds. In particular, they indicate how candidate gender influences public perceptions, and the role of the media in reinforcing stereotypes. While most of these works focus on candidates at the sub-executive and/or sub-national level, they indicate that some gender stereotypes may have a particular impact for national executive elections. For example, authors such as Alexander and Andersen and Dolan have observed that women are more strongly associated with "soft" policy areas while men are more positively associated with the "hard" policy areas of foreign policy and the economy.[8] While association with "soft" policy areas may be favorable for lower-level office, presidential elections tend to focus on the "hard" policy areas which favor men.[9] Similarly, gendered notions of leadership are more significant at the executive level.[10] Recent studies of Hillary Clinton's presidential bid demonstrate the unique binds and stereotypes associated with the presidency, and illustrate how the same stereotypes which may be beneficial at lower levels of election may be harmful in presidential races.[11]

In addition to studies looking at other types of election, there are also a few comparative studies of women at the executive level. For example, Falk looks at media coverage of eight women presidential candidates throughout U.S. history, from Victoria Woodhull in 1872 through to Carol Moseley Braun in 2004.[12] One of Falk's most interesting findings is the way in which the use of gendered stereotypes and framing by the media has endured despite the many other changes in attitudes towards women over the past 140 years. Jalalzai does a quantitative analysis of all the women who have achieved executive power around the world, providing useful insights into the factors which enable women to reach high office (including fragmented executive power, political instability, and family ties).[13] Jalalzai does not consider campaign effects, nor does she look at unsuccessful candidates, but her study is invaluable for placing campaign and media effects within a broader framework. Finally, Kittilson and Fridkin offer an initial comparative analysis of women candidates in parliamentary elections, looking at gendered media coverage in Australia, Canada, and the United States. They identify "long-standing gender stereotypes ... [which are] common to all three democracies."[14] Their work indicates that these stereotypes may be a contributing factor to women's success in the wider range of case studies examined here.

A NEW COMPARATIVE FRAMEWORK

The existing literature on women in executive office remains limited. The low number of case studies at national executive level, combined with the concentration of research on the single case study of the United States, together result in limited understanding of the issues facing women executive candidates around the world. The theories and observations developed in the existing literature provide useful building blocks for a comparative framework of analysis which is outlined below and tested throughout this book. The findings of this book both highlight, and seek to overcome, the limitations outlined above. The conclusion offers suggestions of how the framework can better be adapted to take account of the specificities of elections to executive office as well as the generalities of comparative case studies.

The aim of the framework used in this book is twofold. First, we seek to provide a deeper understanding of the role that gender has played in the elections considered here, in order to separate gender effects from other factors influencing the election campaigns, such as the qualities and features of individual candidates and political systems. This will help us to explain why so few women have won executive elections, and why some women have succeeded where others have lost. Second, we shall offer an indication of the role that gender might play in future executive elections.

Our framework focuses on three main areas: gender stereotyping, media framing, and external factors. By gender stereotyping, we refer to pervasive attitudes about men and women within politics, and the way these are translated into gendered expectations about candidate traits and issue positions. For example, women may be considered as more gentle and nurturing, while men may be considered as tougher and more aggressive. By media framing, we refer specifically to the role played by the media in its coverage of women and men candidates. For example, women candidates may receive different coverage than men, including greater emphasis on stereotypical traits and issues, even when these are not in keeping with the candidate's message. In other words, the media may change a candidate's message and frame a candidate in ways which correspond to traditional stereotypes rather than the campaign actually undertaken by the candidate.

We illustrate how the combined effects of gender stereotypes and media framing create a series of "double binds," whereby the demands of executive office are incompatible with social expectations about women's abilities and duties. We then put forward a new hypothesis which highlights how these cumulative effects make executive elections particularly difficult to win for women candidates from left-wing parties. Finally, we consider external factors such as the political environment, and the way in which these interact with gender to influence the overall outcome of the election. Each of these themes is explored in greater detail below.

GENDER STEREOTYPES

The literature on women candidates indicates that voters and commentators continue to hold stereotypical views about gender roles and attributes, which may be damaging to women candidates. The impact of these stereotypes may be particularly powerful when applied to elections for the masculinized and personalized office of the presidency.[15] As executive office is usually the final glass ceiling to be broken, public perceptions of executive office-holders may be more gendered than perceptions of politicians at lower levels, as the job will always have been identified with a man. The male norms which underpin executive office make it very difficult for women to succeed in executive elections. The women who have succeeded have often benefited from a particular set of circumstances, such as a political crisis, which have made qualities perceived as "feminine" (like honesty and renewal) more attractive to the electorate. Here, we consider how gender stereotypes inform voters' perceptions of candidate traits, ideological positioning, and issue strengths.

Traits

Women and men candidates are perceived to bring different personal qualities to the political process. For example, Huddy and Terkildsen argue that "a typical woman is seen as warm, gentle, kind, and passive, whereas a typical man is viewed as tough, aggressive, and assertive."[16] Dolan presents comparable qualities that voters identify with women candidates ("warmth, expressiveness, gentleness, compassion, and emotion") and men candidates (who are "perceived as strong, competent, rational, aggressive, and knowledgeable").[17] While both sets of traits may be deemed positive, the masculine traits are considered more appropriate for executive office.[18] Duerst-Lahti argues that "because so much of what is perceived as contributing to presidential capacity is strongly associated with men and masculinity, presidential capacity is gendered to the masculine; as such, women who dream of a presidency must negotiate masculinity, a feat much more difficult for them than for any man."[19] This places women in a very difficult position. First, they are associated with the wrong skill set for being president. Second, even if they possess and promote the masculine traits associated with being a president, they may still be viewed unfavorably because it is assumed that these traits come more naturally to a man. Third, women may be penalized for straying too far from expected gender roles. This is what Jamieson refers to as a "competence/femininity" double bind, and it is explored in greater detail below.[20] The associations of masculinity with executive leadership are so strong that even men may be disadvantaged if they are not considered "manly" enough, as was the case for Democratic candidates Al Gore and John Kerry.[21]

Ideology

A second way in which voters make gendered assumptions about electoral candidates is that, all other things being equal, they perceive women as being more liberal and men as being more conservative. While there is some evidence to suggest that women may, on the whole, be more liberal than men, the stereotype exceeds any actual gender difference. Alexander and Andersen and Huddy and Terkildsen both find strong evidence that women candidates are perceived as more liberal, while Koch finds that the stereotype is based both on truth and exaggeration:[22] "citizens' generalization that women candidates are more liberal than male candidates was in fact true. However . . . citizens perceive female candidates as being more liberal than they are."[23] As we will discuss below, the stereotyping of women as more liberal than men is particularly disadvantageous to left-wing candidates. We also consider in subsequent chapters whether this stereotype works internationally, with the argument put forward that women in South American countries may actually be perceived as more conservative than men.

Issues

There is substantial evidence that men and women politicians are seen as being stronger on different issues. Alexander and Andersen found that women candidates were positively associated with issues such as child-care, health care, education, the environment, civil rights, and controlling government spending.[24] Conversely, men candidates were positively associated with military spending, foreign trade, agriculture, and taxes. Huddy and Terkildsen concur, arguing that the areas on which women are seen as strongest are what they term "compassion issues."[25] This can be problematic for women executive candidates, because "compassion issues were seen as much less likely to confront a good president than a good member of Congress" while " 'male' policy issues such as the military and economy were seen as more likely to arise at higher levels of office."[26] Kahn found strong evidence of issue stereotyping, while Jalalzai found that the extent of issue stereotyping has diminished somewhat in the past decade.[27] Nonetheless, Jalalzai did find clear trends for women to be more heavily associated than men with certain issues, including those listed above as well as unemployment, welfare, poverty, and women's rights.

Interestingly, although Dolan uses a similar list of issues to Jalalzai which are seen as stereotypically male or female, with both authors considering crime to be a male issue, Dolan lists gun issues as a male issue while Jalalzai considers gun control a female issue.[28] Similarly, Dolan sees budget and deficit control as strengths for men, whereas Alexander and Andersen had coded these as strengths for women. These differences highlight not only the shifting nature of gender stereotypes, but also the difficulty in determining what is meant by "women's issues." Indeed, while some policy domains (such as abortion) might be deemed of particular interest to women, many (such as guns) may be an issue associated with both men and women but in different ways, with Dolan arguing that men are associated with the right to bear arms, while Jalalzai identifies women with gun control. These build on Sapiro's arguments that men and women have different perspectives on gun control, with men focusing on gun control as a way to reduce crime (or bear arms) and women focusing on gun control as a matter of public safety.[29] These nuances indicate that there may be two interlinked sets of gendering at play here—one which considers women's "issues," and a second which considers their "perspectives." If women are perceived as more liberal than men, voters may assume that women take more liberal stances on particular policy issues, such as favoring abortion rights, supporting welfare measures, and regulating gun ownership.

Although the traits, ideology, and issues on which women are stereotyped may appear fairly neutral—after all, both men and women are identified with strengths, albeit different ones—they actually serve to disadvantage women candidates in a number of ways. First, women are identified more positively with softer traits, while men are identified with the tough leadership skills expected of a president. Second, women are viewed more positively on domestic issues, whereas the presidency is most identified with the masculine issues of foreign policy and the economy. Finally, the assumption that women are more liberal than men may be particularly damaging to left-wing candidates. These factors combine with additional forms of stereotyping that are provided by the media, and serve to frame women as trivial and unviable candidates. We consider media framing below, and then illustrate how gendered stereotypes and media coverage combine to create a series of double binds for women, culminating in a particular trap for women presidential candidates that we label the "Mommy Problem."

MEDIA FRAMING

Many of the gender stereotypes considered above have been assessed through experiments using student or voter opinions and hypothetical candidates. Conversely, gender stereotyping in the media is measured through coverage of actual candidates, and it extends above and beyond simple stereotypes of traits and issue positions. The media reinforce traditional stereotypes in a number of ways. First, there is evidence that media coverage of candidates focuses on the traits and issues presumed to correspond to the candidate's gender, even if a candidate has actually tried quite hard to promote herself in non-stereotypical ways, thus reinforcing stereotypes and preventing candidates from breaking the mold.[30]

Second, the media may accord different amounts of coverage and prominence to men and women candidates.[31] While more recent work[32] has pointed to a reduction in the gender gap in media coverage, other recent research suggests that it is still ongoing. For example, Heldman et al found that Elizabeth Dole received significantly less media coverage than John McCain in the 1999 Republican presidential primary, even though Dole was polling significantly higher than McCain throughout this period.[33] Under-reporting of women candidates is significant because candidates rely on media coverage in order to be considered viable; lack of visibility can kill a candidate's campaign.

Third, the media may frame men and women candidates in different ways, with men receiving more coverage of the issues while women are framed predominantly in terms of horse-race coverage (that is, coverage of the candidates' relative leads).[34] This can make it harder for voters to become sufficiently well informed about a woman candidate's policies. Additionally, negative horse-race framing ("losing her lead," "catching her up," "falling behind," and "out of the running") can all be highly detrimental to a campaign, and this is accentuated if it is not accompanied by sufficient issue coverage.

Finally, and importantly, the media use a number of gendered frames for covering women candidates, all of which can be very damaging. These include excessive coverage of a woman candidate's appearance; greater use of her first name relative to her male opponents; an emphasis on her "newness"; greater coverage of her family relationships; and framing of women candidates as more emotional and irrational than their male counterparts. Each of these is considered in more detail below. As Norris argues, "gendered news frames may combine and thereby reinforce a range of sex stereotypes."[35] This can have electoral consequences for women candidates, with agendas and voter perceptions both shaped by media coverage.[36] Heldman et al argue that "differences in election coverage along the lines of gender can shape public perceptions and, ultimately, influence the fate of a candidate's campaign."[37] Falk adds that a further disadvantage of gendered media coverage is that it may dissuade women from running in the first place, thus creating a vicious circle of women as a novelty category in politics.[38]

GENDERED NEWS FRAMES

Appearance

Women candidates receive disproportionate attention to their appearance relative to their male opponents, with media coverage focusing on a range of trivial issues such as clothes and hairstyle. This trend is both historic (Falk observed the trend for every woman presidential candidate in the United States including the first, Victoria Woodhull, in 1872) and contemporary. Recent studies all confirm a trend which is already evident to the casual observer.[39] For example, in the nineteenth century, Woodhull was described as "arrayed in a plain black dress,"[40] while her twenty-first century successors fared little better, with ABC News running a feature on September 7, 2008 questioning whether "Palin's rimless eyeglasses are the new Hillary Clinton pantsuit?" This widespread phenomenon is not limited to the United States. French presidential hopeful Ségolène Royal visited Chile in February 2006 to celebrate Michelle Bachelet's election as president (and, presumably, to remind French voters that a woman president was possible). The dominant frame surrounding coverage of her trip was the fact that she wore high heels. Similarly, Theresa May made a landmark speech to the British Conservative party conference while serving as the party chairman [sic], telling the party that it needed to modernize or die, only to find coverage of her speech subsumed by commentary on her footwear.

There are several problems with this focus on appearance. Time spent discussing appearance is time not spent discussing issues of substance. If a woman's campaign is constantly trivialized by reverting to what the candidate wore rather than focusing on her ideas and successes, voters will be less aware of her achievements and less inclined to take her campaign seriously. It is also harder for a woman to get her message across if it is buried under comments about her hairstyle. Finally, the media objectify women and frame them as sexual and visual rather than powerful and intellectual. For example, much attention was paid to the fact that Irene Sáez and Sarah Palin were former beauty queens, while Ségolène Royal was placed sixth in the French issue of FHM's 100 sexiest women (2006).[41] Women who are not considered sufficiently desirable are subjected to negative comparisons about their appearance, as exemplified by the SNL skit at the start of this chapter, or by the following comment in a British newspaper:

> Ségo, as we call her in France, is a different, altogether more seductive creature than the dumpy hausfrau Angela Merkel, the new German Chancellor. This is a woman who wouldn't look out of place on a catwalk despite what she lacks in stature (she's just 5 ft 2) and has been dubbed the "Socialist in Stilettos."[42]

Appearance therefore becomes a double bind, as discussed below; women are either trivialized for being pretty or ostracized for being plain, and women who have tried to reduce this unwanted focus by minimizing changes to their appearance have still received undue comments about their clothes and hair. Conversely, appearance is less prominent in the media coverage of men candidates.

First Name

Another noticeable tendency is the use of a woman candidate's first name, either alone or in conjunction with her surname, whereas men are more often referred to only by their surname. The use of a woman's first name has two damaging effects. First, if used alone, it implies familiarity and warmth rather than authority and gravitas. Second, and perversely, it may also indicate unfamiliarity if used repeatedly with the woman's surname, as if to suggest that the candidate is new and still requires introduction to the voters. Conversely, the use of just the surname indicates someone who is both well known and respected, and this is the dominant frame for viable male candidates. Falk also notes that women candidates are less likely than men to be referred to using an official title, such as senator, rather than Ms. or Mr.[43]

"First Woman"

Alongside the usage of the first name comes the "first woman" frame. Irrespective of how many other women candidates may have come before, women are still framed as being the first woman executive candidate.

As Falk argues, "[a]lthough the 'first woman' frame may help candidates in the short term by increasing the perception of their novelty and resulting in more press coverage, the effects of reinforcing the notion of women as out of place and unnatural in the political sphere may be longer lasting and have important political consequences."[44] This reflects a wider pattern, observed by Jamieson, of deleting women's legacy from public consciousness and forcing each new generation to reinvent the wheel.[45]

Change

In keeping with the idea that every woman who stands for executive office is the first woman to do so, the media portray women candidates as representing change and a break from the past. This frame is not always negative—indeed, we discuss below how, in a country with a tainted past, this frame has helped women to succeed—but it does come at a price. A woman who is new and different is, by definition, lacking in the experience and networks which are expected of a leader. Even when a woman possesses the necessary experience, this may be underestimated due to the emphasis on the woman's newness and difference.

"Wife of"

The role of family and relatives is framed differently for men and women candidates. For men, having a family is an asset, and men are often willing to use their wives and children as props in publicity and campaign materials. For women, the reverse is true—husbands and children may be viewed as a liability, and women are more likely to be presented alone in their campaigns. There are two reasons for this. The first links back to stereotypes—societal norms assume that women will undertake the majority of caring and domestic duties. Therefore, a married man is expected to benefit from his wife's supporting role, while a married woman may be viewed as carrying the burden of domestic obligations on her shoulders. Women are also framed repeatedly as mothers, whereas fatherhood is a less prominent trait for male candidates. Family is linked to the masculinity/femininity double bind explored below—women with families are assumed to be burdened by them, while women without families are treated with suspicion for failing to conform to societal expectations of heterosexuality and maternity. For example, in the Peruvian presidential elections of 2006, Martha Chavez said of her female rival Lourdes Flores that it was not enough to be a woman, she also had to be a mother.[46] Similarly in Nicaragua, "Miriam Argüello, a career politician who was once jailed by the Sandinistas, who openly campaigned for the UNO nomination for president, and who was elected to the National Legislature and served as its president, has been ridiculed in the popular media for being a spinster."[47]

For some women politicians, however, family relations go beyond simple stereotypes. Many women have entered politics as a result of family ties, for example, through following a husband or father into political office. More recently, women may build up a political career over time alongside a political spouse. The gendered rules of the game have meant that the male spouse has often been the first to succeed at high office, even within a marriage of equals. When his female partner then steps up for her turn, she risks being dismissed as a "wife of" rather than a qualified politician in her own right. The "wife of" frame implies that a woman who has a family or sexual tie to a powerful man must therefore owe her success to him rather than to her own qualities, thus dismissing the capacity of women candidates to be competent and autonomous individuals. Cristina Fernández de Kirchner, Hillary Rodham Clinton, Ségolène Royal, and Elizabeth Dole are all prominent examples of this phenomenon. As Duerst-Lahti argues, "it is hard to be perceived as the 'single great leader alone at the top' if one is always mentioned in connection with a husband."[48]

Emotions

Another negative way in which the media frame women is through the depiction of women as highly emotional. This framing often has historic and sexist undertones linked to menstruation and menopause. The suggestion is that women are irrational and at the mercy of their hormones during these times. They may be subject to fluctuations in mood and temperament, and such instability is not befitting of someone who has to make difficult decisions in moments of crisis. Women who succumb to their affective, indecisive, or even hysterical sides are not capable of holding executive office. This framing of women resonates with what Jamieson labels the "womb/ brain" double bind, whereby it is assumed that women's reproductive functions somehow erode their mental capacity. For example, a Peruvian legislator made a speech in which he claimed that Peruvian presidential candidate Lourdes Flores must be "on her days."[49] Despite the many advances that women have made, they still remain trapped within clichés which portray them as weak and irrational (or, at best, as "angry feminists"[50]).

DOUBLE BINDS

Women candidates are subjected to ingrained gender stereotypes about women in public life which are supplemented and reinforced by gendered media coverage of political candidates. The combination of these two sets of barriers results in a particular set of "double binds," or lose-lose scenarios, which confront women standing for executive office. We include here a number of "double binds" identified by Jamieson[51] and Lawrence and Rose,[52] such as those of femininity/competence and equality/ difference (which we combine to consider femininity/masculinity), too young/old, experience/change, connectedness/independence, and silence/ shame.

Too Masculine or Too Feminine

As noted above, the traits most positively associated with executive office are the same traits which voters stereotypically associate with men. Therefore, in order to be seen as competent and credible, women have to be masculine. However, in order to avoid being punished for subverting gender norms, women also have to be feminine. When the femininity/competence double bind is at its most potent, it "defin[es] femininity in a way that excludes competence. By this standard, women are bound to fail."[53] While physical attractiveness can be an asset for male candidates—indeed, it is common for men candidates to emphasize or even enhance their physique—a similar approach may backfire for women. Beauty in women is associated with superficiality and fragility rather than power. Heldman labels this the "smart/attractive dichotomy."[54]

Expectations surrounding femininity, from appearance to demeanor, run counter to expectations of the strength and assertiveness associated with executive office. While Alexander and Andersen do not necessarily view the double bind as intractable, they do recognize that it places an additional burden on women candidates: "successful women candidates feel the double bind of having to be both feminine and masculine. They are welcomed into the political fray, as long as they bring with them their traditional skills, capabilities, and vestiges of their roles as mother and spouses. At the same time they have to demonstrate their power, toughness, and capacity to win, traits assumed by most voters to be inherent in most male candidates."[55] Sczesny et al concur, stating that "[i]n the context of leadership of women, the violation of their traditional gender role results in the dilemma of either being 'too feminine or too masculine.' "[56] For men, masculinity is more easily assumed and less contradictory, although male candidates have also been punished if they are presented by opponents as straying too far from the alpha male model (as was the case for Al Gore in 2000 or John Kerry in 2004). Men may find it easier and more desirable to combine masculine and feminine traits when facing a woman opponent, as was the case for Barack Obama in the 2008 Democratic primary.[57]

Women may be subjected to particular types of stereotyping if they do not conform sufficiently to social expectations of femininity. In a society which still views women as the primary home-makers and care-givers, it can be very challenging for women to combine the commitment required for a political career with domestic obligations. Yet if a woman candidate is not sufficiently ensconced in domesticity—and especially if she does not have children—she runs the risk of having her sexuality called into question. Jamieson and Trimble and Arscott have both noted numerous instances of women candidates being accused of being a lesbian if they are seen as being too masculine, or not feminine enough.[58] Tarja Halonen, the president of Finland, was framed in this way despite having a male partner (whom she subsequently married).[59]

Women who promote themselves as possessing the masculine traits expected of political leaders may also be labeled as a "bitch." Rebecca Stafford complained that "if you're tough, you are considered to be nasty and mean and if you are not tough then you are too emotional. Women are not called tough leaders, they are called bitches." Dr. Pam Douglas concurs: "A woman is bitchy, and a man knows what he wants. A woman is aggressive and harsh, and a man is directed and goal-oriented."[60] Hillary Clinton, who was criticized for being too masculine, was so frequently referred to by commentators as a "bitch" that there was little doubt as to the reference made by Barack Obama's campaign when he entered a victory party following the Iowa primary to the sound of Jay-Z rapping "I got 99 problems but a bitch ain't one."[61] Similarly, when a voter asked John McCain during a campaign rally, "How do we beat the bitch?" McCain paused for a moment and then replied, "That's an excellent question."[62]

Too Young or Too Old

The emphasis on women's appearance and experience creates a particular age-related double bind. Younger women candidates are assumed to be inexperienced, unviable, and are expected to be at home raising children. Younger candidates with children, such as Palin or Royal, have faced questions about who would look after their children if they were elected into office (a question never asked of men as it is assumed that a female partner would look after the family on their behalf). Women without children, such as Helen Clark, have had question marks drawn over their sexual orientation. However, waiting until children have grown up before running for political office is not necessarily a solution, due to negative perceptions of older women. By the time women are no longer trapped within stereotypes of motherhood, they face new stereotypes based on visions of older women as unattractive, menopausal, weak, and past their prime. Ellen Johnson Sirleaf was repeatedly referred to as a "grandmother," while conservative radio host Rush Limbaugh asked, in reference to an unflattering photo of Hillary Clinton, "Will this country want to actually watch a woman get older before their eyes on a daily basis?"[63] The window of opportunity within which to build a political career is so narrowly defined for women as to prevent most women from succeeding.

Experience or Change

It was noted above that the default frame for women is that of "change." While this frame may be positive in certain scenarios, it tends to come at the expense of experience. However, a woman who opts to emphasize her experience risks losing the benefits of the "change" frame, as was the case for Hillary Clinton. By contrast, men have far more flexibility in choosing to emphasize experience or renewal. Barack Obama successfully framed himself as the candidate of change without being too heavily penalized for lack of experience, while Nicolas Sarkozy (Royal's opponent) successfully promoted himself as the candidate of political renewal despite being a key member of the incumbent government and leader of the incumbent party.

Connected or Independent

The difficulties that many women politicians have in gaining sufficient prominence and viability mean that relatively few women make it to the executive level without the boost provided by a prominent male relative. This results in the "wife of" frame described above (or in some instances, the "daughter of" frame such as Gloria Macapagal-Arroyo or Benazir Bhutto[64]). Women who are connected to a prominent man risk remaining forever in his shadow and lacking independence and credibility, while those without family connections struggle to get noticed. Women candidates with prominent husbands also face media speculation about whether the "First Husband" will continue to run the show once his wife is in office.

Silence or Shame

The heavily gendered coverage of candidates for executive office has not gone unnoticed, either by the public or by the candidates themselves. Journalists have occasionally written pieces criticizing their peers for sexist comments and coverage. However, exposing sexist comments may serve only to draw attention to them and to frame women candidates as victims. This places women candidates in a catch-22 situation—if they remain silent, gendered coverage goes unchallenged and negative stereotypes continue to undermine women's campaigns. But if women complain about sexism in the media, they risk being portrayed as victims and sore losers.

THE "MOMMY PROBLEM"

In addition to the "double binds" listed above, the various issues facing women candidates for executive office combine to create a particular effect which we label the "Mommy Problem."[65] Men and women are viewed by voters as possessing distinctive traits and issue strengths, with women seen as stronger on "compassion" traits and issues while men are favorably associated with being tough, assertive, decisive, and strong on issues such as the economy and foreign policy. While "feminine" qualities may be advantageous for certain elections, executive office is the most masculine of all political positions.[66] Nearly all executive incumbents have been men, and both the traits and issues associated with the job are masculine. In addition, the "masculine" issues associated with executive office—such as foreign policy, taxes, and defense—are the same issues which tend to be "owned" by parties of the right.[67] The association of right-wing parties with tough policies and left-wing parties with compassionate, nurturing policy stances led Chris Matthews (anchor of MSNBC's Hardball) to coin the phrases "Mommy Party" (to describe the Democrats) and "Daddy Party" (to describe the Republicans) in 1992. Since then, the phrase has stuck in the public consciousness and has been developed both by scholars (such as George Lakoff) and by the media.[68]

This pigeonholing creates a particular dilemma for women candidates, the majority of whom come from left-wing parties.[69] Left-wing women are doubly stereotyped on gender and party lines to be weaker on the very issues that are associated with executive office. Additionally, women are persistently framed by the media in personal terms, with undue focus on their appearance, first name, and families. The presentation of women candidates as familiar, sexual, and maternal all run counter to the dignity and authority required of a presidential figure. Last but not least, the stereotypes about women's ideology combine with the above factors to place an extra burden on left-wing women candidates. As Koch argues, "[f]or female Democratic candidates, who are perceived as more liberal than they actually are, the application of gender stereotypes increases the ideological distance between them and most voters, reducing their chances for securing elected office. In contrast, Republican female candidates appear to benefit from gender stereotypes; they are perceived as less conservative than they actually are, reducing the ideological distance between them and most citizens and increasing their electoral prospects."[70]

The combined effect of all these factors results in the following dilemma: the mommies from the Mommy Party aren't man enough for the job! In other words, the culmination of different types of gender stereotypes and media framing make it very difficult for left-wing women to win executive office. Women on the right may therefore stand a better chance of winning executive elections, as they are better able to balance the masculine stereotypes associated with right-wing candidates and the feminine stereotypes associated with women and left-wing candidates. They may also be better placed to tackle "women's issues," as their ideology protects them from being pigeonholed as feminists. Just as "only Nixon could go to China,"[71] so it may be easier for non-feminist women to break glass ceilings. This might explain why the three women leaders of the G8 thus far—Margaret Thatcher (United Kingdom), Kim Campbell (Canada), and Angela Merkel (Germany)—have all been from conservative parties.

HOW CAN A WOMAN WIN?

The numerous obstacles which lie in the path of women seeking executive office make it almost surprising that any women have succeeded in breaking through the ultimate glass ceiling. It might be tempting to wonder whether women have succeeded only where gendered stereotypes and media framing have been absent. However, the case studies explored in this book demonstrate most clearly that gender stereotypes are universal and omnipresent. Farida Jalalzai provides a number of alternative insights into the factors enabling some women to reach executive office.[72] These include the nature of the political system, nepotism, and opportunities generated by crisis and upheaval.

Easier to Be a Prime Minister than a President

It was noted at the beginning of the chapter that women have succeeded more often as prime ministers than as presidents. First, this is due to the reduced emphasis on individual candidates within a parliamentary system, with more emphasis being placed on the party ticket. Second, the prime minister is usually the leader of the party which wins the most seats in a legislative election. As voters chose party representatives within their constituency rather than directly electing the leader, it is usually the case that the majority of votes cast for the victorious party were directed at male parliamentary candidates, and based on the party's platforms as a whole. These two factors reduce the impact of gender stereotyping in parliamentary systems.

However, it should not be assumed that prime ministerial candidates are not subjected to media scrutiny. Party leaders in parliamentary systems are subjected to sustained media attention which intensifies in the build-up to an election, and campaigns are frequently driven by the image and personality of the party leader. In many respects, media coverage of executive candidates in presidential and parliamentary systems is comparable.

Low Power

To the extent that women have succeeded in holding presidential office, this has often been in countries with a dual executive where the president is a ceremonial figurehead and power is concentrated in the hands of the prime minister. Women have also served as prime ministers within systems where presidents are the more powerful figure—in some cases as a result of nomination by a male president. Women have figured far less frequently in the most powerful executive office within a country.[73]

Family Ties

We argued earlier that many women in politics are wives or daughters of powerful male figures. While this route is certainly not used exclusively by women—many men, not least George W. Bush, have benefited from family ties—greater emphasis is placed on family ties for women candidates due to the low number of women entering executive office through alternative routes. As other opportunities for women become more available, the dependence on family ties is likely to become less prominent.

Crisis and Upheaval

Some of the countries where women have won elections to high executive office have been marked by some form of political or economic crisis. Crisis offers two particular benefits for women candidates. First, if previous leaders have been discredited (for example through scandal, corruption, or failure), an opening is created for a new candidate to emerge. This helps alleviate the problem of entrenched old boys' networks. Second, in times of crisis, gender stereotypes may actually work in women's favor. The association of women with "change" and "renewal" is particularly advantageous, and women also benefit from being seen as more honest and less corrupt than men. For example, Violeta Chamorro won the presidency of Nicaragua in 1990 as Nicaragua emerged from a devastating civil war in which Chamorro's husband (a famous journalist) was assassinated. Chamorro capitalized on an image of female martyr-dom, dressing all in white and presenting herself as a woman who was pure, noble, and able to unite and heal the war-torn nation. Gender stereotypes are no less prevalent during crisis than elsewhere, and may be no more accurate, but they do provide a rare advantage for women candidates in these scenarios.

Considered together, these enabling factors have helped to explain why some of the women studied in this book have broken through the highest glass ceiling, and also why some of the women studied have not. Some women, such as Angela Merkel and Helen Clark (and before them, Margaret Thatcher, Jenny Shipley, and Kim Campbell) have succeeded in part thanks to parliamentary systems. Women in less powerful countries, such as Ellen Johnson Sirleaf, have succeeded thanks to crisis. There were also enabling factors not yet accounted for in the literature that are examined in this book. But Hillary Rodham Clinton, Sarah Palin, and Ségolène Royal were all targeting high power through presidential elections in stable systems. Even though Clinton, Royal, and Fernández had family ties, these were not enough. In the absence of enabling factors, the glass ceiling has proved to be remarkably resilient. As Caroline Heldman observes of the United States, the barriers to a woman president "seem insurmountable at the present time."[74]

BOOK OVERVIEW

The book uses the framework outlined above to examine the campaigns of nine women standing for executive office around the world. Each chapter illustrates the history of the campaign in question, before examining the media coverage of candidates and evaluating the extent to which the gender stereotyping discussed above was present. The first section considers women who were not successful in cracking the highest glass ceiling: Irene Sáez (Venezuela), Ségolène Royal (France), Hillary Rodham Clinton (United States), and Sarah Palin (United States). These four chapters consider the ways in which gender stereotypes may have prevented women from winning elections in these countries. Although Palin was a vice-presidential rather than presidential candidate, she provides a very interesting contrast to Clinton, in that they were both subjected to gender stereotyping but in very different ways, based on different "versions of gender."[75] Palin was also the first Republican woman to be on a presidential ticket in either position.

The second section of the book looks at women who have succeeded in winning elections to executive office. These women include Helen Clark (New Zealand), Angela Merkel (Germany), Ellen Johnson Sirleaf (Liberia), Michelle Bachelet (Chile), and Cristina Fernández de Kirchner (Argentina). While these women share their success in common, their paths to victory were varied. Each of these candidates had to negotiate gender stereotyping in some form. Every chapter considers the extent to which gender stereotypes, framing, and double binds were present, and the reasons why the candidates succeeded in winning in spite, or even with the aid, of gendered assumptions about their abilities.

The book then concludes by re-evaluating the framework outlined in this chapter, and considering the extent to which our current knowledge—which is based largely on studies conducted in the United States—is relevant to case studies worldwide. Some notions about women candidates appear to be universal, while others are less relevant in different contexts. A more comparative framework, based on the insights of this book, is offered as a means for evaluating the role of gender in executive elections around the globe.

Acknowledgments

I would like to thank Dianne Bystrom, Magda Hinojosa, Jennifer Piscopo, Melody Rose, and Gwynn Thomas for their helpful comments on an earlier draft of this chapter.

NOTES

1. It is not known exactly what "flirge" stands for. It is believed that the term was invented by the writers of "Saturday Night Live." One polite interpretation is that it stands for "First Lady I'd Rather Get Elected."

2. Transcript from "Saturday Night Live," September 13, 2008. Source: http://featuresblogs.chicagotribune.com/entertainment_tv/2008/09/saturday-night.html, accessed November 6, 2009.

3. Erika Falk, *Women for President: Media Bias in Eight Campaigns* (Chicago: University of Illinois Press, 2008).

4. Mary Ellen Egan and Chana R. Schoenberger, "The World's 100 Most Powerful Women," Forbes, http://www.forbes.com/2009/08/18/worlds-most-powerful-women-forbes-woman-power-women-09-angela-merkel_land.html, accessed November 18, 2009.

5. Farida Jalalzai, "Women Rule: Shattering the Executive Glass Ceiling," *Politics & Gender* 4, no. 2 (2008): 205–232.

6. The G8 is the group of the eight richest countries in the world. Its members are Canada, France, Germany, Italy, Japan, Russia, the United Kingdom, and the United States.

7. For example, Dianne G. Bystrom, Marcy C. Banwart, Lynda Lee Kaid, and Terry A. Robertson, *Gender and Candidate Communication: VideoStyle, Web-Style, NewsStyle* (London: Routledge, 2004); Susan J. Carroll and Richard L. Fox, eds., *Gender and Elections: Shaping the Future of American Politics* (Cambridge: Cambridge University Press, 2006); James Devitt, "Framing Gender on the Campaign Trail: Women's Executive Leadership and the Press," Report to the Women's Leadership Fund, 1999; Kathleen Dolan, *Voting for Women: How the Public Evaluates Women Candidates* (Boulder: Westview Press, 2004); Kathleen Dolan, "Do Women Candidates Play to Gender Stereotypes? Do Men Candidates Play to Women? Candidate Sex and Issues Priorities on Campaign Websites," *Political Research Quarterly* 58, no. 1 (2005): 31–44; Leonie Huddy and Nayda Terkildsen, "Gender Stereotypes and the Perception of Male and Female Candidates," *American Journal of Political Science* 37, no.1 (1993a): 119–147; Leonie Huddy and Nayda Terkildsen, "The Consequences of Gender Stereotypes for Women Candidates at Different Levels and Types of Office," *Political Research Quarterly* 46, no. 3 (1993b): 503–525; Kim Fridkin Kahn, "Does Being Male Help? An Investigation of the Effects of Candidate Gender and Campaign Coverage on Evaluations of U.S. Senate Candidates," *Journal of Politics* 54, no. 2 (1992): 497–517; Kim Fridkin Kahn, "Gender Differences in Campaign Messages: the Political Advertisements of Men and Women Candidates for U.S. Senate," *Political Research Quarterly* 46, no. 3 (1993): 481–502; Kim Fridkin Kahn, "Does Gender Make a Difference? An Experimental Examination of Sex Stereotypes and Press Patterns in Statewide Campaigns," *American Journal of Political Science* 38 (1994): 162–195; Kim Fridkin Kahn, *The Political Consequences of Being a Woman: How Stereotypes Influence the Conduct and Consequences of Political Campaigns* (New York: Columbia University Press, 1996); Kevin Smith, "When All's Fair: Signs of Parity in Media Coverage of Female Candidates," *Political Communication* 14 (1997): 71–82.

8. Deborah Alexander and Kristi Andersen, "Gender as a Factor in the Attribution of Leadership Traits," *Political Research Quarterly* 46, no. 3 (1993): 527–545; Dolan, "Candidate Sex."

9. Huddy and Terkildsen, "Consequences of Gender Stereotypes"; Farida Jalalzai, "Women Candidates and the Media: 1992–2000 Elections," *Politics and Policy* 34, no. 3 (2006): 606–633.

10. Huddy and Terkildsen, "Consequences of Gender Stereotypes."

11. Regina Lawrence and Melody Rose, *Hillary Clinton's Race for the White House: Gender Politics & the Media on the Campaign Trail* (Boulder, CO: Lynne Rienner Publishers, 2009); Susan J. Carroll, "Reflections on Gender and Hillary Clinton's Presidential Campaign: The Good, the Bad, and the Misogynic," *Politics & Gender* 5, no. 1 (2009): 1–20.

12. Falk, *Women for President.*

13. Jalalzai, "Women Rule."

14. Miki Caul Kittilson and Kim Fridkin, "Gender, Candidate Portrayals, and Election Campaigns: a Comparative Perspective," *Politics & Gender* 4, no. 3 (2008): 385.

15. Prime ministerial office is also masculinized but, we argue here, somewhat less personalized than presidential office.

16. Huddy and Terkildsen, "Perception of Male and Female Candidates," p. 121.

17. Dolan, *Voting for Women*, p. 60.

18. Ibid., p. 4.

19. Georgia Duerst-Lahti, "Presidential Elections: Gendered Space and the Case of 2004," in Carroll and Fox, eds., *Gender and Elections: Shaping the Future of American Politics* (Cambridge: Cambridge University Press, 2006), p. 15.

20. Kathleen Hall Jamieson, *Beyond the Double Bind: Women and Leadership* (Oxford: Oxford University Press, 1995).

21. Georgia Duerst-Lahti, "Masculinity on the Campaign Trail," in Lori Cox Han and Caroline Heldman, eds., *Rethinking Madam President: Are We Ready for a Woman in the White House?* (Boulder: Lynne Rienner, 2007), pp. 87–112.

22. Alexander and Anderson, "Gender as a Factor"; Huddy and Terkildsen, "Perception of Male and Female Candidates"; Jeffrey Koch, "Do Citizens Apply Gender Stereotypes to Infer Candidates' Ideological Orientations?," *Journal of Politics* 62, no. 2 (2000): 414–429; Jeffrey Koch, "Gender Stereotypes and Citizens' Impressions of House Candidates' Ideological Orientations," *American Journal of Political Science* 46, no. 2 (2002): 453–462.

23. Koch, "Do Citizens," p. 426.

24. Alexander and Anderson, "Gender as a Factor."

25. Huddy and Terkildsen, "Consequences of Gender Stereotypes."

26. Ibid., p. 512.

27. Kahn, "Experimental Examination of Sex Stereotypes"; Jalalzai, "Women Candidates and the Media."

28. Dolan, "Candidate Sex."

29. Virginia Sapiro, "When Are Interests Interesting? The Problem of Political Representation," *American Political Science Review* 75 (September 1981): 701–716.

30. Kahn, "Political Advertisements"; Kittilson and Fridkin, "Candidate Portrayals."

31. Kahn, "Experimental Examination of Sex Stereotypes"; Kahn, *Political Consequences*.

32. Kittilson and Fridkin, "Candidate Portrayals"; Jalalzai, "Women Candidates and the Media"; Smith, "When All's Fair."

33. Caroline Heldman, Susan J. Carroll, and Stephanie Olson, "She Brought Only a Skirt: Print Media Coverage of Elizabeth Dole's Bid for the Republican Presidential Nomination," *Political Communication*, 22, no. 3 (2005): 315–335.

34. Jalalzai, "Women Candidates and the Media"; Kahn, "Experimental Examination of Sex Stereotypes"; Kahn, *Political Consequences*; Pippa Norris, ed., *Women, Media and Politics* (Oxford: Oxford University Press, 1997).

35. Norris, *Women, Media and Politics*, p. 8.

36. Shanto Iyengar and Donald R. Kinder, *News That Matters: Television and Public Opinion* (Chicago: University of Chicago Press, 1987); Kahn, "Experimental Examination of Sex Stereotypes"; Kahn, *Political Consequences*; Norris, *Women, Media and Politics*.

37. Heldman et al., "Only a Skirt," pp. 316–317.

38. Falk, *Women for President.*

39. Bystrom et al., *Gender and Candidate Communication;* Dianne G. Bystrom, "Advertising, Web Sites, and Media Coverage," in Susan J. Carroll and Richard L. Fox, eds., *Gender and Elections: Shaping the Future of American Politics* (Cambridge: Cambridge University Press, 2006); Heldman et al., "Only a Skirt"; Kittilson and Fridkin, "Candidate Portrayals."

40. Falk, *Women for President*, p. 90.

41. FHM is a men's magazine which compiles an annual list, voted for by its readers, of the world's 100 sexiest women.

42. Helena Frith Powell, "How the Socialist in Stilettos Became the Sixth Sexiest Woman in the World," *The Telegraph*, June 15, 2006.

43. Falk, *Women for President.*

44. Ibid., p. 37.

45. Jamieson, *Beyond the Double Bind*, p. 11.

46. *La Primera*, "Karp Pide a Lourdes Dar a Luz para que Aprenda," March 4, 2006 (available here: http://weblogs.elearning.ubc.ca/peru/archives/023673.php, accessed November 10, 2009).

47. Michelle A. Sainte-Germaine, "Women in Power in Nicaragua: Myth and Reality," in Michael A. Genovese, ed., *Women as National Leaders* (Newbury Park, CA: Sage Publications, 1993), p. 97.

48. Duerst-Lahti, "Presidential Elections," p. 37.

49. Sainte-Germaine, "Women in Power in Nicaragua."

50. Falk, *Women for President*, p. 58.

51. Jamieson, *Beyond the Double Bind.*

52. Lawrence and Rose, *Hillary Clinton's Race.*

53. Jamieson, *Beyond the Double Bind*, p. 18.

54. Caroline Heldman, "Cultural Barriers to a Female President in the United States," in Cox, Han, and Heldman, eds., *Rethinking Madam President*, p. 28.

55. Alexander and Anderson, "Gender as a Factor," p. 542.

56. Sabine Sczesny, Janine Bosak, Daniel Neff, and Birgit Schyns, "Gender Stereotypes and the Attribution of Leadership Traits: a Cross-Cultural Comparison," *Sex Roles* 51, no. 11/12 (2004): 633.

57. Lawrence and Rose, *Hillary Clinton's Race*, pp. 212–213.

58. Jamieson, *Beyond the Double Bind*; Linda Trimble and Jane Arscott, *Still Counting: Women in Politics Across Canada* (Peterborough, ON: Broadview Press, 2003).

59. Liesbet van Zoonen, "The Personal, the Political and the Popular: A Woman's Guide to Celebrity Politics," *European Journal of Cultural Studies* 9, no. 3 (2006): 287–301.

60. Both citations from Jamieson, *Beyond the Double Bind*, p. 122.

61. *New York Post*, "Hillary, Barack Rap and Rock," January 14, 2008.

62. Mark Santora, "Pointed Question Puts McCain in a Tight Spot," *New York Times*, November 14, 2007.

63. www.rushlimbaugh.com, accessed December 17, 2007.

64. Gloria Macapagal-Arroyo is President of the Philippines and daughter of the former President Diosdado Macapagal. Benazir Bhutto was the former Prime Minister of Pakistan and daughter of former Prime Minister Zulfikar Ali Bhutto.

65. This phrase is the title of an episode of the TV series *The West Wing* (series seven, episode two). The phrase is used to tell the (male) Democratic presidential candidate that he was likeable and strong on domestic policy such as education, but was seen as weak on foreign policy.

66. Georgia Duerst-Lahti, "Reconceiving Theories of Power: Consequences of Masculinism in the Executive Branch," in MaryAnne Borrelli and Janet M. Martin, eds., *The Other Elites: Women, Politics, and Power in the Executive Branch* (Boulder, CO: Lynne Reiner, 1997), pp. 11–32; Jalalzai, "Women Rule."

67. Huddy and Terkildsen, "Perception of Male and Female Candidates"; Dolan, "Candidate Sex."

68. Patrick Healy, "A Mom Running to Lead the Mommy Party," *New York Times*, May 14, 2007; Robin Toner, "Women Wage Key Campaigns for Democrats," *New York Times*, March 24, 2006.

69. Miki Caul, "Political Parties and Candidate Gender Policies: A Cross-National Study," *Journal of Politics* 63, no. 4 (2001): 1214–1229.

70. Koch, "Do Citizens," p. 415.

71. The extent of Nixon's anti-communist sentiment protected him from accusations of being soft on communism when he visited China while president.

72. Jalalzai, "Women Rule."

73. Ibid.

74. Heldman, "Cultural Barriers," p. 39.

75. Lawrence and Rose, *Hillary Clinton's Race*, p. 222.

PART 2

Glass Ceilings Cracked but Not Broken

CHAPTER TWO

"She's Not My Type of Blonde": Media Coverage of Irene Sáez's Presidential Bid

Magda Hinojosa

When Irene Sáez announced her bid for the presidency of Venezuela in early 1998, she led in the polls, ahead of a dozen male competitors. A former Miss Universe, Sáez had garnered support as mayor of the municipality of Chacao, and had gained a reputation for being an honest and efficient politician. Twelve months later, Sáez finished a very distant third in the December 6th elections with only 3.1 percent of the vote. Political commentators pointed to her association with the nation's two most powerful parties, a volatile staff, and sugary campaign slogans to explain Sáez's dramatic drop in the polls. However, the role that the media may have played in discrediting Sáez's presidential bid went largely ignored, despite sexist comments such as these, from Andrés Galdo, a columnist for the Venezuelan daily *El Nacional*: "Irene passes her time constantly changing her clothes, her hairdo, her make-up. She hasn't been able to come up with a single idea that could impress voters."[1]

The following section outlines the unique situations present in this elections: the loss of credibility of the two major political parties, the existence of a "coup candidate" with enormous name recognition, and the dominance in the polls by independents. The gendered news frames described in the introduction to this book are discussed in the qualitative analysis section of this chapter, while the quantitative analysis section highlights the importance of media framing in explaining the results of the 1998 Venezuelan presidential elections. Like other women who have vied for the presidency, Irene Sáez was viewed through a gendered lens; the gender stereotypes that she faced were reinforced by her role as a former beauty queen. The media seemed trapped into gendered news frames, emphasizing the candidate's appearance, undermining her authority by referring to her by her first name, and repeatedly focusing on her femininity. The quantitative analysis offered here indicates that Sáez may have received as much media coverage as her male competitors, but that the type of media coverage that she received served to undermine her candidacy, especially in conjunction with the qualitative coverage.

THE 1998 ELECTIONS

Venezuela had long been a model of stable democracy for the Latin American region. The Venezuelan political system was dominated by two political parties: Acción Democrática (AD) and Comité Organizado por Elecciones Independientes (COPEI). Though originally characterized by differences in class appeal (AD represented the interests of the lower classes and was considered a populist party, while COPEI, a more conservative party, received greater support from the upper classes), ultimately "the parties converged programmatically and were transformed into multiclass, catchall electoral parties."[2] The state of affairs in Venezuela would soon be dubbed a *partyarchy*[3] due to the enormous influence that political parties held; these "hierarchically controlled, bureaucratically organized parties so thoroughly dominated electoral campaigns, legislative proceedings, and civic organizations that they destabilized democracy and generated disillusionment by blocking off most of the informal channels through which citizens voice their demands (1994, 158). When combined with presidentialism at the regime level, this *partidocracia* undermined democratic accountability and flexibility while encouraging unprincipled political factionalism within the parties."[4]

To understand the presidential elections of 1998, it is important to note that democracy, though once the "expected and customary state of affairs" in Venezuela, deteriorated rapidly after the 1988 election of Carlos Andrés Pérez to the presidency.[5] Economic crises had undermined both the AD and COPEI political parties. The power-sharing that these two parties had engaged in for so long and the enormous hold they had over all aspects of Venezuelan life made them both responsible for the economic situation in the eyes of citizens. Both were seen as culpable for their inability to turn the economic situation around. Pérez had reigned over Venezuela during the oil-rich days of the late 1970s, and Venezuelans mistakenly believed that returning Pérez to the presidency would bring back those prosperous times.[6] Pérez's unexpected reforms, including dramatic market liberalization and unannounced price hikes, led to mass rioting, looting, and over three hundred deaths.[7]

It was in this context of political upheaval that Hugo Chávez Frías was able to capture the nation's attention on February 4, 1992 when he co-led a coup attempt against President Pérez. In his nationally broadcast and now famous *por ahora* (for now) speech, Chávez asked rebel troops in the interior of the country to lay down their arms, accepted personal responsibility for the coup, and implied that while his group's objectives had failed "for now," Venezuela would soon be undergoing political change.[8] Moisés Naím writes of that live television message:

> He was a compelling and uncommon sight for television viewers accustomed to the verbal and political maneuverings of traditional politicians: a public figure who acknowledged that he personally had failed while others had done a great job; who maintained an unfaltering position even after failure and defeat; who faced responsibility and did not try to evade the repercussions of his action.[9] His televised image conveyed the possibility of change, a break from the political and economic schemes usually blamed for the country's problems. A new face unrelated to the traditional power structures and offering to guide the nation back to prosperity, equality, and integrity was an item that, regardless of its packaging, was bound to appeal to a mass audience.[10]

The appeal would be quite evident more than six years later on December 6, 1998, when Venezuelans would catapult Chávez to the nation's highest office with nearly 57 percent of the vote. As Norden explains, "The leaders of the coup, particularly the charismatic Chávez, were lauded as heroes, long-awaited knights who had come to rescue Venezuelans from a stagnating system."[11] Polls revealed that about half of Venezuelans thought the political situation might be improved by a coup.[12] That first coup attempt was followed by another in November 1992 by factions within the air force, and though the sight of low flying military aircraft over downtown Caracas was daunting, this coup attempt also failed.[13]

In May of 1993, with national elections quickly approaching, Pérez was forced from office by a corruption scandal that ended with his impeachment. After 40 years of stable democracy, Venezuelans were disgruntled with a system they perceived as corrupt, and were hostile towards politicians. The two major parties, AD and COPEI, which had held power for so long,[14] were discredited.[15] The collapse of the party system was evidenced by the election of Rafael Caldera to the presidency. Caldera had founded COPEI, but recognizing the lack of appeal of the traditional parties, broke from his party in 1993 and ran for the presidency under the banner of a number of small parties representing the left, the center, and the right.

In this context, it was not surprising that the elections of 1998 were dominated by three independents, each representing a segment of the political spectrum: Hugo Chávez (a leftist), Henrique Salas Römer (representing the center-right), and Irene Sáez (occupying the center).[16] Chávez, who had been arrested but later pardoned by President Rafael Caldera for his actions in February of 1992, appealed to millions of Venezuelans who were tired of politics as usual, and wanted an end to a system they viewed as corrupt. Democratic watch dogs worried that Chávez's calls for a constituent assembly that could disband Congress and veiled threats against political opponents signaled an end to one of Latin America's most enduring democracies.[17] Promises by his Movimiento V República (MVR) and the Patriotic Pole coalition to stop the free market reforms that the Pérez administration had put in place increased support for Chávez among the poor, who had seen drastic drops in their standard of living over the last decade. Chávez's economic platform, which included a moratorium on debt payments and a re-nationalization of key industries, caused a panic among the international financial community and decreased investments in the nation during 1998.

Businessman Henrique Salas Römer, who ultimately finished second in the elections with 39.5 percent of the vote, had earned political respect as an independent governor from the industrial state of Carabobo, but early in the campaign suffered from a lack of name recognition—a problem that neither Sáez nor Chávez faced. Salas Römer ran for the presidency under his own *Proyecto Venezuela* (Venezuela Project) party label.

Irene Sáez initially came to national prominence as the winner of the 1981 Miss Universe pageant,[18] but gained political respect as a two-time mayor of Chacao, the richest municipality in the country and one of five municipalities that make up the city of Caracas. Sáez initially forged an independent campaign and ran under the IRENE party, an acronym formed by the Spanish words *integración* (integration), *representación* (representation), and *nueva esperanza* (new hope). The political party COPEI, encouraged by extreme public support for Sáez, later picked up Sáez as their own candidate. Shortly before the election, Sáez agreed to a coalition with AD, the country's other major political party. Irene Sáez's *Changing Venezuela* platform called for an end to corruption, an avoidance of a currency devaluation, a declaration of a state of emergency in education, a reduction in the size of the national bureaucracy, and a refinancing of the public debt.[19] Sáez also emphasized her commitment to increased female participation in government and to feminist ideals. Sáez, in a conference entitled *Commitment to Women*, promised that if elected president, her administration would boast unprecedented numbers of women, spoke enthusiastically about recent statistics indicating that women now represented 50 percent of Venezuelan voters, and reiterated her support for domestic violence legislation.[20]

Sáez lost her substantial lead in the polls by April of 1998 to Chávez, as Figure 2.1 indicates, and was soon surpassed in the polls by Salas Römer.

This pattern, as noted in the introductory chapter, of women candidates starting out strong, but ultimately losing, may be attributable to excitement around a woman candidate, and in this case, an extremely well-known and well-liked woman who had made a name for herself as a beauty queen. The drop in support that took place may be partly attributable to media coverage of her campaign, which may have undermined public support for her candidacy, as I explain in later sections of this chapter.

A poll commissioned by the newspaper *El Universal* asked respondents why they would not vote for Sáez. Nearly 47 percent of the respondents indicated that Sáez lacked experience. As Sandy Tucci wrote, "I feel no apprehension in saying that Irene Sáez is a great woman, whom I admire profoundly, and without envy. She has already won a place in Venezuelan history and I would be pleased to give her my vote, but not now."[21] Another 28 percent said that they disapproved of her alliance with the political party COPEI.[22] Almost 11 percent of respondents reported that they believed Sáez lacked the determination and fortitude to confront the current crisis. According to 4.5 percent of those polled, Sáez's economic policies would only benefit the business community. Though nearly half of poll respondents believed that Sáez lacked experience, she certainly had more political experience than Chávez, who had never held public office. The concern by over one-tenth of respondents that Sáez was incapable of confronting the crisis may have been a result of the media's extreme focus on the candidate's feminine traits and gender stereotyping, which is discussed in detail in the section that follows.

Sáez's association with COPEI signaled her drastic drop in the polls; her union with COPEI and particularly her debate with Eduardo Fernández for COPEI sponsorship discredited her status as an independent, although Sáez had received backing from both COPEI and AD during her mayoral runs and still maintained her identity as an independent at that time. Having positioned herself as a centrist, it was not surprising that the two major political parties, who had long before converged programmatically, wished to support her candidacies. According to de la Cruz, Sáez's campaign team commissioned polls to decide the question of affiliation with COPEI and found that Sáez would suffer a 28 percent drop in popularity if she was supported by COPEI and about a 19 percent drop if she was given support by AD.

As the election neared, more and more voters said that they would not vote for Sáez if she were affiliated with COPEI. Although Sáez had received support from both COPEI and AD during her mayoral campaigns and still was perceived as independent, the voters were unwilling to believe (despite her assertions to the contrary) that she would be able to maintain her independence if affiliated with COPEI. This was partly an issue of sexism; according to de la Cruz, many male voters believed that as a woman Sáez would be unable to stand firm against the COPEI male leadership. This was especially true of males between the ages of 25 and 45, whose support for Sáez dropped most substantially after she was adopted by COPEI.[23] Her association with AD before the November national elections further tarnished her image as an independent.

The unique situation in Venezuelan history disadvantaged Sáez, who might have been able to gain support from the two major parties and maintain her status as an independent were it not for Chávez. Chávez was the ultimate outsider and by virtue of competing against him, Sáez appeared as a political insider with connections to both of the discredited parties. After her decline in the polls, both parties rescinded their support and backed Salas Römer in an effort to keep the presidency from Chávez, the obvious front-runner.[24] Despite her unexpectedly renewed status as an independent in the last weeks of November, Sáez remained in the race, stating: "Irene Sáez will not give up, I will keep fighting to show that the women of this country have strength."[25] Two opinion pieces during the last week of November stated that Sáez would win the respect of the nation if she were to withdraw from the race, and thus increase Salas Römer's chances of winning the presidency.

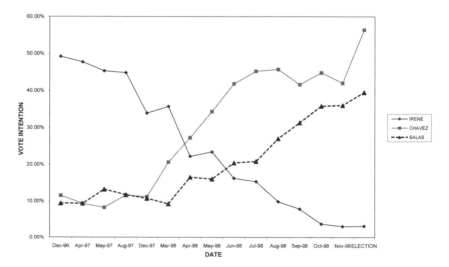

Figure 2.1   Vote Intention for 1998 Presidential Elections: 1996–1998

METHODOLOGY

To gauge the effect that the news media may have had on the presidential bid of Sáez, I analyzed the coverage that Sáez, Salas Römer, and Chávez received from the daily newspaper *El Universal*. Although the 1998 elections featured a dozen presidential candidates, these three were strategically chosen because they ultimately took the largest percentages of the vote and were from the beginning of the election cycle the most viable candidates according to opinion polls and the press. *El Universal*, a nationally-available daily, was analyzed because of its large circulation (together with *El Nacional*, they are the most widely-read newspapers in the country) and its availability.[26] In 2005, *El Universal* had a circulation of 300,000 and the largest adult readership rate (1.7 million) among the top dailies.[27] Thus, *El Universal* would likely impact a large number of voters in Venezuela.

Although the campaign did not officially begin until August 8th, every issue of *El Universal* from January 1, 1998 to December 6, 1998 was carefully read, and all articles pertaining to or simply mentioning Sáez, Salas Römer, or Chávez were more thoroughly analyzed for both the qualitative and quantitative analyses presented below.[28]

For the qualitative analysis, careful attention was paid to the manner in which the candidates were described in *El Universal*. For the quantitative analysis, coverage for these three candidates was placed into one of four categories: issue, event, horse-race, or name. Issue coverage was that which discussed a candidate's position on a particular issue or which discussed a candidate in relation to an issue which was part of the campaign. For example, articles that mentioned Chávez's stand on the nation's debt repayment were coded for issue coverage. When news of a candidate's campaign was printed, it was considered event coverage. Event coverage would include mentions of Salas Römer making a campaign stop in his home state of Carabobo. Horse-race coverage mentioned how the candidates were doing in the polls; a paragraph that stated that Chávez led in the polls by 10 percent would be considered horse-race coverage. Paragraphs or articles that were coded for name coverage simply made mention of a candidate without further analysis. A paragraph might then state that the governor of Carabobo, Henrique Salas Feo was the son of presidential candidate and former governor of Carabobo Henrique Salas Römer or note Irene Sáez's favorite meal. All candidate coverage was measured in paragraphs.[29]

Because women candidates may be seen as less newsworthy or their candidacies taken less seriously by the press, the placement of articles was noted. *El Universal* placed articles into the *News of the Day*, *Nation and Politics*, *Opinion*, *Economic*, *Sports*, *Society*, and *Caracas* sections. Letters to the editor were not analyzed for this project.

SHE'S NOT MY TYPE OF BLONDE: A QUALITATIVE ANALYSIS

Irene Sáez's presidential bid was distinguished in the media by comments about the presidential contender's hair, weight, and clothing, all of which served to both shift attention away from campaign issues and highlight stereotypical notions about appropriate gender roles. In particular, the emphasis on Sáez's beauty and sexuality prevented her from being taken seriously as a presidential contender, despite her initially high popularity rates. The news media "frame" campaigns for voters by arranging "key concepts, stock phrases, and stereotyped images to reinforce certain common ways of interpreting developments,"[30] giving the media power to reinforce traditional views.

Gender stereotypes may play a more important role for presidential elections, an office which is overwhelmingly associated with men. The stereotypes about and expectations of the gender role that Sáez should have played may have been even more pronounced because of her association with beauty pageants. Sáez was known because of her role in the hyper-feminized context of beauty pageants, while Chávez emerged from an overtly masculine context; not only was he a military officer, but he was a coup leader who had been arrested for his actions. Her identification as "female" was only reinforced in comparison to his role as "male" and vice versa. Ultimately, this would serve to disadvantage Sáez because of the executive post's identification with male gender stereotypes, as explained in the introductory chapter of this book.

Because Sáez initially gained national prominence as a Miss Venezuela who went on to win the Miss Universe pageant,[31] her looks automatically drew attention. The "smart/attractive dichotomy" (see the introductory chapter) undermined Sáez's political ambitions, as Sáez was repeatedly treated as a contender for a beauty pageant title, not for the presidency. The emphasis on Sáez's looks proved detrimental to her candidacy; while the novelty of a woman and a beauty queen running for the nation's highest office may have originally served to draw media attention, ultimately, the focus on her appearance diverted attention from issues of importance and called into question whether she was a serious candidate. One columnist referred to this presidential contender as "the girl whom every man dreamt of sleeping with once."[32] It was certainly the case here, as Murray notes in the introduction to this book, that women are "trivialized for being pretty."

The candidate's appearance attracted much media attention,[33] perhaps because as Diego Bautista Urbaneja wrote, "They thought that a person who was so pleasing to the eyes could not be the center or base of anything."[34] Columnist Ibsen Martínez announced that he would not vote for Sáez "because she's not my type of blonde."[35] Omar Estacio, in a piece for *El Universal* wrote, "Héctor Alonso López said it last week: the mustache, the eyebrows, but more than anything the double chin of ex-president Herrera Campins have begun to show on the face of Irene Sáez."[36] In one of her pieces, Elvia Gómez quoted Marcial Mendoza Estrella, president of the IRE party, who commented that Sáez is "a beautiful 37-year-old woman who could once again compete in a beauty pageant, but should not run for the Presidency of the Republic."[37]

More startling was the fact that these references were not limited to the opinion section of the paper. Luisana Colomine, the *El Universal* reporter assigned to cover Sáez's presidential campaign, asked the candidate about her hairstyle in a May 13th news article.[38] Earlier that week, Colomine had written of Sáez, "Again, the hairstyle mimicking Evita's, dressed in black, much too classically for the festive, informal environment."[39] José Vicente Rangel simply entitled one of his columns "The Hairstyle."[40] The emphasis on Sáez's hairstyle indicates the double-bind that Sáez faced. Rather than wear her hair in loose waves as she had always done, Sáez started wearing her hair in a bun which proved to be a failed attempt to decrease focus on her looks and sexuality. The issue of her hair proved to be a lose-lose situation; while her loose locks had probably inspired the media to refer to her as a Barbie doll or simply as a blonde, wearing her hair in this new style met with criticism from the media, even more attention on her appearance, and accusations that she was attempting to emulate Eva Perón.

The ways in which Sáez was referred to in the media certainly undermined her campaign, by leading voters to question her authority and doubt her abilities. While Chávez was frequently addressed as the Coup Candidate, Sáez was referred to as a Barbie doll, as an ex-Miss Universe, and, in one column by Marta Colomina, as Miss Narcissist. Even in items located in the *Nation and Politics* section of the newspaper, Sáez was referred to as an ex-Miss Universe, a former beauty queen, or simply as a blonde. Like other women presidential candidates discussed in this book, Sáez was referred to not by her last name, but rather by her first name. This was the case in all sections of the newspaper. When polls were published in the newspaper, the accompanying charts would list all candidates by last name, with the exception of Sáez who almost always was listed as Irene.[41] The use of Sáez's first name, however, was complicated by her choosing IRENE (an acronym, but also her first name) as the name of her political party. The use of IRENE may have encouraged others, including the media, to refer to the candidate by her first name. The use of her first name, when others were being addressed by their surnames, made her appear less serious than her competitors.

The news media called attention to the candidate's femininity in both expected and unexpected ways. *El Universal* devoted one page of a special election section of the newspaper to a discussion of the candidates' dress, which would have been surprising had no woman been running for the office. The newspaper played with expected gender norms in its coverage of Sáez, as when it took a routine campaign shot of Sáez holding a baby at an event, placed it in the *Nation and Politics* section, and captioned it, "Irene will have her baby after the elections."[42] Sáez was not pregnant at the time and had not mentioned that she intended to have a baby in the near future. The media appeared intent, however, on turning a woman without children and casting her in the frame of mother. Columnist Colomine introduced a quote by the candidate with the following clause: "With that habit of referring to herself in the third person, as if it wasn't about her. . . . "[43] News articles made reference to Sáez's tardiness, noting if a meeting was started late because the candidate failed to arrive on time. Further, the candidate was compared to other Latin American women who had been or were then active in politics, including both Isabel Perón and Eva Perón (especially after Sáez adopted a hairstyle that resembled that of Eva Perón), but also to Noemí Sanín and María Emma Mejía of Colombia.[44]

Newspaper articles reported the sexism that Sáez endured from the other political candidates while emphasizing the candidate's gender. One news article co-authored by two women[45] read in part: "The candidate of the Patriotic Pole received his colleague the way she deserves to be treated: with flowers. She moved the bouquet out of the way and he took a rose and offered it to her."[46] While Sáez may have been attempting to downplay the feminine role Chávez was casting her in by offering her flowers, the news media reports of this event called more attention to her feminine role. Hugo Chávez, angered by Sáez's comment that those who had violated the constitution did not deserve the presidency, sent this message to Sáez: "Mayor, my message to you is this: how ill-fitting are the words of Carlos Andrés Pérez on your lips, and to your beautiful face. . . . "[47] Rather than engage Sáez's point, Chávez dismissed it by referencing the candidate's beauty instead. Sáez was certainly aware of the differential treatment that she was receiving from other candidates and from the press. Women can be seen as "sore losers" if they challenge sexism in their news coverage and treatment by voters. This proved a challenge for Sáez. For instance, in an opinion article, Américo Martin wrote, "Irene, perhaps because she is a woman, *as she says*, they will not forgive her for trading her loose Barbie locks for Eva Peron's aggressive hairstyle. . . . "[48] Sáez's complaints about her coverage by the news media may have provoked a backlash.[49]

The quality of attention that the news media lend to female candidates may reinforce public sentiments about the inability of women to hold political office and thus, undermine their likelihood of winning office. Norris has written that journalists' preoccupation "with the attire and hair styles of women candidates instead of their issue positions" both discourages women from running for office and discourages voters from taking women seriously.[50] Certainly the type of coverage that Sáez received served to undermine her candidacy; she was portrayed as a blonde sex object, making it difficult for her to be taken seriously as a presidential candidate.

MORE THAN HER FAIR SHARE: A QUANTITATIVE ANALYSIS

The results of this quantitative analysis do not suggest that Sáez received less media attention than her male counterparts.[51] In January 1998, as Table 2.1 indicates, Sáez received a total of 139 paragraphs of coverage in *El Universal*, more than twice the amount of paragraphs devoted to the candidacy of Salas Römer and a total of 49.3 percent of all the coverage given to these three candidates. As late as May 1998, Sáez continued to outpace her competitors in amount of news coverage. By June, however, as the chart demonstrates, the amount of coverage Sáez was receiving from *El Universal* dipped suddenly. By this point, the public may have been unwilling to believe that the Barbie doll, as she was often referred to in the press, had a real chance of winning the presidency. The novelty of her campaign may have also begun to wear off, especially given that Sáez had been considered a contender for the presidency for a few years. In July, Sáez and Chávez received virtually identical amounts of coverage; she received 342 paragraphs of coverage and he received 325 paragraphs of coverage. As late as August, Sáez and Chávez differed little in the amount of coverage they were receiving from *El Universal*, but by September 1998, dramatic

Table 2.1 Media Coverage of the 1998 Presidential Election: Number of Paragraphs by Candidate, January–November 1998[1]

Date	Chávez	Salas Römer	Saéz
January	80	63	139
February	172	81	228
March	273	148	280
April	230	75	256
May	399	156	498
June	559	174	240
July	325	208	342
August	400	263	386
September	475	218	280
October	408	275	231
November	428	420	192

[1]Please note that this analysis reflects only totals from the *Nation and Politics* section of *El Universal*. Total paragraphs of coverage for each of the three main competitors in other sections of the paper are available via request.

differences were evident in the coverage that Sáez was receiving relative to her main competitors.

While Sáez may not have been disadvantaged by the *amount* of coverage that her campaign received, it does appear that the *type* of coverage that Sáez received may have harmed her candidacy. An analysis of the issue coverage devoted to these three candidates revealed that Sáez received less issue coverage than her male competitors. While on average 38 percent of the paragraphs devoted to Chávez focused on issue coverage, only 33 percent of the paragraphs devoted to Sáez were issue coverage. Slightly over 35 percent of the paragraphs devoted to Salas Römer were issue coverage. Lack of issue coverage was indicative of the media's inability to take Sáez's candidacy seriously; by focusing less attention on her issue positions, the media could effectively lead voters to believe that Sáez had few or no issue positions.[52]

Sáez also received less horse-race coverage than her male counterparts. Candidate viability becomes more salient when the media devote considerable attention to horse-race coverage. Though Kahn explains that voters who are exposed to more horse-race coverage "may weigh viability concerns more heavily when developing overall evaluations of these candidates," she adds that "the actual content of the horse race information is also consequential."[53] Lazarsfeld et al explain that voters tend to vote for the candidate they expect to win;[54] this bandwagon effect could disadvantage women candidates when they lag behind male candidates in the horse-race coverage. While 13 percent of Chávez's total coverage for the 11-month time period was devoted to the horse-race coverage as was 16 percent of Salas Römer's, Sáez's percentage of horse-race coverage was 11 percent. Although Sáez received positive and abundant horse-race coverage at the beginning of 1998, by the end of the campaign articles that dealt with this coverage were increasingly negative. This negative information would discourage voters from casting their ballots for Sáez. Similarly, less information about the horse-race coverage in the latter months of her campaign actually made Sáez's candidacy appear less viable to the public.

An analysis of coverage in the *News of the Day* section of *El Universal* revealed similar results.[55] Though Sáez received an average of nearly 21 paragraphs per month of coverage, Chávez obtained nearly 29 paragraphs per month, but Salas Römer garnered less than 16 per month. A disaggregation of these totals by type of coverage, however, reveals that Sáez received less issue coverage than both Chávez and Salas Römer and that Sáez obtained considerably less horse-race coverage than her male counterparts.

An analysis of the coverage devoted to these three candidates in the *Opinion* section of *El Universal* revealed that Chávez was overwhelming featured in opinion pieces. Nearly 70 percent of all paragraphs written about one of the three candidates were on Chávez. Only 11.4 percent of these paragraphs were on Salas Römer, and 19 percent of these paragraphs were devoted to Sáez. Chávez also received a considerably greater proportion of issue coverage than his competitors—954 paragraphs versus 75 paragraphs for Salas Römer and 131 paragraphs for Sáez.

The analysis of the *Economic* section of the newspaper showed that Sáez continued to receive less issue coverage than Chávez and less horse-race coverage than both of her competitors. Considering the "Chávez effect" that panicked the financial community, it was not surprising to find that Chávez received much more coverage in the *Economic* section of *El Universal*.

As other scholars have found when studying media coverage of women in politics, both female candidates and officeholders tend to be featured more regularly in the "fluffy" newspaper sections. This was certainly the case with Sáez who received more coverage than her male competitors in the *Society* section of *El Universal*. During the 11-month time period, Sáez was pictured in the *Society* pages seven times. Salas Römer's photograph graced the *Society* pages only twice, while Chávez was never featured in the *Society* section. Sáez was the only candidate among the three to receive any coverage in the *Caracas* section of *El Universal* which is not surprising considering her occupation as mayor of Chacao; more surprising was the fact that Sáez was also the only candidate to be mentioned in the *Sports* section.

QUALITY AND QUANTITY: CONCLUSIONS

The results of this analysis appear to suggest that although Irene Sáez may have attained as much media coverage as Chávez and Salas Römer, her male competitors, the type of coverage that she received was different. In particular, gender stereotyping was evident in coverage of Sáez. In terms of overall coverage, the amount of media attention that Sáez received appears to be relatively positive—high at the beginning of the campaign because of the "newsworthiness" of a female candidate, dropping in the middle of the year as the novelty of a female candidate wore off, and lower after August when Sáez slips drastically in the polls.

A review of the figures for issue coverage (which show that Sáez received a smaller percentage of issue coverage than either Salas Römer or Chávez) indicate that the media may have contributed to a discrediting of Sáez's presidential campaign. The lower percentage of issue attention that Sáez received from *El Universal* may have impaired her ability to communicate attractive ideas, and so have damaged public perception about Sáez's policy positions. The amount of attention focused on Sáez's appearance contributed to undermining her candidacy; the emphasis on appearance distracted readers from issues of substance. Further, an abundance of horse-race coverage has historically disadvantaged female candidates; the unequal amounts of horse-race coverage that Sáez received may have further harmed her candidacy. Her exceptional start in the polls was atypical. The amount of horse-race coverage devoted to Sáez, however, was unexceptional considering her position in the polls during the early months of 1998, as the graph indicates. Analyses of other sections of the newspaper introduce slightly different results, as previously discussed.[56]

Although these results indicate that Sáez was not forgotten by the media, they also suggest that the quality of news coverage that a candidate receives may be as important as the quantity of it. While blame for the failure of Irene Sáez's presidential bid cannot be placed on the media, this project reveals that the media certainly reinforced gender stereotypes in its coverage of Sáez's campaign, which may have prevented voters from taking her candidacy seriously, and thus undermined her efforts to win the presidency.

Acknowledgments

I gratefully acknowledge the financial support provided by a NOMOS research grant, which allowed me to undertake fieldwork for this project in Venezuela during the summer of 1999. I would also like to thank Rainbow Murray and Melody Rose for their helpful comments on this chapter.

NOTES

1. AP.
2. Kenneth M. Roberts, "Social Correlates of Party Demise and Populist Resurgence in Venezuela," *Latin American Politics and Society* 45, no. 3 (Autumn 2003): 48.
3. Michael Coppedge, *Strong Parties and Lame Ducks: Presidential Partyarchy and Factionalism in Venezuela* (Stanford, CA: Stanford University Press, 1994).
4. Roberts, p. 42, citing Coppedge 1994: 158.
5. Daniel Levine, "Venezuela: The Nature, Sources, and Prospects of Democracy," In Larry Diamond, Juan Linz, and Seymour Martin Lipset, eds., *Democracy in Developing Countries: Latin America* (Boulder, CO: Lynne Rienner Publishers, 1989), p. 247.
6. Michael Coppedge, "Venezuela: The Rise and Fall of Partyarchy," in Jorge I. Domínguez, and Abraham F. Lowenthal, eds., *Constructing Democratic Governance: South America in the 1990s* (Baltimore, MD: The Johns Hopkins University Press, 1994), p. 341.
7. Elisabeth Friedman, "Paradoxes of Gendered Political Opportunities in the Venezuelan Transition to Democracy," *Latin American Research Review* 33, no. 3 (1998): 89; Moisés Naím, *Paper Tigers and Minotaurs: The Politics of*

Venezuela's Economic Reforms (Washington, D.C.: The Carnegie Endowment for International Peace, 1993), p. 10.

8. Naím, *Paper Tigers*, p. 99; *El Universal*.

9. While Hugo Chávez was revered for admitting defeat and his own failures, women in powerful positions who admit failure are not typically treated as generously. For example, following the problematic implementation of a new system of urban public transport (known as *Transantiago*) in the capital city, President Michelle Bachelet admitted failure. Rather than laud her admission of personal responsibility, her acceptance of culpability was interpreted as a sign of weakness and drew serious questions about her ability to govern. I thank Rainbow Murray for pointing out this double standard.

10. Naím, *Paper Tigers*, p. 102.

11. Deborah L. Norden, "Democracy and Military Control in Venezuela: From Subordination to Insurrection," *Latin American Research Review* 33, no. 2 (1998): 155.

12. Ibid.

13. Naím, *Paper Tigers*, p. 10.

14. The power that AD and COPEI had was overwhelming, and led to the labeling of Venezuelan democracy as a partyarchy. "Some say even beauty contests were decided along party lines!" (Coppedge, "Venezuela: Partyarchy," p. 328).

15. Levine, "Venezuela: Prospects of Democracy," p. 260.

16. The minor candidates in this election were: Claudio Fermin, Luis Alfaro Lucero, Gonzalo Pérez Hernández, Godofredo Marín, Ignacio Quintana, Radamés Muñoz León, Oswaldo Suju Raffa, Miguel Rodríguez, and Alejandro Peña Esclusa.

17. These concerns about Hugo Chávez have continued over the course of the last decade. As Roberts writes, "By the end of the 1990s, when Hugo Chávez and his upstart Movimiento V República (MVR) had swept to a series of electoral victories, not only the party system but the entire constitutional order of the post-1958 democratic regime had decomposed in Venezuela" (Roberts, p. 39). Chávez has been routinely accused of having ended democracy.

18. Professor Rafael de la Cruz, one of Saéz's campaign managers and the program coordinator for an eventual Saéz government, stated that Saéz's name recognition rates reached 98 percent (Personal Interview, July 23, 1999).

19. The *Changing Venezuela* platform might have been useful to Saéz because, as noted in Chapter One of this book, women are often seen as representing change. However, in light of her association with the two dominant political parties and, more importantly, because of the kind of anti-system change that her competitor Chávez was advocating, Saéz proved incapable of positioning herself as the candidate of change. She was, therefore, unable to benefit from this association that often occurs between women and change.

20. *El Universal*, August 16, 1998.

21. *El Universal*, October 21, 1998.

22. Newspaper articles were uniform in their belief that the alliance with COPEI and AD would only harm Saéz and that the two major parties were using the candidate in a desperate attempt to retain control of the government. Alvaro Miranda, in an article written for *El Universal* wrote: "Adecos and copeyanos [AD party members are known as *adecos*, while COPEI members are known as *copeyanos*] will

attempt to fix all that has been broken over the last forty years, sacrificing the beauty of Chacao, who will make her path in the December 6 elections, as she once did in the Nuevo Circo during the Press Meeting" (*El Universal*, November 23, 1998). Miranda's reference to the beauty pageant press events held at the grand *Nuevo Circo* stadium of Caracas was an unnecessary invocation of Saéz's background as a beauty queen; though many may have agreed with the greater point that the AD and COPEI were using Saéz, the December 6 elections cannot easily be compared to those media events following Saéz's pageant coronations.

23. Personal Interview, July 23, 1999.

24. Please refer to the graph and note that data for 1/97–3/97, 6/97–7/97, 9/97–11/97, 1/98–2/98 was interpolated.

25. *El Universal*, November 23, 1998.

26. Kahn argues that the largest newspapers may also be the most professional, and therefore less likely than smaller newspapers to treat male and female candidates differently in their coverage of campaigns (Kim Fridkin Kahn, "The Distorted Mirror: Press Coverage of Women Candidates for Statewide Office," *Journal of Politics* 56 [1994]: 158). We would therefore expect to find fewer gender differences in campaign coverage for men and women in large national newspapers, such as *El Universal*.

27. World Press Trends 2005: p. 686.

28. All coding was done by the author; for this reason, no intercoder reliability statistics are provided.

29. Each paragraph of coverage was coded as either issue coverage, event coverage, horse-race coverage, or name coverage; this allowed the researcher to avoid double counting coverage. Otherwise, a paragraph mentioning that the frontrunner [coded as horse-race] was making a campaign stop on Margarita Island to discuss economic policies with business owners [coded as event coverage] would be coded as both horse-race coverage and event coverage. There was a need to determine how a paragraph of coverage that included elements of more than one type of coverage would be coded. These four different types of coverage were placed on a scale, with issue coverage being most important, then event coverage, horse-race coverage, and finally name coverage. When one paragraph mentioned more than one category of coverage, the paragraph was placed into the higher category.

30. Pippa Norris, *Politics and the Press: The News Media and Their Influences* (Boulder, CO: Lynne Rienner, 1997), p. 275.

31. Venezuelans are known to be quite passionate about beauty pageants and take tremendous national pride when they are able to win titles such as Miss Universe or Miss World.

32. *El Universal*, June 27, 1998.

33. Newspapers in the United States also seemed to delight in mentioning Saéz's appearance, regularly noting that Saéz was a 5 foot, 10 inch strawberry blonde.

34. *El Universal*, June 11, 1998.

35. *El Universal*, July 15, 1998.

36. *El Universal*, January 12, 1998.

37. *El Universal*, July 15, 1998.

38. *El Universal*, May 13, 1998.

39. *El Universal*, May 10, 1998.

40. *El Universal*, May 17, 1998.

41. Claudio Fermín, who finished fifth in the December elections, was sometimes referred to by his first name, but certainly less frequently than Saéz. Fermín, because of his dark skin, was sometimes simply referred to as *El Negro*.

42. *El Universal*, July 29, 1998.

43. *El Universal*, November 13, 1998. Campaign managers Aníbal Romero and Rafael de la Cruz both mentioned Luisana Colomine and Marta Colomina's coverage of Saéz. Both Romero and de la Cruz believed that Colomine and Colomina's columns damaged Saéz's candidacy (Personal Interviews, July 23, 1999 and July 28, 1999).

44. This seems to be a common strategy when using the "first woman" frame that Norris writes about (Norris 1997). A woman campaigning for office is compared to other female firsts; in this case, to other first women in other national contexts.

45. Kahn and Goldenberg's 1991 study found that female journalists gave women political candidates in the United States more positive news coverage. For this reason, Kahn and Goldenberg urge more equal representation not only in the nation's political bodies, but also across the country's newsrooms (see also Sally J. Kenney [1996]. "New Research on Gendered Political Institutions." *Political Research Quarterly* 49, no. 2: 445–466). My own analysis revealed that slightly over 31 percent of the articles analyzed for this research project were written by women.

46. *El Universal*, November 27, 1998.

47. *El Universal*, April 21, 1998.

48. *El Universal*, Date Unknown. Author's emphasis.

49. Saéz's concern with the role of the news media was not unique. The vast majority of women politicians across the globe cite the news media as an obstacle on their route to political office (Inter-Parliamentary Union, *Democracy Still in the Making: A World Comparative Survey. Series Reports and Documents, no. 28* [Geneva: IPU, 1997]).

50. Norris, *Politics and the Press*, p. 65.

51. In keeping with the historical pattern, de la Cruz insisted that Saéz received more media coverage than both Chávez and Salas Römer during the first months of 1998 because of her gender. She certainly received more media attention "than one would expect" (Personal Interview, July 23, 1999).

52. Though initially Saéz was criticized by many for expressing vague and "sugary" positions on major issues, she and her team of advisors were able to recognize this as a problem and soon formulated a more solid platform.

53. Kahn, "The Distorted Mirror," pp. 162–163.

54. Paul F. Lazarsfeld, Bernard Berlson, and Hazel Gaudet, *The People's Choice* (New York, NY: Columbia University Press, 1968), p. 108.

55. News of the Day coverage in *El Universal* would be the equivalent of front page coverage in most newspapers.

56. The novelty (and threat) of a coup leader running for office became evident in the analysis of the *Opinion* section of the newspaper.

CHAPTER THREE

Madonna and Four Children: Ségolène Royal

Rainbow Murray

I n 2006, Ségolène Royal won the Socialist Party (PS) primary to become the party nominee for the 2007 presidential election. In so doing, she became the first woman with a credible chance of being elected the president of France. Throughout the primary campaign and for the remainder of 2006, Royal was extremely popular. She triumphed over her male opponents in the Socialist Party (PS) primary and looked strong against Nicolas Sarkozy, the candidate from the center-right *Union pour un Mouvement Populaire* (Union for a Popular Movement or UMP) party. Her sex appeared to be an advantage, as she symbolized political renewal in a country hungry for change. However, as the campaign hit full swing in 2007, Royal experienced a sharp reversal of fortune. The gender stereotypes and framing present in the campaign media coverage were accompanied by growing doubts about Royal's competence and credibility. Her opponents carefully sowed seeds of doubt about her ability which were amplified by gendered media reporting, creating a number of double binds from which Royal could not escape. These problems were compounded by a number of political problems facing the Socialist candidate. Hampered by a disloyal party, a disparate Left, and a disorganized campaign, Royal could not compete with the slick electoral machine run by Sarkozy. Her narrow lead in 2006 was gone by January 2007 and did not return; in May 2007, Sarkozy achieved a comfortable victory in the second round of the election.

This chapter begins by looking at the background to the election and the defining moments of Royal's rise and subsequent fall. The media coverage of Royal is then explored in more depth, and is contrasted to the media coverage of Sarkozy to demonstrate disparities in treatments of the two candidates. The analysis focuses on print media coverage of two televised debates, with each debate drawing a large audience and representing a pivotal moment in the campaign. Many of the gender stereotypes considered in the introduction to this volume were present in the French case study, including a focus on "masculine" traits and issues for Sarkozy and "feminine" traits and issues for Royal. The emphasis placed on Royal's motherhood, combined with gendered stereotyping about her competence in "social issues" and her alleged ignorance of foreign policy and economics, presented a strong example of the "Mommy Problem."

Royal was also framed in very different ways from her male opponents. She was frequently referred to by her first name, with a popular juxtaposition of "Ségo" to her opponent's "Sarko." Her attractive appearance and her relationship with the party leader were framed in such ways as further to erode her credibility. As a result, Royal found herself caught in a number of double binds which worked to the detriment of her campaign. If these double binds had been accompanied by sufficiently favorable circumstances, they might not have sounded the death-knell of her campaign. Instead, they combined with the other difficulties faced by the candidate to ensure her defeat.

BACKGROUND: THE 2007 ELECTIONS

France is a semi-presidential system, with a strong and directly elected President who shares power with an autonomous legislature. When the President and Parliament are of the same party, the President is the key political figure; when the President and Prime Minister are of different parties, power is more evenly shared between the two offices. France has a multi-party system, although two parties (the Socialists [PS] on the left, and the *Union pour un Mouvement Populaire* [Union for a Popular Movement or UMP] on the right) are the dominant players. French presidential elections are held over two rounds; with the exception of the 2002 elections, the second round is a stand-off between the candidates from the PS and the UMP.[1]

Ségolène Royal had been an active member of the PS for nearly thirty years. As she informed a member of the public when asked whether she had enough experience to run for president, "I spent seven years working for François Mitterrand, I know all the ins and outs of the French presidency and government, I have been a minister three times, a deputy[2] four times, I am currently the president of a region, I know all the workings of the State."[3] From 2004 onwards, Royal was included in IPSOS polling of potential presidential candidates, and she immediately became the highest-ranked of the Socialist hopefuls.[4] Despite these strengths, she was viewed as an outsider candidate for the Socialist primary; various male candidates (including her partner, François Hollande, the leader of the party) were considered to be more viable candidates. The revered journalist Alain Duhamel published a book in 2006 detailing the twenty most likely candidates for the presidency, and omitted to include Royal.[5]

Royal built up her campaign momentum "both organizationally and ideologically" from the outside, raising support amongst the grassroots.[6] She was assisted in these efforts by the media, who appreciated her novelty value as a potential woman candidate. Her rise throughout 2006 was meteoric, and sexist attempts to discredit her by her male rivals backfired. For example, Laurent Fabius infamously asked who would look after Royal's children if she were elected; such comments served only to boost her popularity and present her opponents in a bad light. By August 2006, three months before the primary was to be held, newspapers had begun pitting Royal as the likely Socialist Party (PS) candidate against Sarkozy as the likely Union for a Popular Movement (UMP) candidate. Their confidence in Royal's victory was justified; she won the primary with more than 60 percent of the vote, leaving her male rivals, Fabius and Dominique Strauss-Kahn, with less than 20 percent of the vote each.

For the remainder of 2006, Royal's star was still in the ascendant. Her status as the first credible woman candidate for the presidency seemed to boost her popularity, to the extent that the UMP pondered how to overcome the advantage that being a woman appeared to bestow upon their socialist rival.[7] A senior woman within the UMP, Michèle Alliot-Marie (known as MAM), even claimed on her blog that only another woman candidate could "neutralize the female advantage" of Royal.[8] MAM was trying to encourage her own party to consider her as an alternative candidate to Sarkozy. When Sarkozy emerged as the undisputed nominee, MAM did not retreat from the campaign; instead, many of the most sexist insults towards Royal came from MAM, perhaps in the belief that these would be more acceptable if uttered by another woman.

From early 2007, Royal's fortune declined. She was implicated in a range of costly blunders on foreign policy; despite her pleas of being misquoted or entrapped, her credibility was damaged on the most important aspect of the presidency.[9] Her party failed to mobilize firmly behind her, with costly snipes at her from within the party and the public defection of her finance minister, Eric Besson, to the Sarkozy camp. The launch of her manifesto proved under-whelming; eager to deflect claims that she had no ideas, Royal put forward a proposal of one hundred policy initiatives, resulting in a lack of theme or direction to her campaign. Meanwhile, Sarkozy went from being the presumptive to the official nominee of his party, and immediately benefited from the full support of the party machine. Royal afterwards lamented the lack of resources and organization within her own campaign compared to the wealth and efficiency of the Sarkozy campaign, noting that the UMP were much better at maintaining good relations with the press.[10] Sarkozy, who had openly been preparing his campaign for years and was now reaping the rewards, carved out a firm lead for himself in the polls.

As Royal began to flounder, the third candidate, centrist François Bayrou, was propelled into the spotlight. Polls indicated that while Royal was more likely to qualify to the second round of voting than Bayrou,[11] Bayrou was more likely to defeat Sarkozy in a second-round stand-off. Some voters on the left, motivated more by their dislike of the temperamental Sarkozy than out of loyalty to Royal, began to shift their votes towards Bayrou in the hope that Bayrou would beat Royal to qualify to the second round, and then defeat Sarkozy in the final vote. Fears that Royal would fail to qualify to the second round, just like her Socialist predecessor Lionel Jospin in 2002, proved to be unfounded. Indeed, Royal never slipped below second place in the polls, so the growing rumors that she would not qualify may themselves have been gendered interpretations of her viability as a candidate. Nevertheless, the refocusing of attention on the fight for second place revealed the underlying belief that the fight for victory had already been won by Sarkozy. Although Royal qualified comfortably to the second round and fought tenaciously until the end, the final result confirmed what the polls had indicated for a long time—a decisive victory for Sarkozy.

The causes of Royal's defeat were numerous. In addition to the problems outlined above, there were the problems faced by a Left in disarray. French voters have long favored the Right in France, with François Mitterrand being the only left-wing president since the founding of the Fifth Republic in 1958. The fragile coalition of left-wing parties which formed the government in 1997 had largely disbanded by 2002. To win an election, a left-wing candidate would need to unify voters ranging from those in the center, who might otherwise vote for Sarkozy or Bayrou, to the significant portion of voters located to the left of the French Communist party. Attempts by Royal to speak to different sectors of the left-wing electorate at different times resulted in claims that her message was incoherent; yet she was faced with an impossible task. The ideological debates on how best to reconcile the different portions of the left-wing electorate continue to plague the PS today. The likelihood is that any Socialist candidate would have struggled, despite the advantage of facing a candidate who was a senior member of an unpopular government. In addition to these difficulties, Royal faced particular problems as a result of gendered stereotyping and media coverage. As demonstrated below, these served to erode her credibility and prevented her from overcoming the other problems that she faced.

GENDER STEREOTYPES IN THE CAMPAIGN

Methodology

One of the central features of the 2007 presidential elections was the use of televised debates, where the candidates appeared individually and answered questions from a live studio audience. Although it is traditional to have a head-to-head televised debate between the two final candidates before the second round of voting, the interaction of individual candidates with a studio audience was a new feature in 2007. The most prominent of these audience debates were those shown on the channel TF1 under the title "J'ai une question à vous poser" ("I have a question for you"). Hosted by broadcasting veteran Patrick Poivre d'Arvor, these debates were key moments in the campaign. Sarkozy was the first to appear, on February 5, 2007, attracting a mean audience of 8.24 million viewers (out of a population of 61.5 million people). These impressive viewing figures were then surpassed by Royal a fortnight later when she attracted a mean audience of 8.91 million viewers. The debates were important to the campaign; Sarkozy's appearance came at a point where his lead over Royal was becoming stable, while Royal's performance was seen as a last chance to resurrect a campaign in trouble.

The use of these debates for the analysis in this chapter is twofold. First, the content of the debates is of intrinsic interest; the questions asked reflect some of the stereotypical assumptions held by the public about both candidates, and the responses gave each candidate the opportunity to discuss a range of policy areas. Second, the press act as a filter, framing expectations of the debate beforehand and then influencing public evaluations of the candidates' performance afterwards.[12] The press coverage therefore illuminates any gendered framing and stereotypes employed by the media. For each debate, a Nexis search was conducted of all French newspapers in the fortnight surrounding each debate. The search terms were "Sarkozy" for the first debate and "Royal" for the second debate. This generated a total of 438 articles, of which 245 focused on the first debate and 192 focused on the second. These articles were subjected to a qualitative analysis; they were coded according to the codeframe outlined in the appendix, with an emphasis on tone and framing rather than on quantifying the number of times each theme was explored. These articles were used alongside a more general survey of media coverage throughout the campaign.

Traits

Royal and Sarkozy were portrayed as possessing very different gendered traits. In keeping with the stereotypes outlined in the introductory chapter, Royal was characterized as possessing various "feminine" traits, such as being emotional, maternal, compassionate, and empathetic. *Le Figaro* (a right-wing newspaper) described her as "the Madonna of welfare: she cajoles, she approves, she shows sympathy, she makes promises ... she feels sorry for each person's misfortune ... Who cares about figures and finances as long as suffering humanity has found its savior?"[13] Implicit within this quote is the notion that the caring qualities attributed to Royal came at the expense of the financial competence required to be a president. Others echoed this sentiment, labeling Royal a "care worker"[14] and a "nanny"[15] while questioning her stature as a potential head of state. Her reluctance to campaign negatively against her opponents through personal attacks, which she saw as contrary to the spirit of "doing politics differently," was interpreted as a lack of toughness. Her emphasis on listening to the people, through participatory rallies and through a consultative Web site, was used to portray her as someone who could not lead. The mixed messages she used to try and woo different sectors of the electorate were taken as indications that she was indecisive and irrational. The credit that she received for feminine traits was not sufficient to compensate for the perception that she lacked important masculine traits such as aggression, toughness, rationality, decisiveness, competence, and intelligence. Indeed, the perception that Royal was neither intelligent nor competent persisted throughout the campaign, despite her qualifications from elite, highly competitive universities (Sciences Po Paris and the Ecole National d'Administration, a graduate school for top civil servants).

The impression of Royal's incompetence was partly a result of increased focus on her campaign errors compared to those of Sarkozy.[16] As one person pointed out in a letter to the newspaper *Le Monde* (following coverage of errors made by Royal in her TF1 performance), "Ségolène Royal, as a woman, is automatically incompetent. Nicolas Sarkozy, in the single program on TF1 on February 5th, can talk about half of French workers being on the minimum wage (the correct figure is 17%), of a barrel of oil costing $90 (it has never exceeded $78), of inflation once being 24 percent in France (it has never exceeded 14%), and yet no-one would treat him as incapable."[17] (Following this accusation, *Le Monde* admitted that the author's claims were correct and that the errors of Sarkozy had gone unreported while those of Royal had been closely scrutinized.) The consequences of excessive emphasis on Royal's mistakes compared to those of other candidates were not trivial: she polled favorably on questions such as "Which candidate most understands your needs?" and was seen by voters as "nice," but she performed poorly on polls about competence and presidential stature.[18] As a result, she struggled to maintain credibility with voters on the traits most valued in a presidential candidate.

While Royal confronted gendered stereotypes which worked against her favor, Sarkozy was largely a beneficiary of media coverage. He was depicted as intelligent, ambitious, energetic, and hard-working. He portrayed himself as healthy and virile by being photographed while jogging, and downplayed potential challenges to his virility such as his choice not to drink alcohol, or his wife's very public affair with another man in 2005.[19] He also possessed some "masculine" traits which were not to his favor, such as being aggressive, uncouth, arrogant, and quick to lose his temper. The media covered these negative traits extensively, and they were certainly damaging to Sarkozy's campaign. Had he faced a male candidate, he might have been punished even more severely for these traits; instead, they may have emphasized his masculinity against the portrayal of Royal as his weak and incompetent opponent.

Ideology

The main challenge to Royal on the ideological front was not her sex, but her need to reconcile an electorate ranging from the far left to the center. Sarkozy faced a similar problem, with the far-right National Front Party (FN) siphoning off votes from the right of the Union for a Popular Movement (UMP) while Bayrou presented a challenge from the center. Sarkozy and Royal may both have benefited in this respect from the events of 2002, when the left-wing vote was split across many candidates in the first round, resulting in a higher score for the National Front Party (FN) candidate (Jean-Marie le Pen) than for the Socialist Party (PS) candidate (Jospin). Royal had benefited through a greater concentration of the left-wing vote on the Socialist candidate in 2007, while Sarkozy benefited from a significant reduction in the FN vote as protest voters returned to the mainstream. Sarkozy wooed far-right voters with promises of being tough on immigration and law and order. At the same time, he played a smart tactical game of *ouverture* or "openness," indicating his willingness to work with actors drawn from all political and social backgrounds. Royal was less successful at appealing to the center and the margins at the same time, and while both candidates used mixed messages for different audiences, Royal was more likely to be labeled as "incoherent" for doing so.[20]

Issues

As with traits, France provided a good example of issue stereotyping. Royal's strengths were very much seen as those of the domestic and social domains, such as welfare policy, which are traditionally associated with women. Royal declared that her first act of office, if elected, would be to strengthen domestic violence policy. An evaluation of her performance on TF1 by *Libération* (a left-wing broadsheet newspaper which was mostly supportive of her campaign) spoke of her positions on education, welfare, and healthcare. It then identified the three focal points of her debate (which actually encompassed a range of policy areas); first, concrete policy proposals such as employment and the minimum wage; second, values such as "dialogue, respect, education, parental responsibility"; and third, her ability to reach out and listen to people.[21] While voters recognized Royal's strengths in these areas, they did not necessarily consider social policy to be important in a presidential election. The dual executive in France comprises a president, primarily responsible for foreign policy, and a prime minister, primarily responsible for domestic policy. Hence, domestic policy is of lesser importance in a French presidential election. One commentator remarked that the range of questions put to Royal during the debate "sometimes led one to think that one was watching a minister for Welfare or for Healthcare, rather than a potential future president of the Republic."[22] The "feminized" policy areas with which Royal was associated most positively did little to reinforce her credibility as a presidential candidate.

On the key areas of foreign policy and the economy—both of central importance in a French presidential election, and both traditionally "masculine" policy areas[23]—Royal was portrayed as ignorant, weak, and incompetent. The series of foreign policy gaffes in January 2007 did much to erode her credibility in this area, while opponents—both within and outside her party—tried to discredit her economic policies. Her finance minister, Besson, caused great damage when he defected from her campaign to that of Sarkozy on the grounds that she had no "clear answers" on issues such as "the 35-hour working week,[24] how to fund social security and welfare, progressive taxation, or nuclear power."[25] Meanwhile, one of MAM's many attacks on Royal declared that "she has not detailed how much her promises will cost because she is incapable of calculating the cost. . . . " MAM then continued by criticizing Royal's "lack of perspective" on "France's place in the world," citing Royal's stance on aircraft carriers as an example of her "inadequacies."[26]

Although Sarkozy was not an expert on foreign policy—his main ministerial experience was as Minister of the Interior—he was not called upon to prove his credentials in the same ways as Royal. Nor was he criticized as strongly for the mistakes that he made. Royal's concerted efforts to be taken seriously were not sufficient to counteract public assumptions of her incompetence in these areas—assumptions which were nurtured by the right. For the first time, the Defense Secretary in the outgoing government was a woman, which should have increased public confidence in a woman's ability to handle issues of defense, security, and foreign policy. However, this woman was MAM, and she greatly assisted Sarkozy by discrediting Royal on issues of defense. As MAM was both a woman and the official government authority on matters of defense, her critiques of Royal were particularly damning, and enabled her to appeal to traditional gender stereotypes while avoiding the appearance of sexism.

MAM's attacks were combined with negative media reporting on Royal's foreign policy efforts. In 2006, Royal travelled to Chile to congratulate newly-elected president Michelle Bachelet, presumably in the hope of reminding French voters of the feasibility of a woman president. Yet the story of the day became Royal's choice of high-heeled shoes, leading to Royal's frustrated retort to journalists: "Are you fetishists?"[27] A year later, Royal was subjected to a series of negative reports on diplomatic issues. For example, she was criticized for failing to respond to an inflammatory remark made by a Hezbollah representative (she claimed that she had not heard the remark).[28] Her much-criticized praise for the swiftness of Chinese judicial decisions was reported without mentioning that she was referring to commercial litigation; meanwhile, her lobbying for human rights while on a visit to China went unreported.[29]

The combination of an over-emphasis in coverage of typically "feminized" policy issues, combined with negative media coverage of Royal on matters of foreign policy and repeated attacks from all sides on her competence at handling "masculine" issues, gave the impression of a candidate who was not well-suited to the demands of the presidency. This impression was compounded through the use of gendered media frames, as explored below.

MEDIA FRAMING

The gendered media frames explored throughout the book were all applicable to varying degrees in the French case. In most instances, these frames worked to Royal's detriment, undermining her stature and credibility as a presidential candidate.

Appearance

Royal's appearance was a constant source of interest to the media. In the early days of her campaign, her attractiveness added to her appeal; she looked photogenic on the cover of magazines. In the summer of 2006, she was pictured in a bikini, an image juxtaposed with

Sarkozy in beach shorts. The image was taken by a paparazzo without her knowledge or consent; she threatened to sue, but did not pursue the case, perhaps out of reluctance to draw further attention to the sexualized image.

As the campaign continued, there was a great deal of comment on Royal's choice of clothing, and in particular her preference for white jackets. Her choice of white clothing led to her being called a "Madonna," the "Woman in White," and the "Virgin Marie-Ségolène"[30] (a strange choice for a mother of four children!). In the articles surrounding Royal's debate, there were twelve references just to the color of her jacket (compared to two references to any aspect of Sarkozy's appearance in the reporting on his debate). For example, the coverage of Royal's performance by the newspaper *Aujourd'hui en France* began, "The usual white jacket over a black dress, standing straight in her pumps. . . ."[31] While not directly harmful, the interest in Royal's appearance was trivializing, and may have detracted from her gravitas as a presidential candidate.

First Name

Royal was widely referred to throughout the campaign by her first name, either with or without her surname. She was also given the nickname of "Ségo," a play on her first name which was contrasted with "Sarko," a play on Sarkozy's surname. The use of a candidate's first name was not unheard of in French politics; Arlette Laguiller, a (female) politician on the far left, and a candidate in every presidential election since 1974, is affectionately known as "Arlette." However, male politicians are frequently referred to by surname alone, especially if they are well known, and it is uncommon to refer to men by their first name only.

Several studies have demonstrated that Royal was more commonly referred to by her first name than were her male opponents.[32] This trend is confirmed by a content analysis of the articles used in this study. As can be seen in Table 3.1, Royal was at least six times more likely than Sarkozy to be referred to by her first name alone.[33] While the use of both names was the most common style for both candidates, Sarkozy was referred to only by his surname nearly 40 percent of the time, compared to just 27 percent of the time for Royal.[34] The use of Sarkozy's surname is fairly consistent, whether or not he is the main focus of the story; conversely, Royal is even more likely to be referred to with both names in stories which focus on Sarkozy.[35] De Singly argues that the use of "Ségolène" contributed to the impression of Royal as warm, "close to the people," but lacking presidential stature.[36]

Table 3.1   Media Use of Different Names for Sarkozy and Royal

	First Name Only	First and Last Name	Last Name Only	Nickname	Total
Sarkozy (NS Stories)[1]	0.76%	57.55%	39.74%	1.95%	921
Sarkozy (SR Stories)[2]	0.90%	56.33%	39.14%	3.39%	442
Sarkozy Total	0.88%	57.15%	39.55%	2.42%	1,363
Royal (SR Stories)[1]	5.88%	62.24%	29.82%	2.07%	919
Royal (NS Stories)[2]	4.08%	73.98%	19.44%	2.51%	319
Royal Total	5.42%	65.27%	27.14%	2.18%	1,238

[1]This refers to newspaper stories collected using the search term Sarkozy.
[2]This refers to newspaper stories collected using the search term Royal.

"First Woman"

The novelty value of Royal as the first woman candidate with a realistic chance of winning the election was present throughout the campaign. The qualifier of "with a realistic chance" is necessary; Laguiller was the first woman to stand in a presidential election, and a number of women have stood since, including three other women candidates running in 2007.[37] However, none of these women stood any hope of qualifying to the second round. As the nominee of the main party of the left, Royal was the first woman to be seen as a potential president. In the build up to the primaries, the hype surrounding Royal as the "first woman" worked in her favor, as it increased public and media interest in her candidacy. By the main campaign, the frame was less dominant within the French press, and was sometimes used to criticize the sexist treatment received by Royal, as in this example: "Clearly, no attacks have been spared against the first woman with a chance of becoming the president of the Republic. . . . She is endlessly forced to prove her educational qualifications, her experience, and to show that she was not born yesterday. . . . Even Arlette Laguiller has not been subjected to a trial for incompetence. This is unsurprising, as there is no risk that she will be elected."[38]

Change

In the early days of her campaign, Royal personified change in at least three ways. First, her ideas were innovative and placed her outside the PS mainframe; she openly acknowledged that she drew inspiration from then-Prime Minister of Britain, Tony Blair. Second, her style of campaigning was new. She was the first candidate to harness the power of the Internet as a campaign tool through the use of her Web site, "Désirs d'Avenir."[39] (Indeed, Royal later claimed that Barack Obama had taken inspiration from her campaign.)[40] Third, as the "first woman," she was a physical embodiment of change. Royal's association with change was an asset which assisted her in the build-up to the primary. The incumbent government was unpopular, and Jacques Chirac's twelve years as president had left the country thirsty for something different. One PS member argued in 2006 that "we need someone who embodies a different way of doing politics. Who else but her?"[41] By contrast, Sarkozy could be considered the candidate of continuity. He was the second most powerful member of the outgoing government, and the chairman of the UMP.

It is perhaps surprising, then, that Sarkozy succeeded in reframing himself, rather than Royal, as the candidate of "change." The reasons for this are twofold. First, Royal herself was not eager to emphasize the "change" frame, as it was accompanied by the double binds of novelty and inexperience. The gender and politics literature counsels running on a mandate of "experience" rather than "change," as women find it harder to establish their credibility when running for an office that has only ever been held by men. Second, Sarkozy was keen to promote his distinctiveness from the outgoing administration, and had nurtured this image for some time. As party chair, he began to steer the party away from Chirac, and Chirac's public support for Dominique de Villepin[42] as a rival candidate for the party's presidential nomination only underlined the rift between Chirac and Sarkozy. Having distanced himself from Chirac, Sarkozy then promoted himself as the candidate of *rupture tranquille*, or "peaceful severance" with the past: someone who could shake up and modernize government without ruffling too many feathers. In stealing the "change" mantel from Royal, Sarkozy overcame the burden of association with an unpopular government, while neutralizing one of Royal's biggest advantages in the campaign. This is to Sarkozy's credit, and the parliamentary elections which followed a month after the presidential elections were the first to see the re-election of the incumbent government since 1978.

"Wife of"

Technically speaking, Royal has never married. She was the partner of François Hollande, with whom she has four children, for nearly thirty years, but they did not wed. Royal met Hollande in college, and in the following years they both rose to prominence in the PS, with Royal's career equaling and sometimes surpassing that of Hollande. In 2006, Hollande enjoyed slightly greater prominence than Royal because he was the leader of the PS—a position which might have made him the presumptive nominee, had the party not introduced primaries. Royal declared her intention to stand in the primary election in January 2006; Hollande did not immediately respond, but only withdrew himself from contention once Royal's strong showings in the polls made her the clear frontrunner.

As Royal had not been the candidate of choice of the PS old guard, she had been forced to place her campaign outside the party mainstream. Following the primary, Hollande was well-placed to help reintegrate Royal's campaign within the party, and call on the party stalwarts to show their support for her candidacy. However, Hollande's support for Royal was lukewarm, and he did not refrain from criticizing her in public. In January 2007, Royal was forced to suspend her spokesperson after he stated on the record that "Royal's only weakness is her partner."[43] Public opinion of Royal as subordinate to Hollande was strikingly revealed in the questions asked to her by members of the TF1 audience. One member of the audience asked her, "Aren't you really preparing yourself for . . . being the First Lady by François Hollande's side? How do you intend to stand up for yourself against those who were denied power?" Another audience member addressed her as "Mme Hollande." These questions were painful for Royal, both politically and personally. Politically, they reinforced the notion of Royal as weak and dependent. At a personal level, Royal was concealing the fact that her relationship was on the rocks. Hollande was having an affair with a journalist, and Royal announced their separation after polls had closed in the parliamentary elections in June 2007. Royal was probably wise in keeping this rift private, as else it would have dominated headlines and drawn even further unwanted attention to Royal's relationship with Hollande and with her party. Yet the burden of being portrayed as the "wife of" a man who had actually left her was such that, in her book about the campaign written later that year, she struggled to speak of it and did so only sparingly, and in the third person.[44]

Emotions

As very few people knew the turmoil of Royal's private life, she was not given credit for the emotional restraint she showed during this period. Rather, she was portrayed by the media in typically gendered terms, with an emphasis on her "compassion." This frame was particularly dominant in the coverage of the TF1 debate, when Royal was moved by the plight of an audience member in a wheelchair, and walked over to him to place a comforting hand on his shoulder. This one moment (in a two-hour show) received more coverage than any other, prompting one newspaper to report that "the TF1 pre-election program broadcast more emotions and affectivity than information."[45] Another, quoting Sarkozy, stated that "compassion is not a policy."[46] Libération even accused her of "playing the emotion card."[47] Royal was compared in more than one newspaper to "Mary Poppins," amongst other references to her as a nanny or a nurse.[48] These terms are hardly befitting of a serious presidential candidate, and were one of the many factors undermining her stature as a credible contender for top executive office.

DOUBLE BINDS

The various forms of gender stereotyping outlined above contributed to a range of double binds in which Royal found herself. She presented herself as a feminine candidate, both in appearance and persona, perhaps to overcome the criticisms made of Edith Cresson (France's only woman prime minister) that she was too masculine.[49] Although Royal was punished for her femininity (for example, through being portrayed as soft, weak, incompetent, and unable to tackle the "hard" policy issues), she was also punished when she strayed into more "masculine" territory. All her attempts to establish her credibility on foreign policy led to negative reporting, and the aggressive stance which she took against Sarkozy in the final, head-to-head debate was also criticized. (In an interesting contrast, Sarkozy succeeded in overcoming criticisms of his hotheadedness through excessive displays of politeness and chivalry towards Royal during this debate. He smoothly deflected Royal's attacks and left her looking like a nagging woman attacking a weary gentleman.)[50] Royal certainly did not benefit from her "feminine" persona, but the French were not comfortable with any subversion of traditional gender roles. One of the few women who succeeds in straddling the "feminine/masculine" binary is MAM, and she was not successful in contesting Sarkozy for the party nomination.

The double bind relating to age was not applicable in the French case. Royal was almost exactly the same age as Sarkozy, and her age was rarely mentioned except when noting the relative youth of both candidates. Conversely, the "experience or change" paradox was certainly present. Royal was initially presented as a candidate of change, which was certainly beneficial but came at a price, as her experience was belittled or ignored. The encroachment of Sarkozy upon the "change" frame did not enable Royal to reposition herself as an experienced candidate, but rather, neutralized one of Royal's few advantages in the campaign.

Royal was indirectly affected by the bind of connectedness versus independence. Her political trajectory owed very little to Hollande; she was a protégée of Mitterrand who then demonstrated considerable talent in the electoral arena, conquering and holding a difficult parliamentary seat for four terms and being the only woman elected to the coveted position of president of a region in 2004.[51] Her dependence on Hollande in 2007 was less due to their personal relationship than due to his pivotal role, as party leader, in encouraging the party to unite behind her. His reluctance to do so contributed to a particular kind of double bind for Royal. She was portrayed in some quarters as a "wife of," connected to politics at least in part through Hollande. At the same time, she was forced to be independent, as she enjoyed the wholehearted support of neither the party nor her partner.

Last but not least, Royal risked being framed as a victim if she spoke out against sexism in the media. She did not entirely refrain from doing so— for example, Royal would frequently ask journalists, "Would you ask that question of a man?"[52] and she acknowledged during the debate that "It's true that it's much harder for a woman."[53] Most of the complaints about her media treatment, however, came not from her but from journalists themselves and from members of the public. A Web site entitled "One million women got angry" declared that, "we feel, as women, humiliated by what has been said about [Royal]. I am shocked to see this woman endlessly criticized about her personal qualities and appearance ... Everything that is said about her, about her voice, her hair, her earrings, her choice of words, ... her sense of compassion or her harshness, is intended to discredit her, to demonstrate that she does not have a place at the head of the state."[54] Meanwhile, de Singly, writing in Le Monde, argued that "the trap of masculine and feminine stereotypes has closed in around [Royal]."[55]

The "Mommy Problem"

The "Mommy Problem," as outlined in the introductory chapter, theorizes that women on the left face a number of hurdles. First, gender stereotypes relating to policy issues give the impression that women are strong on social policy, but weak on the areas considered most important in presidential elections (such as foreign policy). Second, women are seen as strong on similar issues to those "owned" by left-wing parties, while men are believed to be stronger on the issues "owned" by right-wing parties. Finally, women's attempts to strengthen their credentials may be hampered by the use of gendered frames such as motherhood. All of these hurdles were present for Royal in 2007. As a left-wing, feminine candidate, she struggled to establish credibility on issues beyond those of domestic and social policy. This problem was exemplified in the TF1 debate, where most of the questions put to her were in these "feminized" areas. One newspaper commented that "the accent [is] on social questions. This is no doubt why the predominant sensation ... [was that] the country is looking for a mommy rather than seeking to elect a president. ... It is not a super social worker that the French people will elect on April 22nd and May 6th."[56] In contrast, Sarkozy was naturally assumed—as a man, and as a member of the party more favorably associated with these issues—to be strong on matters of foreign and economic policy.

Royal's "Mommy Problem" was compounded by the strong emphasis placed on her role as a mother. She was referred to by journalists using such patronizing terms as "Mommy Ségolène" and "Big Mommy."[57] A reporter in Libération opined that "Ségolène Royal is not a man but a woman, and not only a woman but a mommy, and a mommy who can speak on equal terms on TF1 to all the mommies in France."[58] The benefits of motherhood are dubious; another journalist argued that "[France] perhaps has more need for a father who forces us to face up to reality than a mother who whispers comforting words in our ears."[59] Royal ended up looking like a micro-manager, ready to handle family affairs and personal problems rather than taking on the broader problems of the country as a whole. This combination of gender stereotypes left many believing that Royal was incapable of running the country.

CONCLUSION

The case study of France and Ségolène Royal has been a classic illustration of many of the gender stereotypes considered in this book. Royal was portrayed as strong on "feminine" traits and issues, and weak on the "masculine" traits and issues associated with the French presidency. Her attempts to prove herself in the domains of foreign and economic policy were not taken seriously; she was frequently discredited and ridiculed. While there was little overt sexism during the main campaign—Royal's opponents had seen in the primary that such a strategy would backfire—there was a more subtle and insidious attempt to discredit Royal through appealing to deeply ingrained stereotypes about women. These stereotypes were nurtured and expanded by the media, from the use of Royal's first name to the portrayal of her as emotional and maternal. The key consequence of all these factors was the over-riding impression of Royal's incompetence. Irrespective of her qualifications, her experience or her policies, Royal could not shake off the growing impression that she was unqualified, inexperienced, and incapable of leading the country. The use of gender stereotypes to erode confidence in her abilities and undermine her authority was effective in contributing to her change of status from front-runner to runner-up.

Gender stereotypes were certainly not the sole factor contributing to Royal's defeat; if other circumstances had been more favorable, she might have been better able to overcome the constant questioning of her ability. A key difficulty was her inability to unite the party around her, which itself was linked partly to the indignation of some senior men in the party that a woman had defeated their preferred candidate. Disunity within the Socialist party, and across the French left more broadly, created circumstances under which any Socialist candidate would have struggled to win. Despite this caveat, gender stereotypes were significant in tarnishing Royal's image, and they illustrated the deeply rooted and ongoing difficulties for the French in accepting women in positions of power.

Acknowledgment

My warm thanks to Sheila Perry who assisted with accessing the data used in this chapter and who provided helpful insights with the analysis.

APPENDIX: CODE FRAME USED FOR DATA ANALYSIS

All articles were coded by the author, so no tests for inter-coder reliability were needed. Phrases within articles were coded according to the categories below. This methodology permitted the identification of the dominant trends in the coverage.

References to each candidate's appearance
References to each candidate's competence
Use of both candidates' first name, surname, and nicknames (this category was measured quantitatively)
References to candidates using explicitly gendered frames
References to each candidate's leadership qualities
References to each candidate's family
References to Royal as a mother/nanny (the uses of these phrases was limited to cases where they were not used in direct reference to Royal's family; this frame was only applied to Royal)
References to each candidate as emotional
References to each candidate's relationship with the media
Direct criticisms of each candidate
Direct praise of each candidate

NOTES

1. France's party system is in constant evolution, and the name and composition of political parties shifts over time. The UMP was created in 2002, combining the Gaullist RPR party with several smaller parties on the right. The 2002 elections were exceptional because, due to a divided left, the far-right National Front

candidate (Jean-Marie Le Pen) qualified alongside the UMP candidate (Jacques Chirac), leaving the Socialist candidate excluded from the second round.

2. "Deputy" is the word for a member of the National Assembly, France's lower chamber of parliament.

3. Ségolène Royal, "J'ai une question à vous poser," TF1, February 19, 2007. All translations in this chapter are the author's.

4. Sheila Perry, "Gender Difference in French Political Communication: From Handicap to Asset?," *Modern and Contemporary France* 13, no.3 (1995): 337–352.

5. Alain Duhamel, *Les Prétendants 2007* (Paris: Plon, 2006).

6. Ben Clift, "The Ségolène Royal Phenomenon: Political Renewal in France?," *The Political Quarterly* 78, no. 2 (2007): 284.

7. Rainbow Murray, "Is the Mere Presence of a Strong Female Candidate Enough to Increase the Substantive Representation of Women?," *Parliamentary Affairs* 61, no. 3 (2008): 476–489.

8. http://mamblog.free.fr, accessed November 30, 2006.

9. For example, a journalist posing as a Canadian diplomat elicited embarrassing comments from Royal about Corsican independence.

10. Ségolène Royal, *Ma Plus Belle Histoire, C'est Vous* (Paris: Grasset, 2007), pp. 64–65.

11. French presidential elections are held in two rounds. All candidates stand in the first round, while only the two front-runners qualify to the second round stand-off.

12. Patrick Champagne, "Qui a Gagné? Analyse Interne et Analyse Externe des Débats Politiques à la Télévision," *Mots. Les Langages du Politique* 20 (1989): 5–22.

13. Michel Schifres, "Sainte Blandine," *Le Figaro*, February 24, 2007.

14. J.-P.L, "Présidentielle: Eléphants, Jaurès, etc," *Midi Libre*, February 24, 2007.

15. Ibid.

16. *Agence France Presse*, "Les Grands Médias et leurs Patrons, Vedettes Malgré eux de la Présidentielle," February 12, 2007; B. Beziat, "Royal à l'Epreuve Médiatique," *Sud-Ouest*, February 19, 2007; Raymond Kuhn, "The French Presidential and Parliamentary Elections, 2007," *Representation* 43, no. 4 (2007): 323–336; Marc de Miramon, "Pourquoi les Médias Votent Sarkozy?," *L'Humanité* February 2, 2007.

17. Elie Arie, quoted in V. Maurus, "Médiatrice; Alerte," *Le Monde*, February 25, 2007.

18. G. P., "Royal Jugée plus Sympathique que Convaincante," *Le Figaro* February 23, 2007; François de Singly, " 'Nicolas et Royal' ou la Domination Masculine," *Le Monde*, March 16, 2007.

19. Cécilia Sarkozy reconciled with her husband following this affair. Tension in their marriage remained visible throughout the election (she did not vote for him), and he divorced and remarried during his first year in office.

20. Examples include the description of Royal's policies as "ambiguous" and "contradictory" (Y. M., "L'élection présidentielle suscite un flot de jugements," *La Nouvelle République*, February 26, 2007), and as "vague" and "confusing" (Dominique Bègles, "Ségolène Royal: le social au régime du donnant-donnant,"

L'Humanité, February 21, 2007; Valérie Sasportas, "Ségolène Royal vous a-t-elle convaincu?" *Le Figaro*, February 21, 2007).

21. Isabelle Roberts (based on an interview with Denis Muzet, director of the Mediascopie Institute), "Elle a Apporté sa Touche, sa Manière d'Être," *Libération*, February 21, 2007.

22. Béatrice Houchard, "Presidentielle," *Le Parisien*, February 20, 2007.

23. Deborah Alexander and Kristi Andersen, "Gender as a Factor in the Attribution of Leadership Traits," *Political Research Quarterly* 46, no. 3 (1993): 527–545; Leonie Huddy and Nayda Terkildsen, "Gender Stereotypes and the Perception of Male and Female Candidates," *American Journal of Political Science* 37, no. 1 (1993): 119–147.

24. The 35-hour working week was a measure introduced by Martine Aubry during the left-wing government of 1997–2002. One of the key themes of Sarkozy's campaign was "work more to earn more," in direct opposition to this policy. Royal supported the policy somewhat unenthusiastically during the campaign in order to keep the party happy, but admitted afterwards that she did not agree wholeheartedly with the policy. Aubry narrowly defeated Royal in 2008 to become the leader of the PS.

25. Ivan Rioufol, "Ebranler le Confort Intellectuel," *Le Figaro*, February 23, 2007.

26. Michèle Alliot-Marie, quoted in *Agence France Presse*, "Alliot-Marie: 'Mme Royal Dit Oui à Tout le Monde,'" February 20, 2007.

27. Isabelle Mandraud, "Ma Vie avec Ségo," *Le Monde*, February 21, 2007.

28. Ben Clift, "The Ségolène Royal Phenomenon: Political Renewal in France?," *The Political Quarterly* 78, no. 2 (2007): 282–291.

29. Royal, *Ma Plus Belle Histoire*, 84.

30. Royal's full name is Marie-Ségolène Royal, although she is more commonly known as Ségolène Royal.

31. Nathalie Segaunes, "Royal Joue la Proximité," *Aujourd'hui*, February 20, 2007.

32. Julian Barnes and Pierre Larrivée, "Arlette Laguiller: Does the Mainstay of the French Political Far-Left Enjoy Linguistic Parity with her Male Counterparts?" (paper presented at a conference entitled "Women, Power, and the Media," Aston University, Birmingham, England, September 15, 2007); Núria Fernández García, "Leader Media Construction: Ségolène Royal Media Treatment Analysis in Opinion Columns in *Le Figaro* and *Libération*" (presented at Women, Power, and the Media, September 2007); Eva-Marie Goepfert, "La Presse People et le Traitement de la Differentiation Sexuée des Candidats à l'Election Présidentielle" (presented at a conference on La Campagne Présidentielle de 2007 au Prisme du Genre, University of Paris XII [Créteil], France, March 14, 2008).

33. Ironically, Sarkozy encouraged familiarity amongst his entourage of journalists, while Royal maintained her distance and asked journalists to address her as "Mme Royal" (Royal, *Ma Plus Belle Histoire*, p. 62).

34. The definition of "surname only" includes the use of the candidate's title followed by their surname, but does not include the use of "Sarko," which is coded separately.

35. The newspaper Nexis search was conducted using the candidates' surnames as search terms.

36. Singly, "Nicolas et Royal."

37. Mariette Sineau, *La Force du Nombre: Femmes et Démocratie Présidentielle* (Paris: l'Aube, 2008).

38. Béatrice Houchard, "Connaisez-Vous Tous les Dossiers?," *Aujourd'hui*, February 25, 2007.

39. This term does not translate easily; one interpretation is "Hopes for the Future."

40. Sylvain Capel, "Ségolène Royal: 'J'ai Inspiré Obama et ses Equipes nous ont Copiés,'" *Le Monde*, January 20, 2009.

41. Isabelle Mandraud, "Si c'est pas Elle, c'est Qui?," *Le Monde*, May 31, 2006.

42. Villepin was the prime minister from May 2005 until the 2007 elections; the bitter rivalry between Villepin and Sarkozy culminated in a court battle over a defamation case.

43. (with Reuters and AFP), "Ségolène Royal Suspend Arnaud Montebourg Pendant un Mois," *Le Monde*, January 18, 2007.

44. Royal, *Ma Plus Belle Histoire*.

45. *Le Télégramme*, February 20, 2007.

46. *Sud Ouest*, "Sarkozy se Bat Maintenant sur Deux Fronts," February 22, 2007.

47. David Revault d'Allonnes, Pascal Virot and Nicole Gauthier, "A la Télé, Royal a des Réponses à Donner," *Libération*, February 20, 2007.

48. J.-P.L, "Présidentielle: Eléphants, Jaurès etc"; Karim Nedjari, "Ovation Chez Jamel," *Aujourd'hui en France*, February 25, 2007.

49. Cresson was prime minister for less than a year, in 1991–1992, making her the shortest serving prime minister of the Fifth Republic. She was appointed by Mitterrand and subjected to widespread gendered criticism throughout her term in office. For example, Perry claims that Cresson was criticized because "she was not 'womanly' or 'feminine' enough" (Perry, "Gender Difference in Political Communication," 343–344).

50. Béatrice Fracchiolla, "Politeness as a Strategy in a Gendered Political Debate—the Sarkozy-Royal Debate" (paper presented at Women, Power, and the Media, September 15, 2007).

51. The position of regional president in France is somewhat comparable to that of state governor in the United States.

52. Patrick Guilloton, "Elle Aime le Débat!," *Sud Ouest*, February 20, 2007.

53. Isabelle Mandraud, "Royal Cherche à Imposer son Style," *Le Monde*, February 21, 2007.

54. www.1milliondefemmessenervent.org, accessed March 20, 2007.

55. Singly, "Nicolas et Royal."

56. Guilloton, "Elle aime le débat!"

57. Fernández García, "Leader media construction."

58. Mathieu Lindon, "Voter Tom! Voter Jerry! Vox Populi," *Libération*, February 24, 2007.

59. Hubert Courdurier, "Sarko Prie pour Ségo," *Le Télégramme*, February 21, 2007.

CHAPTER FOUR

18 Million Cracks in the Glass Ceiling: The Rise and Fall of Hillary Rodham Clinton's Presidential Campaign

Dianne Bystrom

When I was asked what it means to be a woman running for president, I always gave the same answer: that I was proud to be running as a woman but I was running because I thought I'd be the best President. But I am a woman, and like millions of women, I know there are still barriers and biases out there, often unconscious . . . Although we weren't able to shatter that highest, hardest glass ceiling this time, thanks to you, it's got about 18 million cracks in it. And the light is shining through like never before, filling us all with the hope and the sure knowledge that the path will be a little easier next time. That has always been the history of progress in America.[1]

With these words, Hillary Rodham Clinton ended her historic 16-month campaign for the Democratic nomination for U.S. president with a speech on June 7, 2008, before a crowd of supporters packed into the historic National Building Museum in Washington, D.C. In her concession speech—in which she endorsed the eventual Democratic presidential nominee and now U.S. president, Barack Obama, and called for party unity—Clinton referred to the historic significance of her campaign and the nearly 18 million citizens who had voted for her in primaries and caucuses held from January 3 through June 3, 2008. Although her bid had fallen short, she had come closer than any other woman in U.S. history to securing a nomination for president from one of the two major political parties.

"You can be so proud that, from now on, it will be unremarkable for a woman to win primary state victories, unremarkable to have a woman in a close race to be our nominee, unremarkable to think that a woman can be the President of the United States," Clinton said. "And that is truly remarkable."[2]

Did Clinton's campaign for the Democratic nomination for president signal a new era for women presidential candidates in the United States? Or did it confirm that gender stereotypes still exist for women candidates, particularly those who run for the nation's highest executive office, which can not only derail their campaign but also prevent their success?

This chapter sets out to answer the questions outlined in the introductory chapter regarding why women seeking executive office do better in some countries than others, if gender stereotypes continue to exist, and the role of voter perceptions and the media in shaping these stereotypes.

Specifically, this chapter chronicles the rise and fall of Clinton's historic campaign for the Democratic nomination for president from the seemingly inevitable nominee for much of 2007, to her early stumble in the Iowa caucus on January 3, 2008, and through her up-and-down fight with Obama for most of the 2008 primary season. In keeping with the book's comparative framework, this chronicle focuses on her media coverage and, especially, the gender stereotypes she faced as a woman candidate who seemingly possessed the "masculine" characteristics that U.S. citizens say they want in a president. It assesses how the media may have contributed to Clinton's defeat through gendered campaign coverage, but also considers other unique factors at play in the 2008 presidential election. Clinton's media coverage was not only influenced by her gender, but also by her marriage to former President Bill Clinton; the couple's long and often tumultuous relationship with the media; and the youth and race of Obama, who was waging his own historic campaign as an African American candidate.

First, I look at how the public perceived Clinton through an analysis of her job approval ratings and presidential preference, attributes, and issue polls against a backdrop of previous survey research that reveals the gender stereotypes facing women political candidates, especially in seeking the top executive office in the United States. Next, I look at the way in which Clinton was framed by the news media throughout her presidential campaign through content analyses of her newspaper and television coverage, with numerous examples drawn from both quantitative and qualitative inquiries. Finally, I assess the impact of Clinton's historic campaign for president on the future for American women in politics.

GENDER STEREOTYPES IN PUBLIC PERCEPTIONS OF WOMEN PRESIDENTIAL CANDIDATES

Public opinion polls show that voters have viewed female and male political candidates in stereotypical ways, particularly in terms of their personality characteristics, or traits, and in their issue preferences and expertise. A review of recent public opinion polls reveals that voters associate preferred presidential traits and issues primarily with male candidates, but that these gender stereotypes can disappear when they are asked about actual candidates—which seems to have benefited Clinton, at least with public perceptions of her qualifications for president.

Traits

According to a poll conducted by Roper-Starch Worldwide on the viability of women candidates for the U.S. presidency, one-third of the respondents indicated "there are general characteristics about women that make them less qualified to serve."[3] For example, a majority of those polled (51%) indicated that a man would do a better job than a woman leading the nation during a crisis and in making difficult decisions, the top two qualities respondents overall believed were "very important" in a presidential candidate.

Women were favored on the third and fourth most important presidential traits—trustworthiness and honesty—as well as the ability to understand people and moral character. Both women and men were considered equal on intelligence and the ability to forge compromise and obtain consensus. This poll lends further evidence to the observation in the introductory chapter that women candidates are identified more positively with the "softer" traits expected of a U.S. president whereas men are identified with the "tough" leadership traits expected of a U.S. president.

However, when voters are asked about actual—rather than hypothetical—women executive candidates, fewer gender differences emerge in trait associations. For example, a 2006 survey conducted by Lake Research Partners and American Viewpoint of voters in seven states where five women and two men were running for re-election for governor, rated the females higher than the males not only on the attributes of honest, caring, and cooperative but also on tough, problem-solver, and decisive.[4]

Issues

Public opinion polls conducted in the United States reveal gender stereotypical assumptions about female and male issue expertise, which also support the observations detailed in introductory chapter that women are more positively associated with "feminine," domestic, and compassion issues and men with the "masculine" issues such as the economy and foreign policy associated with the presidency.

For example, respondents to the Roper-Starch Worldwide poll said a male president would do a better job than a female president on the top-rated issue of law and order as well as in areas of foreign policy. They said a female president would do a better job on social concerns, such as education, poverty, and homelessness. Although 44 percent of respondents said that there would be no difference on how well a man or woman president would handle the economy—the number two issue overall—more (31%) thought a man would do a better job than a woman (22%).

A more recent poll by CNN/USA Today/Gallup showed similar results when asking respondents whether a female or male president would perform best on issues of national security or domestic policy.[5] Overall, most respondents said a male president would be best in dealing with issues of national security (42%) whereas a woman president would perform better in the realm of domestic policy (45%).

However, this 2005 poll—taken at a time when Clinton was rumored to be considering a run for the 2008 Democratic presidential nomination—showed that most Democrats said a woman president would do the best job in both the area of national security (37%) and domestic policy (62%). Comparatively, 31 percent of Democrats said a male president would do the best job on national security and only 13 percent on domestic policy.

Taken together, these polls show that gender stereotypes could pose roadblocks to women candidates during election cycles where voters are most concerned about foreign policy or national security, such as in 2002 and 2004. But these stereotypes may work in the favor of female candidates when domestic or "women's" issues are more salient, such as in 1992, or when voters are seeking change, such as in 2006. The polls also show that actual women candidates—particularly incumbents—can overcome stereotypical views about gendered traits and issue expertise. That is, they can be seen as tough, caring, and competent on fiscal, social, and global issues.

Within the context of these surveys comparing public perceptions of female and male candidates in general, it is important to consider their opinions on a specific public figure, Hillary Rodham Clinton, particularly as a presidential candidate.

PUBLIC PERCEPTIONS OF HILLARY CLINTON

In the span of her 25-year public persona—from first lady of the state of Arkansas to first lady of the United States, through U.S. senator and presidential candidate, to U.S. secretary of state—Clinton has experienced a rollercoaster of public opinion. A search of the University of Connecticut's Roper Center for Public Opinion Research IPoll databank on

November 1, 2009, revealed that 3,247 polling questions have included Clinton's name.[6] According to Kathleen Frankovic, director of surveys for *CBS News*, "Clinton is the most asked-about woman of all time."[7]

Public perceptions of Clinton can be viewed through opinion surveys assessing her job performance in the various positions she has held in her political life, in presidential preference polls during her campaign for the Democratic nomination for president, and surveys evaluating her qualifications for president in terms of her personality traits and issue expertise. Clinton's job approval ratings show some gendered expectations, as outlined in the introductory chapter, but also show that the public considered her a strong and qualified candidate for president, in both her personality traits and issue expertise, which defies gendered norms.

Job Approval Surveys

One way in which political leaders are evaluated in the United States is by frequent "job approval" surveys of citizens. An analysis of Clinton's approval ratings, especially as first lady, reveals she gets the most favorable reviews by citizens when she is acting within gendered stereotypical role expectations. She gets lower rankings when she violates gendered role expectations.

During her eight-year tenure as first lady of the United States, Clinton's "job approval" ratings ranged from a low of 42 percent favorability in January 1996 to a high of 80 percent in February 1999.[8] She began her tenure as first lady in 1993 with approval ratings in the 60s, which dropped to the low 40s in early 1996 after several scandals—such as the "Travelgate" firings of White House travel office employees and the Whitewater real estate controversy—and Clinton's very public and often controversial role in health care reform. Her approval ratings climbed back to the 70s by 1998, following the public airing of the Monica Lewinsky scandal and impeachment hearings against President Clinton. After President Clinton was acquitted in early 1999, his wife's approval ratings hit the high of 80 percent.

Clinton's job approval ratings as first lady show that the public associated her with the ethical scandals that plagued the Clinton administration during his first term as well as the failure of health care reform. However, the public came to her side when she was wronged by her husband's adultery. After hitting the high of 80 percent in 1999, Clinton's job approval declined to 60 percent favorability by the end of her tenure as first lady, perhaps because of questions over her plans to move to New York state and run for the U.S. Senate, which can be viewed as another gendered stereotypical response.

Clinton became the first woman to win a U.S. Senate seat in the state of New York in 2000, and the first, first lady to run for and become elected to political office, with 55 percent of the vote. She was re-elected to a second term in 2006, with 67 percent of the vote. In November 2007, SurveyUSA showed that her approval rating as a U.S. senator stood at 60 percent overall, with a favorable approval rating of 82 percent by African Americans, 60 percent by Hispanics, and 52 percent of whites. Clinton received slightly higher approval ratings by men (62%) compared to women (59%) and voters 18–54 (62%) compared to voters age 55 and older (57%).[9]

During the course of her campaign for the Democratic nomination for president, Clinton's favorability rating among registered voters ranged from a high of 58 percent in January 2008 to a low of 44 percent in April 2008, according to *ABC News/The Washington Post*.[10] Around the time she announced her intention to run for president on January 20, 2007, 54 percent of registered voters had a favorable opinion of Clinton. By October 2007, her favorability had dropped to 50 percent before rebounding to 58 percent in January 2008. After dropping to 44 percent in April 2008—perhaps due to months of often negative news coverage— Clinton's favorability was back to 54 percent by June 2008 after she withdrew from the presidential race.

Presidential Preference Polls

In addition to the polls that measure the public's favorable or unfavorable opinions of Clinton, surveys of voters' presidential preferences are an important gauge of perceptions toward her candidacy and can reveal gender stereotypes. Analysis of presidential preference polls show that Clinton was the front-running candidate for the 2008 Democratic nomination for president, until the fall of 2007 when studies began showing her negative media coverage in comparison to her male opponents, especially Obama.

Pollsters became interested in Clinton's presidential candidacy as early as 2005. A CNN/USA Today/Gallup poll of registered Democratic voters taken in August 2005 showed Clinton to have an overwhelming 40 percent lead among other likely contenders for the nomination, with Massachusetts Senator John Kerry and former North Carolina Senator John Edwards (who ran together on the 2004 Democratic presidential ticket as president and vice president) tied for second at 16 percent.[11] Obama was not included in the responses to this poll.

A January 2007 USA Today/Gallup poll—taken just as Obama announced his intention to seek the Democratic nomination for president on January 16th—showed Clinton as the frontrunner among

Democrats and Democrat-leaning Independents with 29 percent support followed by Obama with 18 percent. In a February 2007 poll, taken just after Clinton's announcement to seek the Democratic nomination for president, her support among these voters grew to 40 percent with Obama at 22 percent. However, by June 2007, Obama had pulled even with Clinton in the nationwide USA Today/Gallup poll, with 30 percent support compared to 29 percent for Clinton.[12]

Obama also began closing in with likely participants in the January 3, 2008, Iowa caucuses—the first test of presidential candidate strength in the United States. In November 2007, Clinton maintained a 30 percent to 26 percent lead over Obama in a poll of likely Iowa Democratic caucus participants. By December 2007, Obama inched ahead of Clinton with a 33 percent to 29 percent lead over Clinton among Iowa Democrats.[13] Nationally, Clinton held a 45 percent to 27 percent over Obama among Democrats and Democrat-leaning Independents.[14]

Obama went on to win the January 3, 2008, Iowa Democratic caucus, with 34.91 percent support followed by Edwards and Clinton, who finished in a virtual tie with 31.2 percent and 30.43 percent respectively. Despite trailing in the New Hampshire state polls before the nation's first primary contest on January 8, 2008, Clinton won with 39 percent of the vote compared to 36 percent for Obama and 17 percent for Edwards. From January 15th through June 3rd, Clinton won primaries in 20 states— including California, Ohio, Pennsylvania, New York, and Texas—and Obama won 28 primaries, including Illinois, Minnesota, North Carolina, South Carolina, and Virginia.[15]

During the Democratic presidential primary season, Clinton's voter support ranged from a high of 52 percent on February 5, 2008, to a low of 39 percent on May 18, 2008. Between those dates, Clinton and Obama often exchanged the lead in the Gallup Poll's three-day rolling tracking average of Democrats and Democrat-leaning voters nationwide. Obama grabbed the lead for good on May 3, 2008.[16]

Preferred Presidential Traits and Issue Expertise

During her quest for the Democratic nomination for president, Clinton defied most previously identified gender stereotypes found in survey research with strong scores in the roles and attributes associated with the U.S. presidency. For example, a November 2007 poll showed that 73 percent of Americans believed Clinton would work well with Congress; two-thirds or more were positive about the job she would do in proposing new domestic policy legislation, preserving the dignity of the office of the president, and representing the United States abroad; and between 62 percent and 65 percent of Americans expected Clinton to do well in the areas of managing the federal government, the U.S. economy, and U.S. foreign policy. Clinton received her lowest scores—though still more than 50 percent—in the areas of inspiring people and bringing them together and handling the responsibilities as commander-in-chief of the military.[17] Thus, Clinton received strong evaluations on such "masculine" issues of the economy and foreign policy, but lower evaluations on the "masculine" role of commander-in-chief but also on the "feminine" traits of inspiration and unification.

Further evidence of voters' perceptions of Clinton's qualifications as president on typical "masculine" and "feminine" traits and issues can be seen in a January 2007 Gallup poll of Democratic and Democratic-leaning independents and a November 2007 Iowa poll of likely Democratic caucus-goers. According to the Gallup poll, Clinton was widely perceived by Democrats as "having what it takes to do the job of president," with her greatest strength that she was perceived as "the most qualified to be president" by 61 percent of the respondents compared to 13 percent who said Obama was the most qualified.[18] Strong majorities of respondents also perceived Clinton as the strongest leader (59%), best in a crisis (54%), and would manage government effectively (53%)—all "masculine" traits. Clinton was also chosen by respondents as the best Democratic candidate on nine of ten policy issues, with outright majorities preferring her on health care, education, the economy, and energy and the environment and smaller leads on Iraq, terrorism, foreign relations, taxes, and crime.

Interestingly, Obama topped Clinton on only two image attributes, both of which are perceived as stereotypically feminine. For example, Obama was chosen as the most likable candidate by 41 percent of the respondents compared to 31 percent who said Clinton was the most likeable. Obama also topped Clinton—39 percent to 28 percent—as having the highest ethical standards.

Similarly, respondents to the November 2007 Iowa poll rated Clinton the top in a field of eight Democratic presidential candidates on such "masculine" traits as the most knowledgeable about the world (37%), most presidential (27%), and most fiscally responsible (23%) but also the most socially progressive (29%), a "feminine" characteristic. However, her leading opponent, Obama, was rated most likable (33%) and principled (25%), both "feminine" traits.[19]

Taken together, public opinion about Clinton's favorability, support from voters, and qualifications to be president were mostly positive before, during, and after her 16-month campaign for the Democratic nomination for president. Clinton appears to have broken barriers in terms of gender stereotypes held by the public. How did she fare in breaking down gender stereotypes held by the media?

MEDIA FRAMING OF HILLARY CLINTON

Clinton's bid for the 2008 Democratic nomination for president which began on January 20, 2007, with the formation of an exploratory committee—provides yet another opportunity for researchers to analyze gender stereotyping by the media in the quantity and quality of coverage. As noted in the introductory chapter, women political candidates, especially those running for president, often receive less media coverage than their male opponents. Women candidates are more often framed in terms of the "horse-race" of the campaign, sometimes negatively, and receive less issue coverage than male candidates. The media also reinforces gender stereotypes by associating women candidates with certain traits and issues; focusing on their appearance, families, and personality; associating them with their husbands; referring to them by their first names; and emphasizing the novelty of their candidacy as the "first woman."

Academic research centers[20] and studies by scholars[21] in the areas of political science, communication, and journalism have documented that Clinton's media coverage was different—and notably, more negative—than her male opponents. Although Clinton did not lack in the quantity of coverage she received, these studies show that the quality of her coverage was damaged by gendered frames that focused on her campaign strategies,[22] rather than issue emphasis, and attention to her physical appearance and personality, often in a sexist or sexualized way. In addition, Clinton was often associated with her husband.[23]

Although newspaper stories referred to Clinton and her male opponents with similar terms on second reference—e.g., Ms. Clinton and Mr. Obama—Clinton was sometimes called "Hillary" in opinion pieces, whereas Obama was not called "Barack"[24] In addition, the novelty of Clinton's campaign as a serious woman candidate was eclipsed by media attention to Obama's historic run as an African American candidate.[25]

Negative versus Positive Coverage

According to the Center for Media and Public Affairs, on-air evaluations of Clinton by television news programs on ABC, CBS, NBC, and FOX were mostly negative compared to her male opponents from October 2007 through March 2008. Similarly, an October 2007 study by the Project for Excellence in Journalism of 48 different outlets in five media sectors—including newspapers, online news, network television, cable television, and radio—found that Clinton's campaign coverage was 38 percent negative and 27 percent positive compared to Obama's 47 percent positive and 16 percent negative coverage.[26]

The most dramatic difference in television news coverage of Clinton and Obama was seen from December 16, 2007 through January 27, 2008—the months leading up to the January 3rd Iowa caucus, January 8th New Hampshire primary, and February 5th "super Tuesday primaries." During that time, Obama received 84 percent positive coverage compared to Clinton's 51 percent positive coverage. Even after Clinton won the New Hampshire primary, despite polls predicting she would lose, her positive coverage dropped to 47 percent while Obama's positive media coverage held steady at 83 percent.[27]

A content analysis of Clinton's newspaper coverage in Iowa and New Hampshire in the months leading up to the Iowa caucus and New Hampshire primary also revealed that Clinton received significantly more negative coverage and significantly less positive coverage than Obama and Edwards.[28] Of the stories focusing on Clinton, 22 percent were coded as negative. Comparatively, just 2 percent of the stories focusing on Obama were considered negative. And none of the stories focusing on Edwards was coded as negative.

An example of Clinton's negative coverage is illustrated by this December 4, 2007, article in New Hampshire's *Concord Monitor*. The news article begins, "Just call Hillary Clinton kindergarten cop." It goes on to criticize her campaign memo stating Obama's early ambitions to be president as well as being charged by her opponents as "being beholden to special interests."[29]

An opinion column in the November 29, 2007, *Des Moines Register*, criticized Clinton's negative campaigning in response to attacks by her male opponents: "Clinton's attacks just undercut her efforts to change her image as a cold-hearted candidate," implying that strong women candidates are not warm or nice enough. The column also criticized Obama and Edwards for going negative, but not in a gender stereotyped way: "Edwards' negativity mars the sunny, moderate image that served him well in 2004. Obama's attacks distract from the politics of hope he likes to preach."[30]

Of the stories focusing on Edwards, 61 percent were coded as positive. Of the stories focusing on Obama, 66 percent were considered positive. Clinton, on the other hand, received positive coverage in 33 percent of the stories focusing on her candidacy in Iowa and New Hampshire.[31]

Clinton's negative television and newspaper coverage coincided with her drop in the public opinion polls and Obama's rise in popularity among voters. Although we cannot conclude that Clinton's negative media coverage caused her to lose the Democratic nomination for president, we can speculate that it was among the reasons she was not successful.

Horse-Race versus Issue Coverage

Two studies found that Clinton was more likely to receive horse-race coverage—focusing on campaign strategies—by the media rather than attention to her issues. As noted in the introductory chapter, such framing can be highly detrimental to a woman candidate's campaign as it makes it difficult for voters to become well-informed about her policy preferences.

For example, the study of newspapers in Iowa and New Hampshire[32] found that only 8 percent of the stories focusing on Clinton emphasized issues compared to 24 percent of the stories about Obama and 23 percent on Edwards. Clinton was linked most often with health care, an issue that she often touted in her television ads and speeches, but also with the war in Iraq, for which her support in the U.S. Senate was seen as a negative with voters, especially in Iowa.

Clinton also received more horse-race coverage than her male opponents in Iowa and New Hampshire. Of the stories focusing on Clinton, 27 percent were written in the campaign frame—including who's ahead or behind, opinion polls, fundraising efforts, or predictions of outcomes—compared to 17 percent of the stories on Obama and 16 percent of the stories about Edwards.

A study that examined Clinton's media framing in the *New York Times* and *USA Today* between December 31, 2007, and January 14, 2008, also found that Clinton was much more likely to be framed in terms of a "game" —which was defined as a personality contest or strategy, including the tactics of political campaigning—than issues.[33] In fact, 88 percent of the stories about Clinton employed a game frame whereas only 12 percent used an issue frame.

By emphasizing Clinton's campaign strategies over her positions on the issues, the media may not have provided enough information to voters on which to cast their ballots in the Democratic primary for president. In addition, the emphasis on the horse-race aspects of her campaign—e.g., that she was falling behind or losing her lead to Obama in the polls— served to frame Clinton negatively and may have diminished her viability with voters.

Personality, Appearance, and Families

The content analyses of newspapers in Iowa and New Hampshire as well as the *New York Times* and *USA Today* reveal few gender stereotypes in their coverage of Clinton's personality, appearance, and families in comparison to her male opponents.

In the study of newspapers in Iowa and New Hampshire,[34] all three candidates were most likely to be covered in terms of the "candidate" frame—e.g., their personality traits, character and ethics; family; previous record; and experience in office—than their campaign strategies or issues. In fact, 47 percent of the stories focusing on Clinton, 44 percent of the stories about Obama, and 42 percent of the stories on Edwards emphasized their personalities, characteristics, and families. This finding is further evidence of the media's increasing coverage of candidate image—whether the candidate is female or male—over their issues and policy positions.

In the content analysis of the *New York Times* and *USA Today*,[35] Clinton was framed in terms of her appearance in only 12 percent and her family in only 4 percent of the stories. Even though the appearance frame was rarely used to portray Clinton, her clothing was mentioned twice and her hairstyle three times. Similarly, even though the family frame was rarely used, references were made to her family—especially her husband Bill Clinton, whose name was mentioned in 60 percent of the coverage. Clinton was rarely portrayed as a homemaker and motherly figure, with only one reference to her as a mother, seven references to her as a wife, and five references to her daughter Chelsea.

Beyond the general findings of these two content analyses, examples of blatantly sexist references to Clinton's appearance and personality were easy to find in the mainstream and new media. Web sites such as Women in Media and News, http://www.wimnonline.org/, The New Agenda, http://thenewagenda.net/, and Media Matters for America, http://mediamatters.org/; blogs; and newspaper articles documented numerous examples of the sexist attacks launched against Clinton in the 2008 campaign. Some of the more blatant and widely discussed examples of Clinton's sexist media coverage included:

- In a July 20, 2007, article in *The Washington Post*, fashion writer Robin Givhan criticized Clinton for showing cleavage in an outfit she wore while speaking on the Senate floor on July 18th.[36] Other media outlets picked up the story, devoting substantial coverage to Clinton's cleavage as a campaign strategy. According to a report by Media Matters for America, MSNBC devoted almost 24 minutes to segments discussing Clinton's "cleavage" between 9 AM and 5 AM on July 30th.
- Three articles in the September 30, 2007, *New York Times* commented on Clinton's laugh, evoking negative stereotypes about women. Patrick Healy dubbed it the "Clinton cackle,"[37] Frank Rich called her laugh "calculating,"[38] and Maureen Dowd wrote that Clinton was transitioning "from nag to wag."[39] On October 1st, ABC's *Good Morning America*, CNN's *Situation Room*, Fox News' *Hannity & Colmes*, and MSNBC's *Hardball* all included stories about Clinton's laugh, according to Media Matters for America. One reporter who drew attention to the sexist connotations in the coverage of Clinton's

laugh was Joan Vennochi of *The Boston Globe*. "HENS CACKLE. So do witches. And, so does the front-runner in the Democratic presidential contest," she wrote on September 30, 2007, noting that the media's critique of Clinton had moved "from chest to throat, and to a sound associated with female fowl."[40]

- References as a "white bitch" on MSNBC and CNN; a blood-sucking "vampire" on FOX; as the maniac stalker played by Glenn Close in the movie *Fatal Attraction* on CNN, "The McLaughlin Group," and *London Sunday Times*; as an "unkillable" zombie moving "relentlessly forward" in the *London Sunday Times*; as the "wicked witch of the west" on CNN; and as "everyone's first wife standing outside of probate court," a murderous mother trying to "smother infant Obama in his crib," the scheming, manipulative Nurse Ratched in the movie *One Flew Over the Cuckoo's Nest*, as a "she devil," and as the castrating Lorena Bobbitt, all on MSNBC.[41]

"Wife of"

The introductory chapter notes that women political candidates with ties to powerful men are often covered by the media in the "wife of" frame, which questions their capacity to be competent and autonomous individuals. Several examples of the "wife of" frame were found in Clinton's negative coverage in the content analysis of newspapers in Iowa and New Hampshire. The media raised concerns about the role of Clinton's husband not only in her presidential campaign, but also in her administration if she was elected president.

For example, a column that appeared in the November 15, 2007, *Concord Monitor* under the headline "Two for the Price of One Will Test the System: Clinton Co-Presidency Could Mean Problems" criticized presidential candidate Clinton's role in health care reform as first lady and raised concerns about the prospects of a dual presidency:

> When Bill Clinton was president, the large policy enterprise that was entrusted to the first lady—health care reform—crashed in ruins ... the awkwardness of having an unelected but uniquely influential partner to the president in charge affected every step of the process ... she was never again asked to take on such a project. And this was simply the confusion sown by having the first lady in charge. Put the former president in the picture—however sanitized or insulated his role is supposed to be—and the dimensions of the problem loom even larger.[42]

A December 15, 2007, article in the *Des Moines Register* quoted an Obama superdelegate from Wyoming that Clinton was "not electable because of mistakes made by her husband when he was president." The delegate went on to say, "We also will be the target of the locker-room jokes that rightfully belong to Bill Clinton" by electing his wife as president.[43]

Media references to Bill Clinton's adulterous "mistakes" while president as well as his power and influence in the marriage and the specter of a co-presidency no doubt hurt voter perceptions of Hillary Clinton. The media (and even a speech by Michelle Obama during the campaign) implied that Clinton could not take care of her own house and husband when he resorted to affairs and also that she was not independent and competent enough to govern on her own as president.

Masculinity versus Femininity

The introductory chapter describes how women political candidates are often caught in the "double bind" of masculinity and femininity. They must exhibit certain "masculine" traits—such as toughness, leadership, and strength—which voters associate with holding executive office, but they also need to have "feminine" characteristics or risk being punished for subverting gendered norms. In Clinton's news coverage, she was often described and framed in masculine terms.

For example, in her coverage in the *New York Times* and *USA Today*,[44] Clinton was most likely to be framed in masculine terms—such as tough, powerful, independent, uncompromising, or authoritative—in 42 percent of the stories. In contrast, Obama's coverage focused on more traditionally feminine traits. For example, Obama was never portrayed as "tough" or "aggressive" whereas Clinton was portrayed as "tough" in 62 percent and "aggressive" in 20 percent of the articles. Some of the other adverbs used to describe Clinton—each mentioned more than once—were disciplined, regal, defiant, private/secretive, methodical, cold, steely, and strong.

This study confirms previous research on the contradictory expectations women candidates face today. Women candidates, like Clinton, need to be tough and aggressive to compete successfully with their male opponents to get elected. But, in exhibiting masculine traits associated with political office, they also run the risk of appearing too unfeminine and therefore unacceptable to voters. As Daniela Dimitrova and Elizabeth Geske observe in their content analysis of Clinton's coverage in the *New York Times* and *USA Today*, "U.S. female politicians today have to walk a fine line between being strong and being feminine at the same time."[45]

First Name and "First Woman"

The evidence is mixed on references to Clinton's first name in comparison with her male opponents. However, the novelty of her campaign as the "first woman" making a strong run for the presidential nomination was actually eclipsed by the novelty of Obama's success as an African American presidential candidate.

The study of the *New York Times* and *USA Today* found that straight news stories referred to Clinton and Obama similarly, based on their editorial style manuals. However, many of the quoted sources and most of the editorialists referred to Clinton as "Hillary" and Obama as "Obama." "This is interesting from a feminist point of view," Dimitrova and Geske observed, "as using first names is a way of 'infantilizing' women, and marking them as 'othered' or 'different.' "[46] None of the news stories coded for this study referred to Obama as simply "Barack."

The use of Clinton's first name and the last names of her male opponents were debated in the media and on political Web sites. For example, National Public Radio's "On the Media" host Bob Garfield interviewed Marie Wilson, executive director of the White House Project, when he was chastised by listeners for referring to Clinton as "Hillary" and her opponents by their last name. In defending his use of "Hillary," Garfield said that producers of the radio show went on Clinton's official campaign Web site and were "struck by the fact that the word 'Clinton' is barely there. She's running as 'Hillary.' "[47]

An August 18, 2009, post on the Web site Jezebel, discussed how women politicians and the media contribute to the use of female candidates' first names in their news coverage. In Clinton's case, using her first name in campaign materials "was probably in part an attempt to make someone perceived as strident and cold seem friendly and relatable," Anna North wrote, adding that "Bill Clinton complicates the issue here—not only might 'Clinton' signs have been confusing to some, but the campaign likely wanted to distance itself from associations with Bill's presidency, and from accusations that the Clintons were trying to build a dynasty."[48]

Although Clinton and other political women may choose to use their first name in a campaign, it is also a decision that the media makes for them. "Again, this makes a certain amount of practical sense in Clinton's case—her husband is still in the news enough that disambiguation is sometimes necessary," North wrote, nevertheless calling for the media to "give female public figures the same respect we give men" by using their last name on second reference.

As for the "first woman" media frame, Clinton received significantly less media discussion of the historic nature of her candidacy as compared to Obama. According to Regina Lawrence and Melody Rose, Clinton was not marginalized—as women candidates before her—as a 'first,' in fact she was upstaged in this regard by the "nation's understandable interest" in Obama. The researchers conclude that Clinton "actually may have benefited from greater attention to her place among 'firsts', but chose to avoid that moniker."[49]

After beginning the twenty-first century with six years of mostly equitable media coverage of female and male candidates for governor and

U.S. Senate in terms of quantity as well as quality (e.g., assessments of their viability, positive versus negative slant, and mentions of their appearance), Clinton's media coverage—as well as that of the 2008 Republican vice presidential nominee Sarah Palin, the former governor of Alaska—certainly can be seen as a setback. (See the chapter by Gina Woodall, Kim Fridkin, and Jill Carle, in this book, for further discussion of biases in Palin's coverage.)

The sexism that Clinton and Palin encountered in the media coverage in the 2008 presidential campaign may entangle with gender biases within the electorate to create an untenable position for women candidates. By reinforcing some of the traditional stereotypes held by the public about men and women and their roles in society, the media may have an impact on the outcome of elections and, thus, upon how the nation is governed.

CONCLUSION

This comparison of Clinton's public opinion polling and media coverage during her bid for the Democratic nomination for president reveals that some barriers and biases toward women candidates were indeed shattered by her campaign. However, while progress was made in terms of favorable public opinion and even voting preferences for a woman presidential candidate, the media coverage of Clinton's campaign indicates a retreat to gender stereotypes and blatant sexism not generally seen in the past six years.

Analyses of Clinton's media coverage by a variety of mediums—newspapers, television, radio, and Internet—in her campaign for the Democratic nomination for president agree that she received more negative coverage than her male opponents and that her coverage was more likely to focus on campaign strategies rather than issues. Although it has been a longtime and common practice for the media to focus on the "horse-race" aspects of a presidential campaign—and to give greater and often negative scrutiny to the frontrunner—the fact that Clinton received more negative coverage focused on her campaign strategies than accorded her male opponents throughout the campaign suggests that the media treated her differently. Her different and perhaps gendered treatment by the mainstream media is underscored by the fact that Obama received often overwhelming positive coverage and less scrutiny once he became the frontrunner for the nomination.

Clinton also received blatantly sexist references to her appearance and personality, both in the mainstream media and, most often, in the new media of blogs, emails, and political and social networking Web sites.

Some of the most negative and sexist comments about Clinton (and Palin) in 2008 first appeared in the new media and then spilled over into the mainstream media in the coverage of their campaigns. The online universe of political commentary operates outside of traditional media editorial boundaries and is often offensive, sometimes incisive, and often unsubstantiated.

Common themes that originated in the new media—and spilled over into the mainstream media—about Clinton in her 2008 presidential campaign portrayed her as psychotic; a power-hungry stalker, killer, or castrator; and questioned her sexuality. New media commentary on Palin often exploited her "feminized" sexuality, comparing her to a Barbie doll and photoshopping her head onto a bikini-clad woman with an automatic weapon.

Like many women before her, Clinton was often associated with the power of her husband. But unlike many female candidates breaking new territory, Clinton was not marginalized as the "first woman," which actually may have hurt her campaign when running against another "first" in Obama.

Although Clinton's media coverage represents a setback—rather than progress—for women political candidates, especially after eight years of mostly equitable coverage, it was just one of many factors that contributed to her defeat. Other factors include the rules under which the Democratic Party selects its presidential candidates, mistakes made by the Clinton campaign within that context, questions and concerns about the influence of Bill Clinton on Hillary Clinton's presidency, and the juxtaposition of gender versus race as presidential firsts.

First, the rules under which Democrats select their presidential candidates favored Obama. Under Democratic Party reforms enacted in 1972, candidates receiving at least 15 percent of support in a primary or caucus are awarded a share of delegates to the nominating conventions in proportion to the vote they receive in each congressional district. Some have questioned whether these rules go too far in awarding delegates to all candidates, instead of focusing on the frontrunners. Clinton and Obama were the clear frontrunners throughout the campaign for the Democratic nomination for president, with candidates at the bottom of the pack siphoning votes from each. Edwards' candidacy hurt Clinton most in the state of Iowa, where the former North Carolina senator and vice presidential candidate had an organization in place since the 2004 presidential campaign.

By contrast, the Republican system for delegate selection varies state-by-state, from "winner-takes-all" states, in which the winner of the state-wide primary receives all of the delegates allocated to a state by the national party, to more complex allocations that consider statewide and congressional-level winners on a proportional basis. According to an analysis by Lauren C. Bell, Obama would have been able to win the Democratic nomination using the Republican's selection mechanism. However, Clinton would have handily won the Democratic nomination for president in a "winner-takes-all" system, as is employed to determine the winners of all but two states (Nebraska and Maine) in the general election.[50]

Second, the Clinton campaign made strategic mistakes within the context of the Democratic Party delegate selection process. In their book on Clinton's presidential nomination bid, Lawrence and Rose summarize several tactical errors made by the campaign—including focusing on primary states, declining to train workers on the intricacies of delegate selection in caucus states, and assuming the nomination would be settled by Super Tuesday on February 5, 2008. Thus, Clinton spent a disproportionate amount of her campaign funds in the months prior to Super Tuesday, draining her coffers as the battle waged on for an additional four months.[51]

Third, as a former first lady running for president, there were questions throughout her campaign about former President Clinton's role in the campaign and a possible Hillary Clinton administration. Polls show that the former president was both a benefit and distraction to her campaign, particularly in southern states where he angered African American voters with some of his comments about Obama. He also was accused of stealing the spotlight and putting Hillary Clinton in the background while campaigning for her nomination. According to a recent analysis of Clinton's campaign, the former first lady had trouble establishing her own authenticity as a presidential candidate because her husband relegated her to a secondary position on the campaign trail and drew harsh criticism from the media and distrust from her advisors.[52]

Fourth, we must consider the historic firsts of a woman running against an African American for the Democratic nomination for president and whether race trumps gender. Although there is no doubt that barriers exist for both women and minority candidates in their election to political office, in this particular contest of presidential firsts, race did trump gender. Several analyses have concluded that the presidency is still defined by voters and the media in very male terms, regardless of race. Polls, taken at the time that both Obama and Clinton were rumored to run for the Democratic nomination for president, indicated that more American voters were willing to vote for an African American candidate than a woman candidate for president. In the end, Clinton received strong support from rural whites while Obama received almost unanimous support from African Americans.

However, most relevant to this discussion, is the conclusion by several analysts that "race trumped gender" in terms of media discussion of the campaign. "Uncomfortable questions about race relations in America formed the backdrop of much campaign coverage," noted Lawrence and Rose. "Discussion of women's struggles in American society were more muted." They found significantly less media coverage of the historic nature of Clinton's presidential candidacy, and her primary victories, than of Obama's campaign.[53]

So, what does this all mean for the future of women in American politics, especially those running for president? I believe that despite her negative and often blatantly sexist media coverage, which could give future women candidates considerable pause, Hillary Clinton emerged as a strong and fierce competitor who ultimately found her voice. Polling data suggests that she was successful in challenging gender stereotypes about a woman serving as the chief executive officer of the United States. The media has been put on notice that their coverage of Clinton was often sexist and unfair. Perhaps, they will do better next time.

Recent polls attest to Hillary Clinton's popularity after her historic run for the U.S. nomination for president. In August 2009, a USA Today/Gallup poll asked adults nationwide if Clinton should run for president again. Overall, 52 percent of respondents said "yes." Among Democrats, 75 percent said they would like to see Clinton run for president again.[54] As U.S. secretary of state, Clinton has received very favorable ratings. For example, a CNN/Opinion Research Poll conducted in March 2009 showed that 71 percent of adults nationwide approved of the way Clinton was handling her job as secretary of state, including 90 percent of Democrats and 50 percent of Republicans. The same public opinion poll put Obama's approval rating as president at 64 percent.[55]

Overall, the future of American women in politics seems better than before Clinton's campaign for the Democratic nomination for president in 2008. Clinton did confront many gender stereotypes, especially from the media. But she did shatter some barriers and biases and perhaps raised consciousness and concerns about sexist coverage of women politicians by the media, which should benefit women who run for legislative and executive office in the future.

Acknowledgments

Dianne Bystrom thanks her undergraduate student assistants—Ashley Margo and Emily Kuster—for their help with the content analysis of Hillary Clinton's early newspaper coverage in Iowa and New Hampshire and graduate assistant, Narren Brown, for his help with the statistical analysis. She also acknowledges the input of Iowa State University colleague, Dr. Daniela Dimitrova, as she conducted her analysis of Clinton's coverage in the national media surrounding her "tearful moment" prior to the New Hampshire primary. And, of course, she acknowledges the support of her husband, Keith Bystrom, who helps keep her life in balance.

NOTES

1. Hillary Rodham Clinton, concession speech, June 7, 2008. Available online at http://www.womenspeecharchive.org/women/profile/speech/index.cfm ?ProfileID=65&SpeechID=643

2. Clinton, concession speech.

3. *Roper-Starch Worldwide*, "Women in Elected Office Survey Identifies Obstacles for Women as Political Leaders," 2000, http://www.us.deloitte.com.

4. *Positioning Women to Win: New Strategies for Turning Gender Stereo-types into Competitive Advantages* (Cambridge, MA: The Barbara Lee Family Foundation, 2006).

5. Jeffrey M. Jones, "Nearly Half of Americans Think U.S. Will Soon Have a Woman President," October 4, 2005, http//www.cawp.rutgers.edu/Facts/Elections/pres08_polls/Gallup_NearlyHalfof America.pdf.

6. Roper Center for Public Opinion Research, search of IPoll databank for polling questions between 1990 and 2009 with "Hillary Clinton," November 1, 2009, http://www.ropercenter.uconn.edu.

7. Kathy Frankovic, "What's in a Name?" July 11, 2007, http://www.cbsnews.com/stories/2007/07/11/opinion/pollpositions/main3043678.shtml.

8. Jeffrey E. Cohen, "The Polls: Public Attitudes toward the First Lady," *Presidential Studies Quarterly* 30, no. 2 (2000): 375–381.

9. Survey USA, November 20, 2007, http://www.surveyusa.com/client/PollReport.aspx?g=92ccc75f-f0b2-4717-8958-bd125e4fbef4.

10. *Polling Report*, "In the News–Hillary Clinton," http://www.pollingreport.com/C2.htm#Hillary (accessed September 2, 2009).

11. Jeffery M. Jones, "Hillary Clinton Easily Paces Democratic Field," August 11, 2005, http://www.gallup.com/poll/17773/Hillary-Clinton-Easily-Paces-Democratic-Field.aspx.

12. Joseph Carroll, "Hillary Clinton, Barack Obama Tie in Latest Democratic Trial Heat," June 5, 2007, http://www.gallup.com/poll/27763/Hillary-Clinton-Barack-Obama-Tie-Latest-Democratic-Trial-Heat.aspx.

13. *Reuters*, "Clinton and Obama Deadlocked in Iowa: Poll," December 9, 2007, http://www.reuters.com/article/topNews/idUSN1955196620071219.

14. Joseph Carroll, "Clinton Maintains Large Lead over Obama Nationally," December 18, 2007, http://www.gallup.com/poll/103351/Clinton-Maintains-Large-Lead-Over-Obama-Nationally.aspx.

15. *New York Times*, "Primary Season Election Results," June 4, 2008, http://politics.nytimes.com/election-guide/2008/results/votes/.

16. *Polling Report*, "White House 2008: Democratic Nomination," http://www.pollingreport.com/wh08dem.htm (accessed September 9, 2009).

17. Lydia Saad, "Clinton Considered Presidential on 11 Dimensions," November 7, 2007, http://www.gallup.com/poll/102508/Clinton-Considered-Presidential-Dimensions.aspx.

18. Lydia Saad, "Clinton Eclipses Obama and Edwards on Leadership," January 31, 2007, http://www.gallup.com/poll/26332/Clinton-Eclipses-Obama-Edwards-Leadership.aspx.

19. "Iowa Poll of 500 Likely Democratic Caucus Participants," *Des Moines Register*, December 2, 2007, p. 2.

20. See "The Invisible Primary-Invisible No Longer: A First Look at Coverage of the 2008 Presidential Campaign," The Project for Excellence in Journalism, 2007, http://www.journalism.org/node/8187 and Donald Rieck, "Media Boost Obama, Bash 'Billary': NBC is Toughest on Hillary; FOX has Heaviest Coverage," February 1, 2008, http://www.cmpa.com/studies_election_2_1_08.htm.

21. See Dianne Bystrom, "Gender and U.S. Presidential Politics: Early Newspaper Coverage of Hillary Clinton's Bid for the White House" (paper presented at the annual meeting of the American Political Science Association, Boston, MA, August 29, 2008); Daniela V. Dimitrova and Elizabeth Geske, "To Cry or Not to Cry: Media Framing of Hillary Clinton in the Wake of the New Hampshire Primary" (paper presented at the annual meeting of the International Communication Association, Chicago, IL, May 24, 2009); and Regina G. Lawrence and Melody Rose, *Hillary Clinton's Race for the White House: Gender Politics and the Media on the Campaign Trail* (Boulder, CO: Lynne Rienner Publishers, 2009), p. 227.

22. See Bystrom, "Early Newspaper Coverage of Hillary Clinton's Bid," and Dimitrova and Geske, "Media Framing."

23. Dimitrova and Geske, "Media Framing."

24. Ibid.

25. Lawrence and Rose, *Hillary Clinton's Race*.

26. "The Invisible Primary-Invisible No Longer."

27. Rieck, "Media Boost Obama, Bash 'Billary'."

28. Bystrom, "Early Newspaper Coverage of Hillary Clinton's Bid."

29. Shira Schoenberg, "Top Democrats Intensify Attacks: Obama's Past Surfaces in Kindergarten Memo," *Concord Monitor*, December 4, 2007.

30. David Yepsen, "When Throwing Flames, Be Careful About Burns," *Des Moines Register*, November 29, 2007.

31. Bystrom, "Early Newspaper Coverage of Hillary Clinton's Bid."

32. Ibid.

33. Dimitrova and Geske, "Media Framing."

34. Bystrom, "Early Newspaper Coverage of Hillary Clinton's Bid."

35. Dimitrova and Geske, "Media Framing."

36. Robin Givhan, "Hillary Clinton's Tentative Dip into New Neckline Territory," *Washington Post*, July 27, 2007, http://www.washingtonpost.com/wp-dyn/content/article/2007/07/19/AR2007071902668.html.

37. Patrick Healy, "The Clinton Conundrum: What's Behind the Laugh?" *New York Times*, September 30, 2007, http://www.nytimes.com/2007/09/30/us/politics/30clinton.html.

38. Frank Rich, "Is Hillary Clinton the New Old Al Gore?" *New York Times*, September 30, 2007, http://www.nytimes.com/2007/09/30/opinion/30rich.html.

39. Maureen Dowd, "The Nepotism Tango," *New York Times*, September 30, 2007, http://www.nytimes.com/2007/09/30/opinion/30dowd.html?_r=1&hp.

40. Joan Vennochi, "That Clinton Cackle," *Boston Globe*, September 30, 2007, http://www.boston.com/news/globe/editorial_opinion/oped/articles/2007/09/30/that_clinton_cackle/.

41. Media Matters for America, search for articles on Hillary Clinton, http://mediamatters.org/issues_topics/search_results?qstring=Hillary+Clinton (accessed September 9, 2009).

42. David Broder, "Two for Price of One Will Test the System: Clinton Co-Presidency Could Mean Problems," *Concord Monitor*, November 15, 2007.

43. Jennifer Jacobs and Jason Clayworth, "Clinton, Obama Campaigns Condemn Personal Attacks, Launch Accusations," *Des Moines Register*, December 15, 2007.

44. Dimitrova and Geske, "Media Framing."

45. Ibid., p. 20.

46. Ibid., p. 14.

47. "Say My Name, Say My Name," On the Media, National Public Radio, November 30, 2007, http://www.onthemedia.org/transcripts/2007/11/30/03.

48. Anna North, "Hillary, Sarah, and Kay: What's Wrong with Female Politicians' Last Names?" August 18, 2009, http://jezebel.com/5340033/hillary-sarah-and-kay-whats-wrong-with-female-politicians-last-names.

49. Lawrence and Melody Rose, *Hillary Clinton's Race*, p. 227.

50. Lauren C. Bell. "Alternative Approaches to Delegate Selection and Their Effects on the 2008 Democratic Primary Election Results," in Theodore F. Sheckels, ed., Cracked But Not Shattered: *Hillary Rodham Clinton's Unsuccessful Campaign for the Presidency* (Lanham, MD: Lexington Books, in press).

51. Lawrence and Rose, *Hillary Clinton's Race*.

52. James M. Schnoebelen, Diana B. Carlin, and Benjamin R. Warner, "Hillary, You Can't Go Home Again: The Entrapment of the First Lady Role," in Theodore F. Sheckels ed., *Cracked But Not Shattered*.

53. Lawrence and Rose, *Hillary Clinton's Race*, p. 216.

54. Jeffrey M. Jones, "Hillary's Stock Still High Among Democrats," August 26, 2009, http://www.gallup.com/poll/109837/Hillarys-Stock-Still-High-Among-Democrats.aspx.

55. Paul Steinhauser, "Poll: Clinton Has High Job Approval Rating," March 25, 2009, http://www.cnn.com/2009/POLITICS/03/25/clinton.poll/index.html.

CHAPTER FIVE

Sarah Palin: "Beauty Is Beastly?" An Exploratory Content Analysis of Media Coverage

Gina Serignese Woodall, Kim L. Fridkin, and Jill Carle

Hottest VP from the Coolest State

> —prevalent slogan on buttons, posterboards, and
> the like at the Republican National Convention,
> September 1–4, Minneapolis, Minnesota

On August 29, 2008, Republican presidential nominee Senator John McCain announced that Alaska Governor Sarah Palin would be his vice-presidential nominee.[1] The news attention following the announcement was intense. Picked for her "grit, integrity, good sense and fierce devotion to the common good," the 44-year-old governor of Alaska was a force to be reckoned with.[2] A self-described "hockey mom," Governor Palin never expected to be running for vice president. Governor Palin recognized the symbolism of being chosen as Senator McCain's choice for the vice-presidential nominee. Just about two months prior to Senator McCain's pick of Governor Palin, Senator Hillary Clinton ended her fiercely fought primary race against Senator Barack Obama. "Hillary left 18 million cracks in the highest, hardest glass ceiling in America. But it turns out the women of America aren't finished yet, and we can shatter that glass ceiling once and for all," Palin noted at the Republican National Convention.[3]

In running as the first female Republican vice-presidential candidate, Governor Sarah Palin needed to increase positive assessments of her candidacy. However, as a female candidate, she faced different obstacles than her male colleagues. To begin, Sarah Palin needed to decide how to manage the "Double bind" created by common gender stereotypes.

In particular, should she emphasize her stereotypical strengths in the campaign or should she try to revise people's views of her stereotypical weaknesses?

Given the prevailing electoral climate, including U.S. involvement in two wars and an emerging economic crisis, we expect that Governor Palin needed to reassure potential supporters that she was competent to deal with economic and foreign policy matters. In particular, we expect Governor Palin to adopt a strategy aimed at revising perceptions of her stereotypical weaknesses. Given the political context of the 2008 election, it is unlikely that Governor Palin focused on her stereotypical strengths by emphasizing her abilities to deal with social issues, like the environment, health care, or education.

Even if Governor Palin sought to emphasize male issues over female issues in her campaign communications, this strategy would only be effective if the news media represented her messages in their campaign coverage. Prior research examining candidates for statewide office suggest a distortion between women candidates' messages and the news media's representation of their messages.[4] In this chapter, we will examine how the news media covered Governor Palin's policy messages in their 2008 campaign coverage.

While issues are an important component of a candidate's "presentation of self," candidates also need to decide which personality dimensions to highlight in their campaigns. According to research on voting behavior, voters weigh assessments of a candidate's competence more heavily than other personal characteristics.[5] For women candidates, this can be problematic since stereotypes lead people to view men as more competent than women. Women candidates often try to revise stereotypes regarding traits by emphasizing their embodiment of male traits, like leadership, intelligence, and experience.[6] Governor Palin may have embraced this same strategy.

However, there are at least three reasons why Governor Palin may have chosen to accentuate her "female" traits in her campaigns. First, Governor Palin's elected experience was limited (first-term governor, small-town mayor), making it difficult to emphasize her qualifications, competence, and experience. Second, running for vice president, as compared to president, may have given her the opportunity to show how her personality complemented her male running mate, leading her to focus on her "female" traits. Finally, prominent ethics scandals during the fall campaign, including the indictment of Senator Ted Stevens of Alaska for failing to report gifts received from a major pipeline company, may have encouraged Governor Palin to emphasize her honesty and integrity. Governor Palin, by depicting herself as someone who would enhance honesty and integrity in government, not only highlights a stereotypical female strength, but also echoes a theme of her running mate, John McCain.

In this chapter, we will examine the news media's representation of Sarah Palin's personality (and thus trait coverage), exploring—when possible—the connection between the candidate's own message and media portrayal of that message.

In addition to examining how Sarah Palin navigated the "Double bind," we also examine how the news media framed her bid for vice president. We know that the news media rely on specific criteria of newsworthiness when deciding how to cover political events and political news.[7] One of these criteria of newsworthiness is "novelty."[8] Sarah Palin, as the first female Republican vice-presidential candidate, clearly met the news media's criteria of "novelty." Given that Sarah Palin was a "novel" candidate, we expect that she received more news coverage than her male counterpart, Senator Joe Biden. In addition, her novelty as a woman vice-presidential candidate may have framed *how* she was covered. In particular, the "first woman" frame may have generated a great deal of attention of her appearance, her family, and her role as a mother.

Finally, we will look at how Sarah Palin's navigation of the Double bind, as well as the news media's framing of the Sarah Palin story, influenced the tone of news coverage. We will see whether the tone of this news attention varied over the course of the campaign. A cursory look at the campaign suggests that the initial announcement of Governor Sarah Palin as Senator McCain's choice for vice president, as well as coverage of her speech at the Republican National Convention, generated mostly positive coverage. However, in the week or two following the speech, the media coverage of Governor Palin appeared to shift, becoming much more critical. News organizations bristled at being denied access to Governor Palin for interviews or news conferences.[9] As part of the McCain campaign's strategy, Governor Palin agreed to three one-on-one interviews and no press conferences during the length of the fall campaign.[10] We will examine how the McCain media strategy influenced the tone of coverage given to Governor Palin during the length of the fall campaign.

SAMPLE AND NEWS SOURCES

In this content analysis of Sarah Palin's media coverage, we used Lexis Nexis to identify and collect every news transcript that aired on NBC, CBS, ABC, FOX, and CNN focusing on Sarah Palin's campaign.[11] Figure 5.1 displays the percentage of stories coded for each of the news outlet. Our sampling procedure produced 131 news transcripts, with an average number of 19 paragraphs.[12] In coding the news transcripts, we treated the paragraph as the unit of analysis within the transcript.[13]

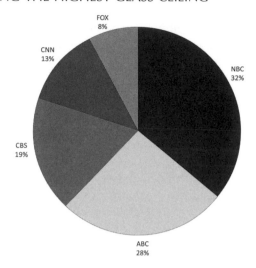

Figure 5.1   Coded News Stories from Network and Cable Television Programs

We began sampling when John McCain announced Sarah Palin as his running mate, August 29, 2008 and continued through Election Day, November 4, 2008. We relied on transcripts because of the sheer amount of coverage about Sarah Palin, and we wanted to obtain coverage from the mainstream news shows, both in the morning and evening (e.g., *The Today Show*, *NBC Evening News with Brian Williams*), as well as the more opinionated, tabloid news shows (*Hannity and Colmes*; *No Bull, No Bias with Campbell Brown*).[14]

We relied on news transcripts, as opposed to newspapers, Internet, or radio due to the fact that the vast majority of citizens still obtain the bulk of their news information from TV.[15] Throughout the long campaign, nearly 80 percent of voters relied on television news programs for their election coverage, while just over 25 percent used the Internet for the same news.[16] Additionally, according to *Nielsen*, although the Internet played a pivotal role in the 2008 presidential campaign, the vast majority of citizens continued to receive their news *only* from the TV on Election Day (135 million), versus those who *only* got their news online (5.2 million).

In short, our goal was to capture the news coverage of Sarah Palin viewed by most citizens. By selecting the major news networks (ABC, CBS, and NBC) as well as the two most popular cable news programs (FOX and CNN), we were able to examine the bulk of Sarah Palin's coverage from late August to Election Day. We coded the articles for both manifest (e.g., number of mentions) and latent (tone) content. We looked at the quantity of Palin's coverage, the attention devoted to her family and her appearance, as well as specific issue and trait coverage. The code sheet employed in the content analysis is presented in Appendix A.

Gender Stereotypes and the Double-Bind

Traits

As presented in the introductory chapter, people's adherence to gender stereotypes is pervasive and persistent, and is the driving force behind the Double bind. Since the late 1950s, research suggests that men are perceived as being bold, rational, and straightforward, while women are perceived as emotional, empathetic, and passive.[17] In a recent study, Jennifer Lawless found that citizens are more likely to view male politicians as assertive, aggressive, and self-confident and female politicians as emotional, compassionate, and compromising.[18] Additionally, people continue to identify male traits (i.e., self-confident, tough, and assertive) as coinciding with important leadership traits more often than female traits. Put simply, traits associated with women generally do not coincide with standard leadership traits. Therefore, women are not perceived as being effective leaders, regardless of the traits they stress in their campaign.[19]

In our analysis, we are interested in examining how the news media described Sarah Palin's personal traits. We expect the media to focus on different types of personality traits for both men and women, based on gender stereotypes.[20] Based on the gender stereotyping literature, we classify the following traits as "female" traits: honesty, authenticity, family-oriented, religious, honorable, inexperienced, unintelligent, unknowledgeable, weak leader, pretty, victim, nagger, incapable, overly ambitious, maternal, opinionated, sassy, and incompetent. The traits categorized as "male" traits are ambitious, articulate, assertive, dishonest, untrustworthy, experienced, intelligent, strong leader, funny, tough, strong, and fighter.

As a point of departure, we look at the traits Sarah Palin chose to emphasize in her own communications. In particular, we examine Sarah Palin's speech at the Republican Convention. While traits were not a focus of her speech, she did mention her personal characteristics a number of times. In particular, in the first twenty-five paragraphs of her speech, eight paragraphs (32%) mentioned her role as mother or discussed her family. For example, Governor Palin explains, "I'm just one of many moms who will say an extra prayer each night for our sons and daughters going in harm's way." And then, a few minutes later, she says, "You know, from the inside, no family ever seems typical, and that's how it is with us. Our family has the same ups and downs as any other..."

And then, a few minutes later, "I was just your average hockey mom and signed up for the PTA . . . So I signed up for the PTA because I wanted to make my kids' public education better."

Sarah Palin definitely focused on her role as mother at the start of her speech. And, while she didn't explicitly discuss her compassion (a female trait), she did discuss her desire to increase honesty and integrity in government. For example, about midway through her speech, Governor Palin explains, ". . . we are expected to govern with integrity and good will and clear convictions and a servant's heart. And I pledge to all Americans that I will carry myself in this spirit as vice president of the United States."

Sarah Palin didn't mention any "male" traits in her speech. However, she did display her "aggressive" side. In particular, she launched a number of personal and policy attacks at her Democratic rivals. For example, she said, "I guess a small-town mayor is sort of like a community organizer, except that you have actual responsibilities." She continues by saying, " . . . in small towns, we don't quite know what to make of a candidate who lavishes praise on working people when they're listening, and then talks about how bitterly they cling to their religion and guns when those people aren't listening. No, we tend to prefer candidates who don't talk about us one way in Scranton and another way in San Francisco."

In her speech, then, Governor Palin may be using her role as mother to highlight her "female" traits. However, Governor Palin also relished her role as an aggressive critic of her opponents. We examine how the news media presented Sarah Palin's personal characteristics. Given common gender stereotypes—stereotypes that members of the press may hold—we expect media coverage to focus more extensively on Sarah Palin's "female" traits than her "male" traits.[21]

When analyzing coverage in the transcripts, we found that the media were much more likely to focus on female traits in their coverage of Sarah Palin.[22] Specifically, the proportion of trait coverage that focused on "female" traits was 64 percent, while 36 percent of the trait coverage focused on male traits. This emphasis on "female" traits in news coverage of women candidates has been found by other researchers looking at different countries and different time periods. For example, Kittilson and Fridkin found that news coverage emphasizing "female" traits like compassion and honesty was much more prevalent for women, compared to men, for candidates running for legislative office in the United States, Canada, and Australia in 2004 and 2006.[23] Similarly, Kahn examined news coverage of women candidates for governor and senator in an earlier time period (1980s–1990s) and found that the news focused more attention on "female" traits when covering women candidates, compared to male candidates. For example, almost half (45%) of the trait coverage devoted to female senate candidates focused on "female" traits, while less than a third of coverage of male candidates emphasized "female" traits.[24]

Issues

People's reliance on gender stereotypes also affects people's views regarding women candidates' policy expertise. Women are viewed as more capable of dealing with issues that are decidedly "feminine," including child care, health care, poverty, and education policies, while men are viewed as more capable of dealing with "masculine issues," such as defense, foreign affairs, and economic policies.[25] And, just as "male" traits are perceived as more important traits for a leader, "male" issues are more likely to coincide with the salient issues of a presidential campaign.[26]

In the 2008 presidential election, two of the most salient issues were decisively masculine issues: the economy and national security.[27] The economic downturn and the wars in Iraq and Afghanistan dominated the political landscape, leaving little room for "female" issues like education and healthcare.

In her convention speech, Governor Palin discussed "male" issues, like spending, foreign policy, and terrorism frequently; these "male" issues accounted for 65 percent of all of her issue discussion.[28] However, Sarah Palin did mention "female" issues, like education, special needs programs, ethics reform, and maintaining honesty and integrity in government in 35 percent of the issue mentions.

Given the political climate as well as the salience of "male" issues in presidential campaigns more generally, we expect male issues to be covered extensively in Palin's coverage. Relying on the gender stereotyping literature, we categorize issues as "male" if they are related to the following issues: defense issues, the economy, the bailout, nuclear arms control, taxes, treaties, foreign affairs, the budget, energy/oil, farm issues, employment/jobs, business, the Iraq War, terrorism, and trade. "Female" issues include welfare, education, religion, poverty, civil rights/women's rights, the environment, gay marriage, healthcare, prescription drugs, childcare, parental leave, family/small town values, gun control, human rights, social security, creationism/evolution, violence against women, women in politics, culture of life, double-standards for men and women, and family/work balance.[29]

The media mentioned male issues 63 percent of the time when covering Sarah Palin, and female issues were discussed 37 percent of the time.[30] This reliance on "male" issues over "female" issues matches Sarah Palin's own emphasis in her convention speech. In addition, issues that are generally important to Republicans overlap with these "male" issues (e.g., economy and taxes, compared to education and health care), so it is very likely that such issues were highlighted more by the McCain-Palin ticket.

While it is difficult to know whether Sarah Palin's gender affected the proportion of coverage given to "male" and "female" issues, we can examine whether the gender of the reporter covering Sarah Palin affected the content of the issue coverage. Male anchors may be more likely to focus on "male" issues and traits when covering Governor Palin, compared to female anchors.[31] Male anchors may be more likely to view male issues (e.g., the economy) as more important in potential leaders and may, therefore, focus more extensively on these dimensions when covering Sarah Palin.

When we examine issue coverage by gender of anchor, important differences emerge (see Table 5.1). Female anchors devote almost half (44%) of their issue coverage to "female" issues, while these same issues account for less than one-third (26%) of the issue coverage discussed by male anchors. Male anchors prefer to focus almost exclusively on "male" issues, with 74 percent of their coverage focusing on issues like the economy (see Table 5.1). Furthermore, the appearance of a female anchor—either as a sole anchor or as a co-anchor with a male colleague—appears to encourage the discussion of "female" issues. For example, "female" issues are discussed 46 percent of the time in stories anchored by both a male and a female reporter.

The coverage of Sarah Palin's issue positions and priorities emphasized "male" issues, like taxes and terrorism, a stereotypical weakness for women candidates. With the data at hand, we cannot be certain whether news coverage echoed Governor Palin's own choice of strategy. And, we don't know whether the strategy was effective. For instance, we do not

Table 5.1   Type of Issue Coverage (Male/Female) Reported by Anchor (Male/Female)

	Male Anchor	Female Anchor	Male and Female Anchors
"Female" Issues	26%	44%	46%
"Male" Issues	74%	56%	55%
	(304)	(63)	(335)

Note: "Male" issues include defense, the economy, the bailout, nuclear arms control, taxes, treaties, foreign affairs, the budget, energy/oil, agriculture, employment/jobs, business, the Iraq War, terrorism, and trade. "Female" issues include welfare, education, religion, poverty, civil rights/women's rights, the environment, gay marriage, health care, prescription drugs, childcare, parental leave, family/small town values, gun control, human rights, social security, creationism/evolution, violence against women, women in politics, culture of life, double standards for men and women, and family/work balance.

know whether the media's focus on "male" issues led people to revise their stereotypes regarding women's abilities to deal with these issues.

However, we do know that some of the coverage Governor Palin received regarding "male" issues was clearly negative. For example, when Sarah Palin was asked by Katie Couric how Alaska's proximity to Russia gives her foreign policy experience, Governor Palin responded, "Well, it certainly does because our—our next door neighbors are foreign countries ... We—we do—it's very important when you consider even national security issues with Russia as Putin rears his head and comes into the air space of the United States of America, where—where do they go? It's Alaska." (CBS interview with Katie Couric, September 24, 2008). This quote received a great deal of critical coverage by news organizations. For example, the following headlines were published regarding Governor Palin's quote about Russia: "Palin talks to Couric—and if she's lucky, few are listening" (*Los Angeles Times*, September 26, 2008), "Sarah Palin: It's just wrong" (*Las Vegas Review Journal*, September 30, 2008), and "Campaign tries to explain Palin's Putin comment" (*USA Today*, September 30, 2008).

With regard to personal traits, the news media focused on "female" traits, like empathy and honesty. These traits correspond to women's stereotypical strengths. However, they are not valued as highly as competence and leadership when evaluating candidates for high political office. Therefore, the focus on these "female" traits may have hurt Governor Palin's electoral prospects.

Media Framing

Novelty

As the first woman nominated to run for vice president of the Republican Party, much of Sarah Palin's initial coverage focused on the historic nature of her candidacy. Sarah Palin generated a great deal of press attention, especially when compared to her counterpart on the Democratic ticket, Senator Joe Biden. In the week of Senator McCain's announcement of Sarah Palin as his running mate (August 25th–August 31st), the "Campaign Coverage Index" compiled by the PEW Center's Project for Excellence in Journalism showed that 12 percent of all the news stories focused on Sarah Palin being named as McCain's choice for vice president.[32] Only 6 percent of the stories focused on Joe Biden being named as Barack Obama's running mate, even though the Democratic Convention was going on during this period.

The focus on Sarah Palin's campaign continued for several weeks.[33] For example, during the week of September 1st–September 7th, 43 percent of all the campaign stories analyzed in PEW's "Campaign Coverage Index"

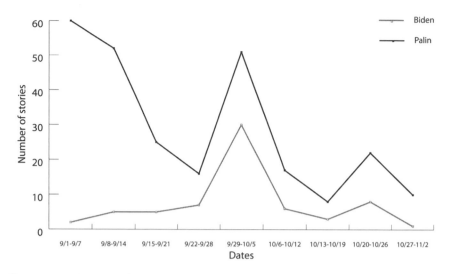

Figure 5.2 Amount of Coverage Devoted to Palin and Biden.
Source: The Project for Excellence in Journalism's Campaign Coverage Index. The amount of coverage used here is measured by the number of stories in which a candidate plays a significant role as a subject (between 25% and 50% of the story) or as a newsmaker (more than 50% of the story). PEJ's weekly Campaign Coverage Index examines the news agenda of 55 different outlets from five sectors of the media: print, online, network TV, cable, and radio.

focused on Sarah Palin. In the following week, Palin's coverage consumed 32 percent of the campaign news show, including her ABC interview with Charlie Gibson. And, during several weeks, Sarah Palin actually garnered more coverage than Senator McCain or Senator Obama. By mid-September, attention to Governor Palin had declined somewhat, accounting for only 13 percent of all campaign coverage.

During the entire campaign period, Governor Palin's coverage always outpaced coverage for Biden. The data in Figure 5.2, based on PEW's measure of "race for media exposure," show that Governor Palin consistently received more press attention than Senator Biden. In some time periods, particularly at the start of the campaign, the differences are quite dramatic. However, even when both candidates participated in the vice-presidential debate (9/29–10/5 period), Governor Palin continued to receive significantly more press attention than Senator Biden.

Appearance

"I think Hillary Clinton was held to a different standard in her primary race. Do you remember the conversations that took place about her, say superficial things that they don't talk about with men, her wardrobe and her hairstyles, all of that? That's a bit of that double standard. But I'm not going to complain about it, I'm not going to whine about it, I'm going to plow through that, because we are embarking on something greater than that, than allowing that double standard to adversely affect us."

—Sarah Palin in an interview with Jill Zuckman
from the *Chicago Tribune*, October 23, 2008,
"Sarah Palin Responds to Wardrobe Flap."
Printed October 24, 2008.

Governor Sarah Palin, as the quote illustrates, was well aware of the unequal treatment of men and women's media coverage, particularly the emphasis on superficiality and appearance. The focus on Sarah Palin's appearance was acknowledged by Campbell Brown, a CNN anchor, who pointed out the double standard during her *No Bias, No Bull* segment in October of 2008. Brown said, "My issue? There is an incredible double standard here, and we are ignoring a very simple reality: women are judged based on their appearance far more than men. That is a statement of fact. There has been plenty written about Sarah Palin's jackets, her hair, her looks. Sound familiar? There was plenty of talk and plenty written about Hillary Clinton's looks, hair, pantsuits. Compare that to the attention given to Barack Obama's $1,500 suits or John McCain's $520 Ferragamo shoes. There is no comparison" (CNN, October 22, 2008).

Scholars examining coverage of Elizabeth Dole during her bid as the first female Republican candidate for president in 2000 also found a great deal of the news coverage focused on her appearance.[34] Perhaps, one of the most negative articles written about Dole was published in *The Washington Post* by Mary McGrory. McGrory wrote that "[d]espite her ... credentials ... she brought only a skirt to the proceedings ... "[35] Adjectives used to describe Dole in the McGrory article included "Stepford wife" and "well-coifed."[36] Although there were a series of problems with Elizabeth Dole's presidential nomination bid, the news media's focus on her appearance may have led voters to question the seriousness of Dole's candidacy.

In our analysis, we look at the coverage of Sarah Palin's appearance in the news media. We simply count the number of times stories about Sarah Palin mentioned her physical features, including her hairstyle, her clothing, and her glasses. We find that 18 percent of the news stories about Sarah Palin mentioned her appearance. Governor Palin's appearance received more press attention than discussion of her policy views regarding the environment (2% of coverage), energy (10%), education (1%), healthcare (7%), the bank bailout (2%), taxes (8%) or government spending (8%).

We also examined whether discussion of Sarah Palin's coverage was more pronounced for male anchors, compared to female anchors. While male anchors may be more likely to make sexist comments (e.g., Keith Olbermann of MSNBC comparing Sarah Palin to Miss South Carolina), female anchors may be more likely to decry the news media's attention to Sarah Palin's appearance (e.g., Campbell Brown's comment above). [37]

We find that stories anchored only by men discuss Governor Palin's appearance less often than stories anchored by only women or stories anchored by both men and women. In particular, about 11 percent of the stories discussed by male anchors mention her appearance, while women anchors are twice as likely (22%) to discuss her appearance, and stories joint-anchored by men and women mention Sarah Palin's appearance 20 percent of the time.

The focus on Sarah Palin's appearance may have hurt her chances of election, according to recent research.[38] Relying on an experimental design, researchers found that subjects who view Governor Palin as attractive were far less likely to view her as intelligent and competent for the job, and thus, were less likely to vote for the McCain-Palin ticket.[39] These new findings suggest a negative relationship between level of attractiveness in women seeking male-dominated jobs and perceptions of competency.

The "Mommy Problem"

According to the introductory chapter of this book, the "mommy problem" stems from gender stereotypes and media framing, making it difficult for left-wing women to win executive office. However, Sarah Palin faced a very specific "mommy problem." In particular, voters and media elites questioned her ability to be a viable vice-presidential candidate given her role as mother of five, including a baby diagnosed with Down's syndrome and a pregnant teenage daughter.

The news media began questioning Sarah Palin's choice to run for vice president, given her family obligations, almost immediately. The weekend after John McCain's announcement of Sarah Palin, John Roberts of *CNN* asked whether it was appropriate for Sarah Palin to accept the vice-presidential nomination given the magnitude of her current family responsibilities. Radio talk show host, Ed Schulz, on *CNN* a few days later said that Governor Palin would not be able to focus on her job given her family distractions. And, *ABC*'s Bill Weir accused her of neglecting her children by running for vice president.[40]

In an opinion article in the *St. Louis Post Dispatch*, Kurt Greenbaum asks, "Should a mother of five children, including an infant with Down's syndrome, be running for the second highest office in the land? Are her priorities misplaced?"[41] And, in a *Vanity Fair* article titled, "Sarah Palin's Mommy Problem," Evgenia Peretz writes, "In this day and age, plenty of women make the decision that they will not be the primary caretaker of their children. That might be hard to swallow for some, but that's progress. . . . But if that's the case, and, if, like Palin, you returned to work three days after your Down's syndrome son was born, you don't get 'hockey mom' bragging rights to boot. You can't have it both ways."[42]

Another young, charming presidential candidate with children (Senator Barack Obama) was never subjected to the same questions regarding the appropriateness of running for office with small children. In Senator Obama's case, it was likely assumed that his wife would care for the children. Would Governor Palin have received as much coverage on her husband and family if she had been Sam Palin? Some research suggests not.[43] Because she was a woman, a mother, and an ambitious politician, she was often questioned how she could manage it all.

When we look at the number of times that Sarah Palin's family is mentioned in her coverage, we find that her marital status is mentioned in more than one-third (34%) of the stories examined and her husband and family are mentioned 26 percent of the time.[44] To put these numbers in perspective, Sarah Palin's ideology was mentioned just as often as her family, 26 percent of the time. And, Sarah Palin's views regarding the wars in Iraq and Afghanistan received sparse coverage compared to the focus on her family. In particular, 8 percent and 5 percent of the stories about Sarah Palin discussed Iraq and Afghanistan, respectively.

The focus on Sarah Palin's family may have taken away from coverage of her qualifications, her experience, and her policy positions and priorities. The media's coverage of the "Mommy Problem" may have hurt Sarah Palin's electability. Furthermore, the negative coverage of her family—and her choices as a mother—may have led to negative coverage of her candidacy. We now turn to an examination of the tone of Sarah Palin's coverage.

Tone of News Coverage

When we examine the tone of Governor Palin's coverage during the campaign, we find only 15 percent of the campaign coverage was classified as positive. However, the coverage was not overly negative either, with fourteen percent of all the news stories classified as negative. In contrast, half of all of the news stories discussing Sarah Palin were mixed in tone, and the remaining coverage (21%) was classified as neutral.

The tone of coverage did change over time, as we expected. As the data in Figure 5.3 shows, the initial coverage of Sarah Palin was relatively positive. But as the campaign progressed, the tone of coverage became more and more negative, with the nadir occurring after Sarah Palin's interview with Katie Couric on September 24th. The valence of coverage began to rebound after the vice-presidential debate and by the end of the campaign, Governor Palin's coverage was more neutral than negative.[45]

When we examine the mean number of criticisms discussed during the television news programs, we see the same pattern. As the data in

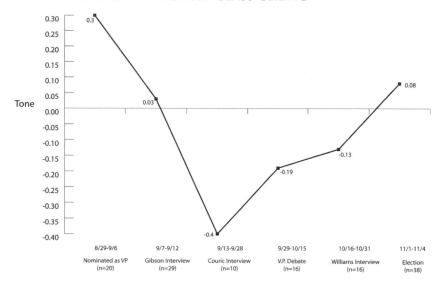

Figure 5.3 Average Tone of News Stories Over Time.
Note: Tone is measured on a three point scale where 1 = positive, 0 = neutral or mixed and, −1 = negative.

Figure 5.4 demonstrate, the criticisms of Sarah Palin were relatively low (an average of about two per story) at the start of the campaign. However, these criticisms grew during the length of the campaign, with the apex of more than five criticisms per story occurring about the same time as the vice-presidential debate. The number of criticisms plummeted near the

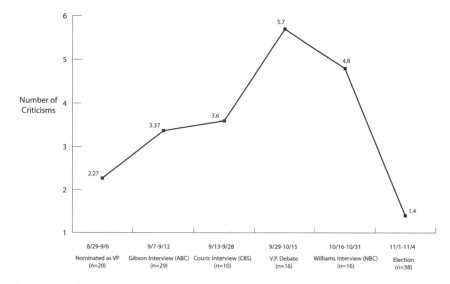

Figure 5.4 Number of Criticisms Per News Story

end of the campaign and by Election Day, stories about Sarah Palin were averaging about one criticism per story.

We also examined the nature of the news media criticisms: substantive (e.g., policy critiques) versus personal criticisms (criticisms focusing on personal aspects of her candidacy) of Sarah Palin. Policy criticisms of Governor Palin were more common, with stories averaging about two policy criticisms versus about one personal criticism per story. Finally, we looked at whether the preference for personal versus policy criticisms varied with the gender of the anchor. We expected female anchors (like Campbell Brown of CNN) to be more sensitive to the focus on personal matters at the expense of policy matters. The data presented in Figure 5.5 provides some support for our hypothesis.

We find that female anchors were more likely than male anchors or mixed gender anchors to focus on policy criticisms, averaging more than three policy criticisms per story. Male anchors also preferred policy criticisms to personal criticisms by about the same ratio (7:1) as female anchors (5:1). However, male anchors leveled fewer policy criticisms at Sarah Palin, compared to their female counterparts. The pattern was strikingly different when stories were anchored by a male and female reporter. In these cases, the proportion of policy and personal criticisms were quite similar. And, reporters appeared to be more at ease at launching personal criticisms when the story was being anchored by both a male and female reporter. At this point, we do not know why stories anchored by male and female reporters generated a greater preference for personal criticisms. However, this preference for personal criticisms may have been problematic since male and female co-anchors reported far more stories than single-sex anchors in our analysis.

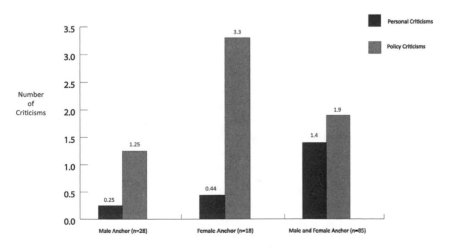

Figure 5.5 Substance of Criticism by Gender of Anchor

SUMMARY AND CONCLUSIONS

Television news covered Sarah Palin, in her historic campaign for vice president, "like a girl." First, the coverage focused more on "female" traits than "male" traits, suggesting that the news media often reinforce gender stereotypes in their coverage of women candidates. While the news media's focus on "female" traits may have echoed Governor Palin's own political messages, we suspect this may not be the case. For example, in her speech at the Republican Convention, Sarah Palin emphasized two alternative traits: her maternal side *and* her aggressiveness. For example, during the campaign, she was described as "family-oriented" or "maternal" three times (13% of the stories) as often as she was described as aggressive (e.g., 4% of the stories described Governor Palin as a fighter, tenacious, or assertive).

The news media's lack of attention to "male" traits when covering Sarah Palin may have created an electoral obstacle. As discussed earlier, voters are most likely to consider "male" traits when evaluating candidates for office. Since coverage of Governor Palin largely downplayed these types of traits, voters may have failed to develop positive evaluations of Governor Palin's embodiment of traits like leadership and competence.

The news media's framing of Sarah Palin's candidacy, especially the emphasis on her appearance and the focus on her "mommy problem," may have also discouraged people from taking her candidacy seriously. For instance, by focusing on Sarah Palin's expensive clothes (purchased by the Republican National Party), her glasses, and her good looks, voters were deprived of in-depth coverage of her issue concerns and her qualifications. Furthermore, the news media's choice of framing may have produced a more negative tone of coverage than an alternative frame.

The coverage of issues, however, focused more on "male" issues. The importance of "male" issues in presidential elections, in general, and the salience of these types of issues in the 2008 campaign was not surprising. Nonetheless, the lack of attention to "female" issues ill-served Governor Palin, given common gender stereotypes. The news media's focus on the economy as well as the Iraq and Afghanistan War in its coverage of Governor Palin may have led to more negative impressions of her candidacy. People view women as less competent on these issues and, given media attention, these issues were likely on the top of voters' agendas during the 2008 campaign. Women anchors may have been an important resource for Sarah Palin since women anchors were much more likely than male anchors to discuss "female" issues when covering Governor Palin.

Overall, this exploratory and descriptive analysis of Sarah Palin's coverage shows that much of the coverage reinforced existing gender stereotypes and covered Senator Palin in a way that overemphasized personal coverage at the expense of substantive coverage. These conclusions are based on an extensive content analysis of television news coverage on the three major networks and two major cable news outlets during the length of the fall campaign. However, we encourage future researchers to build on our study. We offer two suggestions. First, a more extensive examination of Governor Sarah Palin's own campaign messages (speeches, advertisements, press releases) would be worthwhile. With such an analysis, one can see whether the news media simply mirrored Governor Palin's messages or whether the news media's attention distorted her message. Second, more extensive examination of coverage of Senator Joe Biden would provide a useful comparison. For example, is the ratio of "female" to "male" traits significantly different for Senator Biden, compared to Governor Palin? And what percentage of Biden's coverage focused on his appearance, his family, and his spouse? Moreover, was the tone of Senator Biden's coverage similar to Governor Palin's? By comparing Senator Biden's coverage with Governor Palin's coverage, we can better assess whether the nature of Sarah Palin's coverage was indicative of the times or more affected by her gender.

This chapter represents a systematic snapshot of news treatment of a historic candidate. We have shown how Sarah Palin tried to navigate the "Double bind" faced by all female candidates for higher political office. The highlighting of her "female" traits by the television news organizations did not always represent her own choice of strategy. And, the emphasis on "male" issues over "female" issues, most noticeable among male anchors, may have hindered Sarah Palin in her bid to increase positive impressions of her candidacy. Furthermore, the news media's choice of framing Sarah Palin's candidacy as a novelty—focusing on her appearance and her family—may have also hampered her campaign. The focus on trivial issues, like clothes and hairstyle, may have discouraged potential supporters from seriously considering her candidacy. In many ways, Sarah Palin's news treatment during her campaign echoes many of the obstacles women in the United States have faced in the recent and distant past as well as mirroring some of the constraints women face in countries across the world.

NOTES

1. In the United States, a presidential primary system is used to select the Republican (conservative) and Democratic (liberal) nominees. Historically, the respective party conventions chose the vice-presidential and presidential candidates, usually in an effort to "balance" the ticket in terms of geography or ideology. However, for the last 30 years or so, the common practice is to

announce their decision for the vice-presidential nominee a week or so before the national convention. See Morris P. Fiorina, Paul E. Peterson, Bertram Johnson, and William G. Mayer, *The New American Democracy*, 6th edition (Pearson Press, 2008).

2. CNN Online, "McCain Makes Surprising V.P. Pick," *CNN Election Center*, August 29, 2008.

3. Ibid.

4. See Kim Fridkin Kahn, *The Political Consequences of Being a Woman* (New York: Columbia University Press, 1996).

5. Gregory B. Markus, "Political Attitudes During an Election Year: a Report of the 1980 NES Panel Study," *American Political Science Review*, 76 (1982): 538–560; Donald Kinder, "Presidential Character Revisited," in Richard Lau and David Sears, eds., *Political Cognition* (Hillsdale, NJ: Lawrence Erlbaum Associates, 1986): 233–256.

6. Dianne G. Bystrom and Jerry L. Miller, "Gender Communication Styles and Strategies in Campaign 1996: The Videostyles of Women and Men Candidates," in Lynda Lee Kaid and Dianne G Bystrom, eds.. *The Electronic Election* (Mahwah, New Jersey: Lawrence Erlbaum Associates Publishers, 1999); Kahn, *Political Consequences*.

7. Doris Graber, *Mass Media and American Politics* (Washington, D.C.: Congressional Quarterly Press, 1996).

8. Julianne F. Flowers, Audrey A. Haynes, and Michael H. Crespin, "The Media, the Campaign, and the Message," *American Journal of Political Science* 47 (2003): 259–273.

9. Rem Reider, "Searching for Sarah Palin," *American Journalism Review*, October 2008, http://www.ajr.org/Article.asp?id=4600.

10. Joe Garofoli, "Palin: McCain Campaign's End-Run Around Media," *San Francisco Chronicle*, September 30, 2008, http://www.sfgate.com/cgi-bin/article.cgi?f=/c/a/2008/09/30/MNTB1374LU.DTL.

11. We collected data on the major networks (NBC, CBS, ABC), because they are the major non-cable networks that continue to have morning and evening newscasts. We added CNN and FOX to our sample, since, according to the *Nielsen* ratings, they were (and are) the two most watched cable news networks.

12. Intercoder reliability was calculated at 74 percent. The method we used was the average percent agreement across specific content categories. The transcripts were coded by a trained graduate student and an undergraduate Honors student. Reliability checks were done by an author of this paper.

13. Paragraph was defined as each time a new person (i.e., reporter, anchor, guest) would speak on the news program.

14. We collected the transcripts, as opposed to viewing tapes, for efficiency reasons. Moreover, we collected data on *news* sources, as opposed to *non-news* sources in which all the political candidates garnered some attention (e.g., *Saturday Night Live*, The *Daily Show with Jon Stewart*) because (1) we are interested in the tone and content of how the mainstream news outlets covered Sarah Palin and (2) because, for news, most citizens rely on the big three networks and cable TV news shows (Prior 2007, Pew Research 2009).

15. In a study by Pew, the proportion of people who say they have gotten their news "yesterday" from TV, newspapers, or radio has declined since the early 1990s. However, the percentage in the last decade who say they have watched only TV news has been relatively stable, while those for TV *and* radio have fallen steadily (Pew Research 2009).

16. Pew Research 2009.

17. John McKee and Alex Sherriffs, "Qualitative Aspects of Beliefs about Men and Women," *Journal of Personality* 25 (1956): 451–464; John McKee and Alex Sherriffs, "The Differential Evaluation of Males and Females," *Journal of Personality* 25 (1957): 356–371.

18. Jennifer Lawless, "Women, War, and Winning Elections: Gender Stereotyping in the Post-September 11th Era," *Political Research Quarterly* 57 (2004): 479–490.

19. Leonie Huddy, "The Political Significance of Voters' Gender Stereotypes," *Research in Micropolitics* 4 (1994): 169–193; Kathleen Hall Jamieson, *Beyond the Double Bind: Women and Leadership* (New York: Oxford University Press, 1995).

20. Amanda Diekmen and Alice Eagly, "Stereotypes as Dynamic Constructs: Women and Men of the Past, Present, and Future," *Personality and Social Psychology Bulletin* 26 (2000): 1171–1188; Sabine Sczesny, Janine Bosak, Daniel Neff, and Birgit Schyns, "Gender Stereotypes and the Attribution of Leadership Traits: A Cross-Cultural Comparison," *Sex Roles* 51, no. 11–12 (2004): 631–645; Mark Stephen Leeper, "The Impact of Prejudice on Female Candidates: An Experimental Look at Voter Inference," *American Politics Quarterly* 19 (1991): 248–261; Shirley Rosenwasser and Jana Seale, "Attitudes toward a Hypothetical Male or Female Presidential Candidate," *Political Psychology* 9 (1988): 591–598.

21. Kahn, *Political Consequences*; Miki Caul Kittilson and Kim Fridkin, "Gender, Candidate Portrayals and Election Campaigns: A Comparative Perspective," *Politics & Gender* 4 (2008): 1–22.

22. Some traits are considered gender neutral, such as "religious" and "reckless."

23. Kittilson and Fridkin, "Candidate Portrayals."

24. Kahn, *Political Consequences*.

25. Shirley Rosenwasser et al., "Attitudes toward Women and Men in Politics," *Political Psychology* 8 (1987): 191–200; Rosenwasser and Seale, "Attitudes Toward Hypothetical Candidate"; Lawless, "Women, War, Winning Elections."

26. Leonie Huddy and Nayda Terkildsen, "Gender Stereotypes and Perceptions of Male and Female Candidates," *American Journal of Political Science* 37 (1993): 119–147.

27. Lymari Morales, "Americans Prioritize the Economy Over Terrorism," *Gallup Poll*, June 27, 2008, http://www.gallup.com/poll/108415/americans-prioritize-economy-over-terrorism.aspx; Pew Research Center, "Issues and the 2008 Election," August 21, 2008, http://pewforum.org/docs/?DocID=339.

28. A transcript of Sarah Palin's speech can be found at http://www.npr.org/templates/story/story.php?storyId=94258995.

29. Kahn, *Political Consequences*; Kim Fridkin Kahn and Edie N. Goldenberg, "Women Candidates in the News: An Examination of Gender Differences in U.S. Senate Campaign Coverage," *Public Opinion Quarterly* 55 (1991): 180–199.

30. Some issues we considered "non-gendered," such as "Immigration," "Veterans," or "Creationism/Evolution."

31. Typically news anchors in the United States do not write their own scripts, although they often ad lib throughout the newscast.

32. The Pew's Campaign Coverage Index is based on a subset of their News Coverage Index dataset. The CCI includes data on all the news stories that primarily focused on the presidential campaign, from January 1st to November 3rd, 2008. Please go to http://www.journalism.org/by_the_numbers/datasets for more information.

33. Recall that our data collection for Sarah Palin started when Senator McCain announced her nomination (in late August) to Election Day. Since this only encompassed a few short months, we collected our own data during this entire time period, as well as analyzed the PEW data for this same time period.

34. Diane J. Heith, "Footwear, Lipstick, and an Orthodox Sabbath: Media Coverage of Non-Traditional Candidates," *White House Studies* 1, no. 3 (2001): 35–49; Sean Aday and James Devitt, "Style over substance: Newspaper coverage of Elizabeth Dole's presidential bid," *Harvard International Journal of Press/Politics* 6 (2001): 52–73.

35. Caroline Heldman, Susan Carroll, and Stephanie Olson, " 'She Brought Only A Skirt': Print Media Coverage of Elizabeth Dole's Bid for the Republican Presidential Nomination," *Political Communication* 22 (2005): 315–335.

36. Diane J. Heith, *Polling to Govern: Public Opinion and Presidential Leadership* (California: Stanford University Press, 2003).

37. In our analysis, we do not distinguish between anchors discussing Sarah Palin's appearance versus anchors criticizing others for calling attention to Sarah Palin's appearance. We just simply count the number of stories mentioning her appearance.

38. Nathan A. Heflick and Jamie L. Goldenberg, "Objectifying Sarah Palin: Evidence that Objectification Causes Women to be Perceived as Less Competent and Less Fully Human," *Journal of Experimental Psychology* (forthcoming).

39. Heflick and Goldenberg, "Objectifying Sarah Palin."

40. These quotes were reported on the womencount website. See "Sexism and Sarah Palin" at www.womencount.org/blog.

41. Kurt Greenbaum, "Is It Sexist to Criticize Parent Palin for Aspiring to the Vice Presidency?," *St. Louis Post Dispatch*. http://interact.stltoday.com/blogzone/talk-of-the-day/talk-of-the-day/2008/09/is-it-sexist-to-criticize-parent-palin-for-aspiring-to-the-vice-presidency/, accessed September 30, 2008.

42. Evgenia Peretz, "Sarah Palin's Mommy Problem," *Vanity Fair*. http://www.vanityfair.com/online/politics/2008/09/sarah-palins-mommy-problem.html, accessed September 30, 2008.

43. Dianne G. Bystrom, Mary Banwart, and Terry Robertson, "Framing the Fight," *American Behavioral Scientist* 44 (2001): 1999–2013; Heldman et al. (2005), "Only a Skirt."

44. As a point of reference, during the 2000 Republican primary, Elizabeth Dole ran for the Presidential nominee. One study found that her marital status

and personal life was mentioned in 11 percent of news coverage, compared to George W. Bush, whose family was mentioned 15 percent of the time. Although Dole's "private life" was unique in that she is married to Bob Dole, a former Presidential candidate himself, the comparison of these numbers indicates that Palin's coverage on her marital status and family was significantly greater than Dole's. See Heldman et al. (2005), "Only a Skirt."

45. We also examined tone of coverage by news outlet. We found FOX aired more positive stories than the other news programs. In particular, 33 percent of FOX's stories were coded as positive, 20 percent of CBS stories were positive, 11 percent of ABC stories were positive, 17 percent of NBC news stories were positive, and none of the stories aired by CNN was classified as positive.

PART 3

Breaking through the Glass Ceiling

CHAPTER SIX

"Either Way, There's Going to Be a Man in Charge"[1]: Media Representations of New Zealand Prime Minister Helen Clark

Linda Trimble and Natasja Treiberg

INTRODUCTION

Helen Clark is the quintessential political success story. Prime Minister of New Zealand from 1999 to 2008, she is the country's fifth longest serving government leader and the only Labour leader to lead the party to victory in three successive elections. First elected to the New Zealand House of Commons in 1981, at age 31, Clark moved up the ranks of the then governing Labour Party very quickly, with a cabinet appointment in 1987, promotion to Deputy Prime Minister in 1990, and selection as party leader in 1993. After Labour's defeat in the 2008 election, Helen Clark's international expertise and standing were recognized with a prestigious appointment as head of the United Nations Development Program. She continues to be recognized by Forbes magazine as one of the most powerful women in the world.[2] Analysis of Helen Clark's press coverage therefore reveals the nature and extent of gendered news framing of a competitive and highly successful woman, one who enjoyed considerable longevity in the first minister's role.

New Zealand is a unitary state, as befitting its small population of just over 4 million, including a sizeable indigenous (Maori) population.[3] A constitutional monarchy governed with a Westminster-style parliamentary system, New Zealand differs from similar parliamentary systems by including designated Maori seats in the national legislature, the House of Representatives, and by its unicameral nature (the appointed upper house was abolished in 1950). As McLeay notes, New Zealand women who want to have an impact at the national level through conventional politics must seek election to the House of Representatives.[4]

Women were enfranchised early in New Zealand, in 1893, and although the first female member of parliament was not elected until 1933, by 2003 the country boasted an "unusually high number of women in important constitutional positions" including the prime minister, the governor general, and the Chief Justice of the Supreme Court.[5] The adoption of a mixed-member proportional (MMP) electoral system in 1993 helped increase the number of women in the House, at least initially, and it also had an enormous impact on the party system and the nature of electoral competition. Prior to the 1996 election, when MMP was used for the first time, the single-member plurality, or first-past-the-post, electoral formula was accompanied by a two-party system. It produced stable majority governments led by either the conservative National Party or the social democratic Labour Party, although National dominated from 1949 to 1999, holding power for 38 of these 50 years.[6] Ironically, a Labour government introduced free market reforms between 1984 and 1990, and the cost-cutting, de-regulation, and privatization measures adopted by this government were labeled "Rogernomics" and emulated by right-wing regimes in other countries, including several Canadian provinces. Aimer notes that this approach "destroyed the fourth Labour government in 1990," but it set the policy direction for the National-led government that followed and modified the socialism of the Labour Party to the extent that it is now best described as a blend of liberalism and socialism.[7]

Helen Clark became leader of the Labour Party in 1993, when the party was in opposition, still reeling from the electoral fallout of "Rogernomics," and she had to contend with disastrously low poll rankings and an attempted leadership coup. Despite these formidable obstacles, Clark came very close to winning the first New Zealand election contested with the new, MMP electoral system, in 1996. The adoption of MMP fostered a multi-party system and produced electoral results that require the two big parties—Labour and National—to make agreements with one or more smaller parties to form government. Had the party holding the balance of power after the 1996 election, New Zealand First, chosen Labour as its coalition partner, Helen Clark would have been New Zealand's first woman prime minister. However, New Zealand First entered a coalition with National, allowing it to continue as the governing party with New Zealand First's support in the House. Clark prevailed in the 1999 election, defeating National leader and the country's first female Prime Minister Jenny Shipley, to become the first woman *elected* to the prime minister's post.[8] Success in the 2002 and 2005 elections secured Clark's reputation as a winner. However, while she and her party maintained strong support going into the 2008 election, the electorate was in the mood for a change of government and Labour was defeated by National. Helen Clark stepped down from the post of Labour Party leader, having served nine years as prime minister.

Our study contrasts reportage of Helen Clark with that of her primary opponents during the five elections she contested as leader of the New Zealand Labour Party.[9] We focus on election news coverage because elections provide the press with the quintessential political spectacle, and they focus attention on the personalities, leadership styles, and campaign performances of party leaders.[10] Content and discourse analysis methods were employed to address the central organizing question of this book: Does media coverage of female political leaders employ gender stereotypes, thereby reinforcing masculine norms for executive office and implying women do not have the "right stuff" for elite leadership positions? We demonstrate that while some highly personalizing attention was paid to Clark's appearance and marriage, she was not portrayed as too feminine. To the contrary, in fact: Helen Clark's leadership persona was mediated by the norm of "aggressively masterful" and adversarial political leadership.[11] As the title of our chapter indicates, Helen Clark was quite literally represented as a man in news discourses about her campaign performances. While this sort of framing may have helped Clark overcome the perception that women aren't tough enough for the top job, it represented her leadership style and exercise of political authority as unbecomingly belligerent and, ultimately, it failed to disrupt the taken-for-granted notion of political leadership as a masculine domain.

GENDERED MEDIATION OF FEMALE LEADERS

The concept of *mediation* captures the tendency of news coverage to go beyond merely reporting the "facts" by offering analysis and evaluations.[12] Political reporting necessarily involves filtering, selection, and emphasis as no political event can be described in its entirety given the time and space demands of news organizations.[13] Political events and actors are then further mediated when journalists and editors use frames, stereotypes, and short-cuts to ensure the gist of the story is comprehensible to the audience.[14] Framing is a central aspect of mediation as news frames determine what is included, what is excluded, what is seen as salient, and what is regarded as unimportant.[15] Mediation is *gendered* when the news reflects sex-based norms and assumptions by, for instance, using masculine metaphors to describe political events or by highlighting the sex or personal life of a political actor despite its irrelevance to the issue at hand.[16] The most overt type of gendered mediation makes explicit reference to a politician's sex, often suggesting it is as important as her political accomplishments.[17] However, gendered framing goes well beyond noting the sex of the politician to emphasize gender-specific attributes and behaviors, including stereotypically feminine roles, characteristics, and bodily attributes. There is considerable evidence that news media highlight the marital status, sexuality, appearance, and domestic roles of female politicians.[18] New Zealand media studies indicate frequent and consistent references to the looks, wardrobes, hairstyles, family lives, and personalities of women in politics, and sex-stereotypes and gender-based frames have been used to describe and even to undermine the credibility of women in political leadership positions in New Zealand.[19]

Despite the wealth of evidence that female politicians are invariably feminized and de-legitimized by the application of stereotypes and news frames, some studies of elite-level women leaders suggest that they are positioned within intensely masculine scripts. Because male dominance of state institutions is reflected in popular understandings of political power and executive leadership,[20] masculinizing representations may be more prevalent in media treatment of competitive female political leaders. As Sjolander notes, the histories of (male) diplomats, soldiers, and heads of state provide the dominant narratives of the international system, and these stories focus on performances of masculinity on the international stage.[21] Moreover, masculinity and war are strongly associated and war-like imagery pervades descriptions of political life.[22] During election campaigns, masculine-typed skills and behaviors are a taken-for-granted element of a party leader's performance because the dominant game frame for election news coverage is replete with aggressive war-like language and pugilistic imagery, depicting elections as pitched battles between competing parties and leaders.[23] As a result, media representations of political competition construct a prototype of political leadership based on a tough, macho stereotype.[24] Female political leaders, especially successful leaders, are therefore likely to downplay the stereotypically feminine aspects of their identities and focus on the attributes considered important to electoral success, attributes that are typically associated with men and masculinity.[25] Indeed they may have no choice, as once women leaders win the leadership of their parties and contest office, especially at the national level, they are considered "in the game" by the press and framed accordingly. Semetko and Boomgaarden found that horse-race (or game) framing dominated newspaper and television reporting of the 2005 German Bundestag election, particularly in stories that featured both the female and male candidates for chancellor.[26] Similarly, national newspaper reportage of the 1993 Canadian national election, a contest between the incumbent female Prime Minister, Kim Campbell, and male challenger Jean Chrétien, was peppered liberally with pugilistic language and battle metaphors.[27] As a result, we expected to find that the newspaper coverage of Helen Clark followed the dominant electoral script—the game frame—thereby positioning her as strong, combative, and forceful. However, because the specter of a competitive woman stepping onto the "electoral battlefield" disrupts widely held norms of femininity, we anticipated that Clark's political success would foster confused and even contradictory representations of her gendered political persona, thus invoking the "too masculine/too feminine" double bind.

METHODOLOGY

Our study focused on newspaper coverage of the five election campaigns. While most New Zealanders turn to television for news coverage, newspaper readership remains high and "the metropolitan press remains a key source of political information during an election campaign."[28] As well, the large daily newspapers provide "generous 'op-ed' space" for political coverage and debates about current events.[29] New Zealand does not have a national newspaper, thus the three largest circulation dailies[30] were chosen for this study: the capital city (Wellington) papers, the *Dominion* and the *Evening Post*, which merged in July 2002 to become the *Dominion Post*; Auckland's *New Zealand Herald*; and the main South Island paper, Christchurch's *The Press*.[31] The news articles analyzed for this study included hard news, columns, opinion pieces, features, and editorials that offered substantive coverage of Helen Clark and her primary competitors, in each of the five elections Clark contested as leader of the Labour Party (see below). While opinion pieces—columns and editorials—reflect different journalistic standards than do hard news stories,[32] they are equally, if not more likely, to be read by news audiences and thus, strongly shape news representations of party leaders. Moreover, because their purpose is to offer opinions, op-eds are more likely than hard news coverage to reveal commonly-held perceptions about and evaluations of political leaders' personas, behaviors, and levels of political acumen.

> 1996 election: Clark versus National leader, PM Jim Bolger (Clark lost);
> 1999 election: Clark versus National leader, PM Jenny Shipley (Clark won);
> 2002 election: PM Clark versus National leader Bill English (Clark won);
> 2005 election: PM Clark versus National leader Don Brash (Clark won);
> 2008 election: PM Clark versus National leader John Key (Clark lost).

For each election, and each party leader, we examined all news stories over 250 words that mentioned the leader in the headline or lead paragraph and devoted at least 50 percent of the story to that particular leader.

We began the story search from the day the election was called and ended the search on the day after a coalition government was established. This end-point was chosen because a government is not immediately formed after the votes are counted. A feature of the MMP electoral system used in New Zealand since 1996 is that it often takes time for a government to emerge and we wanted our analysis to include the crucial post-vote coalition-building phase of electoral contests. Table 6.1 reports the search dates and number of stories analyzed for each leader, and it maps a jump in the number of stories focusing on Helen Clark in the 2002 election, as well as for the two main party leaders during the 2005 and 2008 elections, indicating an increasingly leader-focused press. That National leader John Key attracted almost twice as many news stories as did Clark during the 2008 election may have contributed to Labour's electoral demise.

Both content analysis and critical discourse analysis were used to examine newspaper coverage of the five elections and six party leaders included in our study. Content analysis employs "objective and systematic counting and recording procedures to produce a quantitative description of the symbolic content in a text"[33] and we used this technique to compare the number of stories for each leader that made reference to the gendered frames and stereotypes itemized in the introduction to this book. The limitations of content analysis were addressed by employing critical discourse analysis to categorize and assess the meanings of gendered discourses.[34] For instance, noting that a certain number of news stories about a leader mention his or her appearance tells us that the press is paying some attention to the

Table 6.1   Search Dates and Number of Stories Analyzed, by Election and Leader

Election	Search Dates	Leader Name	Number of Stories
1996	September 12th–December 11th	Helen Clark	84
		Jim Bolger	81
1999	October 27th–December 7th	Helen Clark	88
		Jenny Shipley	78
2002	June 25th–August 9th	Helen Clark	103
		Bill English	70
2005	August 17th–October 18th	Helen Clark	114
		Don Brash	133
2008	October 8th–November 20th	Helen Clark	127
		John Key	198
Total			**1076**

politician's looks, but it does not tell us what, precisely, is being said and what it implies about gender and norms of political leadership.[35] By producing an inventory of references to each leader's sex, appearance, age, emotions, marital status, and children, as well as any gendered frames and stereotypes used to describe them, we identified differences between representations of Clark and her competitors, as well as changes in Clark's mediation over time. The discourse analysis took account of the fact that gendered news frames have distinct resonances for men and women politicians.

Feminizing Frames and Stereotypes

The gendered frames and stereotypes that tend to feminize, domesticate, or trivialize women politicians—emphasis on their age, newness, sex, femininity, appearance, family life, and emotions—were not typically applied to Helen Clark. In this section, we argue that Clark was not unduly feminized by media representations. To the contrary, with the exception of descriptions of her appearance, she was cast as unusually, and even suspiciously, unfeminine. We begin by showing that many of the feminizing frames documented in the introduction to this volume were not used in reportage of Clark. That others were used more to question her femininity than to reinforce it is demonstrated later in this section.

Helen Clark was no more likely than her male counterparts, the leaders of the National Party, to be called by her *first name*. This is largely because New Zealand journalists follow the protocol of referring to political leaders by their surnames, especially in headlines, or by surname prefaced by Mr., Mrs., Miss, or Ms. When first names only were included in the coverage—which was very rarely—it was typically because other political actors had used them and the newspapers took pains to distance themselves from such a familiarizing approach by putting the names in quotations.[36] The tendency of women leaders to be referenced more often by name than by official position was not evidenced in the coverage of Helen Clark, as she was as, or more, likely than her opponents to be referred to by her position or title.[37]

As Table 6.2 shows, Clark's *age* was not a factor in election news coverage either, as it was mentioned infrequently and in fewer news stories than was the age of her male opponents. Nor was Clark branded inexperienced by the application of an *"agent of change"* frame. She had been in Parliament for twelve years before taking on the Labour leadership. That these years in Parliament included stints as Minister of Conservation, Housing, Health, Labour, and as Deputy Prime Minister undoubtedly allayed any concern that Helen Clark lacked the requisite knowledge or qualifications. Discourse analysis of the newspaper articles revealed that Clark was consistently framed as politically experienced and as extraordinarily competent. For instance, a columnist said this about Clark's experience during her first campaign as Labour leader, in 1996: "as a former deputy prime minister, she is an entirely convincing prime ministerial candidate and has been able to demonstrate on the hustings that she has the qualities needed for the ninth floor of the Beehive", that is, the prime minister's office.[38] Throughout the five campaigns, newspaper articles invariably described Clark as authoritative, formidable, confident, intelligent, competent, experienced, and unmatched in her grasp of a wide range of policy issues.[39]

That Clark is female was certainly noted in the coverage, and the *"first woman"* frame was applied with enthusiasm early in her career as Labour leader. During the 1996 campaign, several stories about Clark included her sex as a point of discussion with most pointing out that she would become New Zealand's first female prime minister if she won the election. Clark lost, and Jenny Shipley became the first woman to assume the post when she took over the leadership of the governing National Party in 1997.[40] The 1999 election between Clark and Shipley was certain to produce New Zealand's first elected female prime minister, and the sex of the women leaders was reported in approximately a fifth of the news stories. News articles highlighted the fact that there were "two strong women" in the running to be the "first woman elected Prime Minister."[41] However, as Table 6.2 indicates, once the first woman frame was passé, Helen Clark's sex was noted *less often* than was the sex of her male National Party opponents during the 2002, 2005, and 2008 elections.

Directly referencing a politician's sex is not the only way of bringing their gendered location to the fore, however, and women politicians are often marked by *feminine stereotypes*. Again, this was not the case for Helen Clark, as she was infrequently described as exhibiting feminine traits or qualities and was no more likely than her opponents to be described with feminine tropes. In fact, three of her male competitors, Jim Bolger, Bill English, and John Key, were described with feminine stereotypes in a higher percentage of news stories than was Clark. So, descriptions of Clark as "stitching together a coalition deal" and giving her cabinet a "makeover" were matched and even bettered by references to Jim Bolger as "vulnerable" and "coy," Bill English as "sensitive" and "choked up," and Don Brash as domesticated enough to "wash his own dirty socks when travelling."[42] While this could be interpreted as evidence of a mutual breakdown of gender stereotypes, we would argue that it actually reflects comfort with male leaders exhibiting a "sensitive side" as well as a perceived need for women leaders to demonstrate that they can fit into the masculine leadership frame.

Table 6.2 Gendered News Frames, by Election and Leader

Election/Leader	Age	Sex	Feminine Stereotypes	Appearance	Marital Status	Children (or Childlessness)	Emotions
1996 Election							
Helen Clark	1 (1%)	11 (13%)*	2 (2%)	9 (11%)*	0 (0%)*	0 (0%)	7 (8%)
Jim Bolger	1 (1%)	3 (4%)*	4 (5%)	1 (1%)*	5 (6%)*	1 (1%)	12 (15%)
1999 Election							
Helen Clark	5 (6%)	21 (24%)	2 (2%)	8 (9%)	7 (8%)	5 (5%)	15 (17%)
Jenny Shipley	2 (3%)	15 (19%)	4 (5%)	9 (12%)	5 (6%)	4 (5%)	7 (9%)
2002 Election							
Helen Clark	1 (1%)*	9 (9%)	2 (2%)	8 (8%)	6 (6%)	2 (2%)*	25 (24%)*
Bill English	5 (7%)*	9 (13%)	2 (3%)	3 (4%)	10 (14%)	6 (9%)*	7 (10%)*
2005 Election							
Helen Clark	2 (2%)*	15 (13%)	8 (7%)	10 (9%)	8 (7%)	1 (1%)	12 (11%)
Don Brash	13 (10%)*	24 (19%)	9 (7%)	18 (14%)	9 (7%)	5 (4%)	17 (13%)
2008 Election							
Helen Clark	3 (2%)	13 (10%)	3 (2%)	12 (9%)	3 (2%)*	3 (2%)*	9 (7%)
John Key	15 (8%)*	25 (13%)	9 (5%)	20 (10%)	19 (10%)*	17 (9%)*	18 (9%)

*Differences between leaders significant at $p < .05$

Helen Clark has argued, as have many other women politicians, that her *appearance* was constantly placed under the media microscope.[43] As Table 6.2 confirms, Clark attracted a consistent level of attention to her looks over the course of the five campaigns, with approximately 10 percent of the news stories about her featuring some discussion of her wardrobe, hair, or make-up. However, during the 2005 and 2008 elections, the looks of the male National Party leaders were more likely to be noted than was Clark's appearance. It appears that the highest level of interest in Clark's looks was during the 1996 campaign, but in fact references to "Cinderella Clark" and observations such as "Clark changes from ugly duckling to canny swan" were really about Clark's transformation from awkward TV presenter to competent, poised, and approachable speaker.[44] During the 2002 election, Helen Clark's looks were mentioned in more articles than were the looks of her male opponent, National leader Bill English. Moreover, the substance of this coverage evidenced traditional sex stereotypes as while the color, line, style, and visual appeal of Clark's outfits was analyzed in exhaustive detail, Bill English's blue ties and "conservative dark blue suits" were merely mentioned.

In the other three election campaigns—1999, 2005, and 2008—Clark's competitors actually endured more articles mentioning their looks than did she (see Table 6.2). However, we maintain that descriptions of leaders' outfits and hair-dos have more trivializing consequences for female leaders than for male politicians. In Helen Clark's case, her appearance provided yet another issue with which to underscore her "unfeminine" political ambition. Her image make-over in 1999[45] and subsequent efforts to polish her appearance were cast as playing the game and looking the part. For instance, an article printed during the 2008 election said: "Sarah Palin she is not—but Labour Party leader Helen Clark certainly has had a bit of a spruce-up for this year's election campaign, sporting new hair styles, make-up regime and snazzy new designer outfits."[46] Reporters reminded New Zealanders that the Labour leader was not normally "the sort who has the time or the inclination to devote to the frivolities of makeup and hairdo."[47] In short, the press was saying that while Clark put in an effort to look good for the cameras during election campaigns, she usually eschewed such womanly interests.

Helen Clark is not a "wife of" a prominent male leader or politician, thus did not have to endure the liability of this domesticating frame. Even without the "wife of" label, media narratives about a female politician's family life represent a privatizing maneuver that can undermine their political legitimacy. Although Table 6.2 reveals that Clark's marriage and family life were given *less* attention than were the wives and families of the male National party leaders, the meanings of these representations were starkly gender differentiated. A male leader's wife and family presents a traditional family trope, thus foregrounding their wives and children is a strategy of normalization for male politicians, one that suggests they "are complete human beings combining caring and working responsibilities."[48] Not surprisingly, then, Jim Bolger, Bill English, Don Brash, and John Key drew media attention to their families by talking about their wives and children with reporters. Attention to Clark's family life, in contrast, highlighted her childlessness and prompted questions about the nature of her marriage and her sexual orientation. For example, in 2002, a newspaper article noted a "whispering campaign that she was a lesbian"[49] and in 2005, Helen Clark told a reporter she was called a "no-kids lesbo" by a hostile audience member during a televised leaders' debate.[50] This sort of reportage went beyond mentioning rumors when, in an election television special, popular TV presenter Paul Holmes asked a series of pointed questions about Clark's physical relationship with her husband, Peter Davis, and even "accused the couple of having an ambiguous marriage."[51]

Fountaine argues that Helen Clark's childlessness has been a constant reference point for the media throughout her political career and our study supports this assertion.[52] That Clark and her husband chose not to have children was raised during the 1999 campaign and reiterated in every campaign thereafter. During the 1999 election, Prime Minister Jenny Shipley played the "mom" card as a matter of credibility and experience. "I'm a politician, but I'm also a Mum," Shipley told reporters, clearly in an attempt to contrast her motherly persona with Clark's childlessness and allegedly cold and formidable leadership style.[53]

We found that although Helen Clark's childlessness was not discussed at all in the 1996 election coverage and was mentioned infrequently in articles printed during the 2002, 2005, and 2008 campaigns, reporters continued to cite Clark's decision not to have children as evidence that she had given up any "normal" semblance of a private life in order to succeed in her political career. For example, that "she has never had children, despite being happily married to her husband Peter for 25 years, is also counted against her by some who feel she is out of touch with "ordinary" Kiwi families."[54] Clark's childlessness was also linked to her emotional persona. "Ms. Clark's greatest weakness is her reserve," said a columnist; "When that is coupled with her braininess . . . *and her childlessness*, ordinary folks sense distance" (emphasis ours).[55]

Once the theme of emotional distance was raised in the 1999 campaign, it appeared in every subsequent campaign. For instance, in 2005, a reporter cast Clark as a "cold, unemotional, purpose-driven woman with a steely determination to succeed against all odds."[56] As Table 6.2 indicates, with one exception Clark's *emotional state* was mentioned in a smaller percentage of newspaper articles than were the feelings of her opponents. Many of these references featured typical emotional responses to campaign events (Clark described as happy, relaxed, in a good mood, ebullient, as well as unhappy and upset) but others positioned her as cold and uncaring,[57] or as frighteningly angry. During the 2002 election, the only one in which press coverage profiled Clark's emotions more often than her opponent's, she was described as "furious" and "angry" throughout the campaign, accused of "losing her rag" and "blowing a gasket" and of finally revealing her "bad temper."[58] As with accusations of Clark's emotional detachment, the framing of Clark as incandescent with rage stuck, and was replayed in subsequent campaigns. As we show in the next section, Clark's leadership style and campaign performances were invariably described as unrelentingly aggressive and adversarial.

Masculinizing Frames and Stereotypes

The majority of the stereotypes applied to Clark and her opponents were masculine. As the title of our chapter indicates, Helen Clark was so emphatically masculinized that she was quite literally referred to as male. Indeed, the newspaper coverage often praised her ability to take it (and dish it out) like a man. However, while it may have benefited Clark early in her career as Labour leader, such framing reinforced the *"too masculine/too feminine"* double bind and ultimately fostered negative assessments of Clark's character and leadership qualities.

Table 6.3 shows that Clark was as, or even more, likely than her male opponents to be described with masculine stereotypes. Stereotypically masculine qualities like strength and assertiveness were seen as hallmarks of Clark's campaign performances, and highly aggressive battle language was used to describe her behavior, especially during party

Table 6.3   Masculine Stereotypes, by Election and Leader

Election	Leader	Number (%) of Stories Describing the Leader with a Masculine Metaphor/Stereotype
1996	Helen Clark	20 (24%)
	Jim Bolger	13 (16%)
1999	Helen Clark	17 (19%)
	Jenny Shipley	24 (31%)
2002	Helen Clark	34 (33%)
	Bill English	19 (27%)
2005	Helen Clark	33 (29%)
	Don Brash	39 (29%)
2008	Helen Clark	43 (34%)[*]
	John Key	38 (19%)[*]

*Differences between leaders significant at $p < .05$

leaders' debates.[59] It is worth noting that the only leader portrayed as more masculine than Clark was another women—Jenny Shipley. Even with two women contesting the 1999 election, the News Zealand news media was intent on staying with a masculine script. Through all five elections, Helen Clark was portrayed as unafraid to launch attacks, and eminently capable of fighting off all challengers. In fact, until her losing campaign in 2008, Clark was assessed as prevailing over her opponents, often as trouncing them. Moreover, she was routinely and persistently represented as a battler, hitting, attacking, and landing body blows on her opponents, unafraid to declare war or play hard-ball.[60] While this sort of hyper-masculine language was used to describe the male leaders as well, it had a different resonance for Clark. As the discourse analysis of Clark's coverage presented below shows, the trope of toughness may have helped her win her first three campaigns, but in 2005 and 2008 it positioned her as oddly unfeminine, even dangerous, and did nothing to challenge the perception of leadership as a masculine performance.

During the 1996 campaign, Clark's campaigning was deemed strong, impressive, and authoritative, and the press pronounced her the clear campaign winner.[61] Clark's "attacks" were described as highly effective, as headlines announced: "Clark Draws First Blood," and "Clark Triumphs in TV Joust with rival political leaders."[62] According to all three newspapers, she handily won the televised leaders' debates and shook up her main opponent, Prime Minister Jim Bolger: "Ms. Clark successfully elbowed her Opposition rivals aside in the battle to take on Mr. Bolger", and as a result "he was on the defensive from the outset." Indeed, reporters called Clark well prepared, media-savvy, relaxed, calm, and authoritative[63] while describing Bolger as "rattled by the drubbing he took," constantly under fire and "looking weak."[64] Reportage of Clark certainly called her tough, referring to her "steely drive"[65] and quoting a colleague's comment that she "doesn't mind who gets steam-rolled in her path,"[66] but it was generally positive and laudatory. A *New Zealand Herald* editorial declared "Prize to Clark before a vote cast" for running the "best campaign,"[67] but National secured the victory by forming a coalition with New Zealand First and, a year later, Jenny Shipley became the nation's first female prime minister.

The Shipley versus Clark contest in 1999 was unprecedented; to rephrase the quotation in our title, either way, there would be a woman in charge. Yet the press did not hesitate to employ the classic pugilistic language of the game frame to describe the performances of the two women leaders. "It's always a prize fight, even when the combatants are the first women to go head to head" declared one article.[68] The "Xena princesses" as Shipley and Clark were called, "crossed swords," "battled," "fought," "cracked the whip," "lashed out," "launched attacks," and "fired salvos."[69] While the press seemed reluctant to say the Labour leader had trounced her opponent, Clark was assessed as the clear victor in one of the televised leaders' debates,[70] and Shipley was described as failing to "land the knockout blow needed to salvage National's fortunes" in another.[71] The trope of toughness was invoked, again with positive overtones, as Clark was labeled a "hardy warrior queen," a "formidable, single-minded, intelligent, and hardworking battler" who "demonstrated coolness under pressure and steely ability to withstand assaults that would have felled most men."[72]

In 2002, Helen Clark sought re-election as Prime Minister, and although this was not a fiercely competitive campaign as National lagged in the polls throughout, it was narrated with highly-pitched and caustic battle language.[73] National leader Bill English delivered "torrid," "furious," and "blistering" attacks on Clark's leadership style and integrity,[74] but he was evaluated as largely unsuccessful. One headline about a leaders' debate declared "English Fails to Land Body Blows."[75] Moreover, English "needed to score a knockout punch but it was never going to happen," thus despite "launching furious attacks" on Clark, he was not "able to dent her."[76] Yet reporters highlighted and perhaps even exaggerated Helen Clark's frustration with the "attacks" which were designed to undermine her integrity. As discussed above, she was depicted as intensely, even irrationally angry, and the toughness theme was intensified. Clark was described as flaying, savaging, and backstabbing her opponents and when an opponent called her a "black widow," the press could not resist applying the label.[77] Its implication was that Clark's sexuality, coupled with her political power and authority, was both irresistible and lethal to men.

The 2005 election once again deployed the dominant game frame for campaign coverage, and yet again Clark was evaluated as stronger, fiercer, and more successful than her opponent, Don Brash. Reportage of this campaign was unique in bringing reporters' views of Clark's gendered identity to the fore, prompted by National leader Don Brash's attempt to rationalize a lackluster performance during a televised leaders debate by claiming he was trying to act the gentleman. It was not "appropriate for a man to aggressively attack a woman" Brash said.[78] Reporters indicated skepticism about the National leader's explanation; "When a Rottweiler is biting your head off, pondering its gender would seem of rather secondary importance" commented one writer.[79] An article quoted the reactions of various pundits, one asserting that the "Prime Minister didn't get to the top of the Labour Party and hold her position within the party by being ladylike" and another suggesting he did "*not think of Helen Clark as a woman* but as a tough political candidate" (emphasis ours).[80] Indeed, Clark was viewed as more masculine than her male opponent; for instance, an opinion writer came right out and said "Helen Clark is more of a man than Don Brash is."[81] In fact, Clark was quite literally deemed male. Signs wielded by students at an election rally called her "da man" and declared "either way, there is going to be a man in charge."[82] Perhaps not coincidentally, the press portrayed Clark as politically and sexually aggressive to the point of extreme ruthlessness by calling her a "political dominatrix—whose regime has been termed 'Helengrad.' "[83] A dominatrix takes a dominant role in bondage, submission, and discipline; similarly, likening her government to Stalin's regime invokes hyper-authoritarian behavior. Thus, this coverage not only associated Clark's political power with her purportedly anomalous performance of femininity, it also framed her as cruel and threateningly dictatorial.

During the 2008 election the Prime Minister remained popular and the press continued to assess her as authoritative, experienced, and in firm grasp of the issues, but the Labour Party lagged the National Party in the polls throughout the campaign and there was a mood for change. The classic game frame script again dominated coverage of the leaders, but for the first time Clark was judged the loser of campaign "bouts" (televised leaders' debates) despite delivering her usual commanding performances.[84] Coverage of National leader John Key was not only more prolific than was coverage of Clark,[85] it was more positive. Key was described as "putting in a plucky performance that was the measure of Clark"[86] and as "resonating better with voters."[87] In contrast, Helen Clark was cast as a poor loser, "punching" and "hitting" her opponent and the press when the media declared John Key the winner of the first TV debate.[88] Clark was called "arrogant," "authoritarian," and "dictatorial" and fears were raised about a ruthless "nanny state" determined to "force their way into the nation's bedrooms" with restrictions on water flow to showers and controversial anti-smacking legislation.[89] "It was as if the state was coming in the front door and telling parents how they should raise their kids," said one commentator about the "smacking bill."[90] While typically the "nanny state" is gendered feminine, in Clark's case it was firmly tied to her masculine persona and war-like approach to campaign politics.[91] "Clark's controlling 'nanny state' "[92] became a locus for criticism of the Labour government, with commentators suggesting Clark's "high handed, ruthless, control-freakery . . . welcome to Helengrad," leadership style and her government's "programme of progressive social change . . . fed an undercurrent of paranoia about 'Auntie Helen' the omnipotent school prefect lecturing us in our own homes."[93] Once again, this placed Clark in a controlling and dominating frame that reinforced her masculine persona.

CONCLUSION

Miss Clark, New Zealand's first elected woman prime minister, is at 58 a battle-hardened warrior. . . . But like Boadicea, her time had eventually run out.[94]

The image of Clark as a "battle-hardened warrior" was prolific in coverage of her last election, illustrating the extent to which her press coverage reflected and reinforced norms of heroic warrior masculinity. Clark was discursively constructed as a tough, powerful, and uncompromising leader who single-mindedly attacked her opponents. In all five campaigns she was described as a willing and enthusiastic political pugilist, eager to enter the battle and, until her losing campaign, as capable of regularly landing the metaphorical "knockout punch." The ubiquity and forcefully masculine tone of the game frame for election coverage is demonstrated by our study, as Clark's portrayal could hardly have been more gladiatorial.

Our findings support van Zoonen's assertion that the "cultural model of politician is much closer to the ideas of masculinity than of femininity, which will make a successful performance more complicated for women."[95] Although she underwent a beauty makeover prior to the 1999 campaign, continued to polish her appearance with each subsequent election, and agreed to an intimate at-home-with-husband television interview in 2005, Helen Clark was unable to successfully counter insinuations that she was strangely unfeminine. Juxtapositions of her choice not to have children against the large families of her opponents served as a reminder of Clark's defiance of traditional gender norms. As a result, Clark's efforts to execute the role of strong and adversarial political leader, while at the same time presenting a normalized version of femininity, were confounded by the "too masculine/too feminine" double bind. Always evident in the coverage, this double bind was amplified when admiring descriptions of Clark's strength, competence, and assertiveness gave way to depictions of the Prime Minister as ruthless and dictatorial. When combined with the specter of the authoritarian "nanny state" in the 2008 election, such representations likely contributed to Labour's electoral defeat by undermining the legitimacy of Clark and her government. Labels such as "political dominatrix" and a "black widow" associated Helen Clark's political power with her allegedly aberrant sexuality and anomalous performance of femininity, framing her leadership as menacing and dangerous and consolidating the perception of political leadership as a masculine performance.

Acknowledgments

This research was funded by a Social Sciences and Humanities Research Council of Canada research grant. The authors are very grateful to Gabrielle Mason and Liz Moore, both of whom conducted seemingly endless microfilm searches to complete the data set for this study. As well, we wish to thank Elizabeth Macve for diligently coding the 2008 New Zealand election news stories.

NOTES

1. Several students brandished placards at a 2005 Labour Party election rally, one of which declared: "Either way, there is going to be a man in charge". In other words, regardless of whether the election was won by Labour's Helen Clark or National's Don Brash, a "man" would be in the top job. See Tracy Watkins, " 'Da man' strikes friendly crowd," *Dominion Post*, August 27, 2005.

2. Forbes magazine http://www.forbes.com/lists/2006/11/06women_Helen -Clark_EXX3.html (accessed August 27, 2009). Clark ranked #20 in 2006; and in August 2009, with her new UN position, she's positioned at #60 out of the world's 100 most powerful women.

3. The Maori population was just under 600,000 as of the 2006 census.

4. See Elizabeth McLeay, "Climbing On: Rules, Values and Women's representation in New Zealand," In *Representing Women in Parliament*, ed. Marian Sawer, Manon Tremblay, and Linda Trimble. London: Routledge, 2006, p. 69.

5. McLeay, "Climbing On," p. 69.

6. See Colin James, "National," in *New Zealand Government & Politics*, ed. Raymond Miller. South Melbourne, Australia: Oxford University Press, 2006, pp. 366–376.

7. Peter Aimer, "Labour Party," in *New Zealand Government & Politics*, ed. Raymond Miller. South Melbourne, Australia: Oxford University Press, 2006, pp. 354–365.

8. Jenny Shipley was New Zealand's first woman prime minister, but she was not elected to the post; rather she assumed this position when she contested and secured the leadership of the National Party, replacing Jim Bolger in 1997.

9. New Zealand was an archetypal two party system prior to the introduction of MMP in the 1996 election, with the Labour and National Parties competing to hold power. Although MMP brought several parties into electoral competition, Labour and National are still the major competitors and they build formal and informal coalitions with the minor parties in Parliament to form the government. See Helena Catt, "Commentary: The New Zealand Election of 27 November 1999." *Australian Journal of Political Science* 35, no. 2 (2000): 299–304; and Jack Vowles, "New Zealand," *European Journal of Political Research* 45 (2006): 1207–1220.

10. For instance, Catt noted that, during the 1999 New Zealand election, TV election specials concentrated on the party leaders. See Catt, "Commentary," p. 300.

11. Heather Nunn, *Thatcher, Politics and Fantasy: The Political Culture of Gender and Nation* (London: Lawrence & Wishart, 2002), p. 13.

12. Paul Nesbitt-Larking, *Politics, Society and the Media* (Peterborough: Broadview Press, 2007), Chapter 13; Thomas E. Patterson, "Bad News, Bad Governance," *Annals of the American Academy of Political and Social Science*, 546 (1996): 97–108.

13. Nesbitt-Larking, *Politics, Society, Media*, pp. 316–317.

14. Pippa Norris, "Introduction: Women, Media and Politics," in *Women, Media and Politics*, ed. Pippa Norris (New York: Oxford University Press, 1997), p. 2.

15. Joseph N. Cappella and Kathleen Hall Jamieson, *Spiral of Cynicism: The Press and the Public Good* (New York: Oxford University Press, 1997), p. 38.

16. Elisabeth Gidengil and Joanna Everitt, "Metaphors and Misrepresentation: Gendered Mediation in News Coverage of the 1993 Canadian Leaders' Debates," *Press/Politics* 4, no. 1 (1999): 48–65.

17. Caroline Heldman, Susan J. Carroll, and Stephanie Olsen, "She brought only a skirt: print media coverage of Elizabeth Dole's bid for the Republican presidential nomination," *Political Communication* 22 (2005): 315–335; Annabelle Sreberny-Mohammadi and Karen Ross, "Women MPs and the Media: Representing the Body Politic," *Parliamentary Affairs* 49 (1996): 109.

18. Dianne G. Bystrom, Mary Christine Banwart, Lynda Lee Kaid, and Terry A. Robertson, *Gender and Candidate Communication* (New York and London: Routledge, 2004); Susan Fountaine, *Women Players: The Game Frame in the 1999 General Election* (Massey University: NZ Centre for Women and Leadership Working Paper Series, 02/2, September 2002); Susan Fountaine and Judy McGregor, "Reconstructing Gender for the 21st Century: News Media Framing of Political Women in New Zealand," www.bond.edu.au/hss/communication/ANZCA/papers/JMcGregorSFountainePaper.pdf (accessed February 6, 2003); Judy McGregor, "Gender Politics and the News: The Search for a Beehive Bimbo-Boadicea," in *Dangerous Democracy? News Media and Politics in New Zealand*, ed. Judy McGregor (Palmerston North: Dunmore Press), 181–196; Gertrude Robinson and Armande Saint-Jean, "From Flora to Kim: Thirty Years of Representation of Canadian Women Politicians," in *Seeing Ourselves: Media Power and Policy in Canada*, 2nd edition, ed. Helen Holmes and David Taras (Toronto: Harcourt Brace), pp. 23–36; Linda Trimble, "Gender, Political Leadership and Media Visibility: Globe and Mail Coverage of Conservative Party of Canada Leadership Contests," *Canadian Journal of Political Science* 40, no. 4 (2007): 969–993.

19. Heather Devere and Sharyn Graham Davies, "The Don and Helen New Zealand Election 2005: A Media A-Gender?" *Pacific Journalism Review* 12, no. 1 (2006): 71–73; Fountaine, *Women Players*, pp. 11–17; McGregor, "Gender Politics," pp. 317–318).

20. Johanna Kantola, "The Gendered Reproduction of the State in International Relations," *British Journal of Politics and International Relations* 9 (2007): 271; J. Ann Tickner 1999, "Why Women Can't Run the World," *International Studies Review* 1, no. 3 (1999): 2; Gillian Youngs, "Feminist International Relations: A Contradiction in Terms?" *International Affairs* 80 (2004): 76.

21. Claire Turenne Sjolander, "Of Playing Fields, Competitiveness, and the Will to Win," in *Feminist Perspectives on Canadian Foreign Policy*, ed. Claire Turenne Sjolander, Heather A. Smith, and Deborah Stienstra (Don Mills: Oxford University Press, 2003), p. 71.

22. Tickner, "Why Women," p. 57.

23. Cappella and Jamieson, *Spiral of Cynicism*, pp. 37–57; Linda Trimble and Shannon Sampert, "Who's in the Game? The Framing of the Canadian Election 2000 by The Globe and Mail and The National Post," *Canadian Journal of Political Science* 37, no. 1 (2004): 51–71.

24. Sjolander, "Of Playing Fields," p. 71.

25. Francis L. F. Lee, "Constructing Perfect Women: The Portrayal of Female Officials in Hong Kong Newspapers," *Media, Culture & Society* 26, no. 2 (2004): 286.

Also see Liesbet van Zoonen, "The Personal, the Political, and the Popular: A Woman's Guide to Celebrity Politics," *European Journal of Cultural Studies* 9, no. 3 (2006): 287–301.

26. Holli A. Semetko and Hajo G. Boomgaarden, "Reporting Germany's 2005 Bundestag Election Campaign: Was Gender an Issue?" *Harvard International Journal of Press/Politics* 12, no. 4 (2007): 166.

27. Linda Trimble, Natasja Treiberg, and Sue Girard. " 'Kim-Speak': Gendered Mediation of Kim Campbell During the 1993 Canadian National Election." *Recherches Féministe* (forthcoming 2010).

28. Simon Cross and John Henderson 2004, "Public Images and Private Lives: The Media and Politics in New Zealand," *Parliamentary Affairs* 57, no. 1 (2004): 143.

29. Tim Bale, "It's Labour, but Not as We Know It," *British Journal of Politics and International Relations* 7 (2005): 389; Cross and Henderson, "Public Images," pp. 143–144.

30. The *New Zealand Herald* has a circulation of 200,000, the *Dominion Post* just over 100,000, and the *Christchurch Press* 90,000. See Bale, "It's Labour," p. 389. New Zealand's population as of the 2001 census was 3,792,654.

31. Two databases were used to gather the articles; Factiva was used for all papers and elections except *The Press* (Christchurch) for the 1996 election, which was searched using LexisNexis.

32. Sean Aday and James Devitt, "Style over Substance: Newspaper Coverage of Elizabeth Dole's Presidential Bid," *Harvard International Journal of Press/Politics* 6, no. 2 (2001): 58.

33. W. Lawrence Neuman, *Social Research Methods: Qualitative and Quantitative Approaches*, 4th edition (Toronto: Allyn and Bacon, 2000), p. 293.

34. Teun A. van Dijk, "Principles of Critical Discourse Analysis," *Discourse & Society* 4, no. 2 (1993): 249.

35. See Liesbet van Zoonen, *Feminist Media Studies* (London: Sage, 1994), p. 73.

36. For example: Audrey Young, " 'Helen' and 'John' deliver spiky broadcast," *New Zealand Herald*, October 15, 2008.

37. The data on this measure are not included in the chapter, but are available from the authors on request.

38. Patricia Herbert, "Out of the bunch and into top gear," *New Zealand Herald*, October 4, 1996. The New Zealand Parliament is called the Beehive because of its unique architecture.

39. See for instance, Christine Langdon, "Clark has more to fear from the worm than from English," *The Dominion*, July 1, 2002; and Colin Espiner, "A woman of substance," *The Press*, November 1, 2008.

40. Clark told a reporter, "When the National Party elected a woman leader, in a sense that was very helpful because it took away gender as an issue." Peter Calder, "Taking tea with the new PM the morning after," *New Zealand Herald*, November 29, 1999.

41. Victoria Main, "Shipley feisty in final TV debate," *The Dominion*, November 25, 1999; Andrew Laxon and Vernon Small, "Support acts outshine big two," *New Zealand Herald*, October 28, 1999.

42. Indeed, the headline for the article read "While Labour dazzles, Brash washes socks." Kim Ruscoe, *Dominion Post*, August 20, 2005.

43. Simon Kilroy, "Clark attacks 'cruel stereotyping' to woo women's vote," *The Dominion*, September 27, 1996.

44. Ruth Laugesen, "Clark changes from ugly duckling to canny swan," *The Dominion*, September 30, 1996; Anna Kominik, " 'Cinderella' Clark can thank media trainers," *The Dominion*, October 10, 1996.

45. Helen Bain, "Trying to look the part," *The Dominion*, November 9, 1999.

46. *Dominion Post*, "Diary," October 28, 2008.

47. Bain, "Trying to look the part," *The Dominion*, November 9, 1999. Clark was described as "a gal who once didn't wear lipstick" in the *New Zealand Herald*, "Third-term-it is makes for hard Labour," November 7, 2008.

48. van Zoonen, "The Personal," p. 298.

49. Tracy Watkins, "Clark lost her rag–Nats," *Dominion Post*, July 12, 2002.

50. Errol Kiong, "Clark hits back over abuse during debate," *New Zealand Herald*, September 5, 2005.

51. Jane Bowron, "Telling chat with spouses," *Dominion Post*, September 1, 2004.

52. Fountaine, *Women Players*, p. 14.

53. *The Dominion*, "Shipley's 'Mum' angle misjudged, says Clark," October 30, 1999; Colin James, "Is it time for a change of woman at the top?"*New Zealand Herald*, November 24, 1999.

54. For instance, Colin Espiner, "A woman of substance," *The Press*, November 1, 2008.

55. Colin James, "Is it time for a change of woman at the top?" *New Zealand Herald*, November 24, 1999.

56. Colin Espiner, "Remember where you came from," *The Press*, August 24, 2005.

57. Patricia Herbert, "Out of the bunch and into top gear," *New Zealand Herald*, October 4, 1996.

58. Vernon Small and Helen Tunnah, "Clark in fury at GM ambush," *New Zealand Herald*, July 11, 2002; Tracy Watkins, "Clark lost her rag–Nats," *Dominion Post*, July 12, 2002; *Dominion Post*, "Juggernaut hits the judder bars, July 13, 2002; Nick Venter, "National stumbles on home straight," *Dominion Post*, July 22, 2002.

59. Linda Trimble, Natasja Treiberg, and Gabrielle Mason, "Beating (Up) the Boys: Newspaper Coverage of Helen Clark in New Zealand Elections, 1996–2005," paper presented to the Canadian Political Science Association Annual Conference, Vancouver BC, June 4, 2008.

60. See Trimble, Treiberg, and Mason; aggressive game language prevailed in newspaper coverage of all of the leaders, with the majority of stories featuring pugilistic discourses.

61. *New Zealand Herald*, "Prize to Clark before a vote cast," October 11, 1996.

62. Ruth Laugesen, "Clark draws first blood," *The Dominion*, September 27, 1996; John Roughan, "Clark triumphs in TV joust with rival political leaders," *New Zealand Herald*, September 27, 1996.

63. Ruth Laugesen, "Clark changes from ugly duckling to canny swan," *The Dominion*, September 30, 1996; Sarah Boyd, "Personal note as Clark gains confidence," *The Evening Post*, September 28, 1996.

64. Patricia Herbert, "Bolger may boycott next leader's joust," *New Zealand Herald*, September 28, 1996; Ruth Laughesen, "Clark draws first blood," *The Dominion*, September 27, 1996; Ruth Laughesen, "Nat caucus criticises PM's performance," *The Dominion*, October 16, 1996.

65. Sarah Boyd, "Personal note as Clark gains confidence," *The Evening Post*, September 28, 1996.

66. Graeme Speden, "Clark, Lange working together again" *The Dominion*, October 7, 1996.

67. *New Zealand Herald*, "Prize to Clark before a vote cast," October 11, 1996.

68. John Roughan, "Clark a clear winner on points," *New Zealand Herald*, November 24, 1999.

69. For example: Victoria Main, "Clark cracks the whip in coalition negotiation," *The Dominion*, December 1, 1999; Audrey Young, "Shipley wields the axe," *New Zealand Herald*, November 25, 1999. A significant number of the articles featured this sort of battle language.

70. John Roughan, "Clark a clear winner on points," *New Zealand Herald*, November 24, 1999.

71. Victoria Main, "Shipley feisty in final TV debate," *The Dominion*, November 24, 1999.

72. Brain Rudman, "Woman of steely resolve in good times and bad," *New Zealand Herald*, November 29, 1999.

73. National only garnered 21 percent of the popular vote in this election.

74. Tracy Watkins, "Blistering words over Paintergate," *Dominion Post*, July 8, 2002; Audrey Young, "PM threatens to sue over 'Paintergate,'" *New Zealand Herald*, July 8, 2002; Colin Espiner, "Gloves off for tirade," *Christchurch Press*, July 8, 2002.

75. Tracy Watkins, "English fails to land body blows," *Dominion Post*, July 23, 2002.

76. Ibid.

77. Vernon Small and Helen Tunnah, "Clark in fury at GM ambush," *New Zealand Herald*, July 11, 2002; Colin Espiner, "Gloves off for tirade," *The Press*, July 8, 2002; Nick Venter, "More suitors vie for hand of 'black widow,'" *Dominion Post*, July 23, 2002; Jonathan Milne, "'Black Widow' steers clear of Peters's web," *Dominion Post*, July 24, 2002.

78. Ainsley Thomson and Ruth Berry, "Gentleman Don affronted by sexist tag," *New Zealand Herald*, August 24, 2005.

79. *New Zealand Herald*, "Don't worry about gender when Rottweiler bites," August 24, 2005.

80. Thomson and Berry, "Gentleman Don," *New Zealand Herald*, August 24, 2005.

81. Tracy Watkins, "I'm no feminist, says Brash," *Dominion Post*, August 25, 2005.

82. Watkins, "'Da man'," *Dominion Post*, August 27, 2005.

83. *New Zealand Herald*, "Helen Clark demonstrated superior debating skills," September 16, 2005.

84. For example, see *New Zealand Herald*, "John gets the people's vote," October 15, 2008.

85. This is confirmed by our data, and also by a study released during the campaign. See Rebecca Todd, "Key gets most media cover," *The Press*, November 7, 2008.

86. Colin Espiner, "Key matches Clark in fiery debate," *The Press*, October 15, 2008.

87. *New Zealand Herald*, "Clark bulldozes over opponent but Key connects with viewers," October 19, 2008.

88. Claire Trevant, "PM comes out punching after Key wins plaudits," *New Zealand Herald*, October 16, 2008; and *The Press*, "Clark hits out at Key, TVNZ," October 16, 2008.

89. *New Zealand Herald*, "Clark fixes the small shower to avoid a bath," October 15, 2008.

90. Emily Watt, "Stick that could yet beat Clark," *Dominion Post*, October 24, 2008.

91. For instance: "For Clark it's open war," Fran O'Sullivan, "Gladiator v. Boadicea," *New Zealand Herald*, October 30, 2008.

92. *New Zealand Herald*, "Clark bulldozes," October 19, 2008.

93. *New Zealand Herald*, "Where to now?" November 9, 2008.

94. Paul Chapman, "New Zealand election: the vanquished Helen Clark," *The Telegraph*, November 8, 2008. Downloaded November 8, 2008 from www.telegraph.co.uk.

95. Liesbet van Zoonen, *Entertaining the Citizen* (Oxford: Rowman & Littlefield, 2005): p. 75.

CHAPTER SEVEN

How the Iron Curtain Helped Break through the Glass Ceiling: Angela Merkel's Campaigns in 2005 and 2009

Sarah Elise Wiliarty

INTRODUCTION

Angela Merkel is one of the most successful of the new female executives. She was elected to the German Chancellorship for the first time in September 2005 and was recently re-elected in September 2009. Merkel is the only woman currently leading a G8 country, the only female head of government in the European Union, and the only woman leading a NATO country. Forbes magazine has ranked Merkel the most powerful woman in the world for the past four years consecutively (http://www.forbes.com). It is therefore particularly interesting to examine how Merkel achieved her success.

This chapter begins by considering the extent to which external factors played a role in Merkel's coming to power. It argues that the most important external factor is that Merkel's career has been helped along by a series of unusual events, which she did not cause or control. The chapter then examines gender stereotyping in terms of candidates' personality traits and the issues they are associated with. It looks at gendered media frames and finds that the most critical one for Merkel—a greater emphasis on appearance—is also ameliorated in the way that her image is considered both a matter of how feminine she appears and how western (rather than eastern) she appears. Finally, the chapter considers whether a series of double binds apply to Merkel, culminating in the so-called "Mommy Problem." A frequent insight throughout is that Merkel is less subject to the usual difficulties faced by female candidates both because she is from a moderate right-wing party and because she is from the former East Germany.

Germany has a parliamentary system with a dual executive. The office of Chancellor (the German name for Prime Minister) is clearly the more powerful one; the presidency is ceremonial. Germany's party system has two large, moderate parties: on the right, the Christian Democrats and on the left, the Social Democratic Party (SPD). The Christian Democrats consist of two "sister" parties, the much-larger Christian Democratic Union (CDU), which campaigns throughout the country with the exception of Bavaria and the small Christian Social Union (CSU), which only campaigns in Bavaria. Once elected to the Bundestag (the German parliament), these two parties caucus together. Three smaller parties are currently represented in the Bundestag: the Free Democratic Party (a liberal party), Alliance '90/the Greens (an environmental party), and the Left Party (formed through a merger of the former Communist party and a splinter group from the SPD). Merkel's party, the CDU, is a moderate Christian Democratic party.

As outlined in the introductory chapter, existing scholarship highlights both the obstacles to women obtaining executive office as well as some factors that can help in overcoming those obstacles. Some of the most important factors in facilitating women's gaining executive office include becoming prime minister rather than president, gaining the lesser office in systems with dual executives, family ties, and coming to power at a moment of crisis.[1] These factors will be explored in more detail below. Only two of them apply to the case of Merkel: becoming a prime minister and coming to office during a crisis or unusual times.

When women are elected to executive office, they are more frequently elected to the less powerful office.[2] In countries with dual executives, women are more likely to be elected to the weaker position. Women are also more likely to be elected in parliamentary systems than in presidential systems because prime ministers are at least theoretically somewhat dependent on the parliament that elected them while presidents are directly elected.[3]

This logic only partially applies in the case of Merkel. As Chancellor, Merkel holds the unquestionably more powerful office in a dual executive system. Obviously, she is not a directly-elected president, so she is beholden to the legislature. On the other hand, the institution of the constructive vote of no confidence means that the Bundestag cannot vote the Chancellor out of office without simultaneously electing a new Chancellor. This institution was put into place to avoid a potential power vacuum in the executive. It serves to empower the office of the Chancellor because the parliamentarians must agree not just on getting rid of the current Chancellor, but also on his or her replacement. Indeed, the office of Chancellor is powerful enough that Germany is sometimes referred to as a "Chancellor democracy."[4] A third factor that can facilitate women gaining executive office is family ties. However, Merkel did not have any family ties to politicians and this factor is not relevant in explaining her rise to power.

Finally, multiple scholars have found that women are more likely to gain executive office during unusual times.[5] "Unusual times" —such as a corruption scandal or a regime transition—disrupt politics as usual and create political openings. Both men and women may benefit from a loosening of the political power structure, but women may come to office more frequently during unusual times both because male rivals may be discredited by the scandal and because of the obstacles in their way during normal times.

Three crises or moments of unusual times have helped Merkel: German unification; internal upheaval within her political party, the Christian Democratic Union (CDU); and the early elections of 2005.[6] Without German unification, Merkel would still be a practicing scientist in East Germany. Unification enabled her political career. Furthermore, German political parties have felt the need to have some easterners represented in their leaderships in order to legitimately claim to be representative of all Germans. Merkel often benefited from the CDU's practice of attempting to create a diverse leadership slate.[7]

Merkel also benefited from unusual times within her political party, the CDU. The CDU had been chaired by Helmut Kohl since 1973. When the party lost the elections in 1998 largely because of dissatisfaction with Kohl, he finally stepped down. Kohl's departure following the electoral defeat led to a leadership overhaul within the party. The new chair of the party, Wolfgang Schäuble, appointed Merkel as his General Secretary. Merkel had been a cabinet member for eight years under Kohl, but the position of General Secretary was a clear promotion in terms of both prestige and power.

The 1998 elections were only the beginning of internal party turmoil for the CDU. In the fall of 1999, a major campaign finance scandal broke. It was discovered that Kohl had accepted millions of Deutschmarks illegally. Because many in the CDU appeared to have known about the illegal money, a series of resignations followed, including that of Schäuble. For the second time in less than two years, the CDU underwent a change of leadership and Merkel became party chair. Multiple disruptions in the leadership of her party helped Merkel ascend the party's internal hierarchy more quickly than would have been feasible during normal times.

Finally, the decision to have Merkel run as the Christian Democratic Chancellor candidate in 2005 was also the product of unusual times. The CDU has a sister party, the Christian Social Union (CSU), which is only active in Bavaria. In 2002, the sister parties chose Edmund Stoiber, chair of the CSU, to run for Chancellor. Having lost once already, Stoiber was unlikely to run again, but with more time, the two parties might have come up with an alternative to Merkel, since she did not have widespread support within the CSU. The governing Chancellor, Gerhard Schröder, used an unprecedented method to call early elections, however, and the Christian Democrats backed Merkel as their default candidate.

Instabilities in the German political system over the past 20 years, then, have been helpful in Merkel's rise to power. As the following analysis argues, German unification facilitated Merkel's rise to power in other ways as well. Because gender relations in East Germany were structured differently than in West Germany, unification disrupted traditional gender norms.[8] As the following analysis reveals, it is not so much that Merkel typified an eastern woman and eastern women are somehow more electable to executive office. Rather the interaction of Merkel's easternness and her femaleness was unpredictable and contributed to a loosening of more traditional expectations surrounding female leaders. The literature on gender and political office reveals that women face a series of double binds when attempting to gain office, particularly executive office. For example, they may be regarded as either too feminine or too masculine. It is not that being from former East Germany made these double binds irrelevant to Merkel, but being from the East meant that sometimes her easternness was more salient than her femaleness and at times this shift of perspective was helpful in facilitating her political rise.

Another factor that has been helpful in Merkel's rise to power is her party affiliation. Merkel is from the CDU, a party of the moderate center-right. Women on the left are more likely to be disadvantaged by gender stereotyping and voters' expectations about female candidates often dovetail with their expectations of left-wing candidates.[9] We refer to this as "the Mommy Problem." If female candidates from left-wing parties are perceived as having political positions on the left, it may put those candidates too far left to be elected. This problem may be especially acute for women running for executive office. Merkel, however, also disrupts these expectations since she is from a party of the right. Indeed, the only women to lead G8 countries (Margaret Thatcher, Kim Campbell, and Angela Merkel) have been from parties of the right.

METHODOLOGY

The following analysis is partially based on content analysis of articles in *Der Spiegel*, Germany's largest and most prestigious weekly news magazine. The time frame under examination for the content analysis is the four weeks prior to the elections on September 18, 2005 and September 27, 2009. This is generally considered the "hot phase" of the campaign.

One researcher coded all observations. Any item in *Der Spiegel* that mentioned either candidate was coded, including news articles, editorials, and columns. Each candidate mentioned in each article is counted as an observation. That is, if an article mentions both Merkel and her opponent, it is counted for each of them.

In 2005 Angela Merkel challenged incumbent Chancellor Gerhard Schröder. Merkel's Christian Democratic party finished with 35.2 percent of the vote while the Social Democratic Party (SPD) under Gerhard Schröder obtained 34.2 percent. Neither party had enough seats in the Bundestag to form a governing coalition with their preferred partner so they formed a Grand Coalition with Merkel as Chancellor. In 2009 the SPD ran Frank-Walter Steinmeier and Merkel ran as the incumbent. This time around the Christian Democrats received 33.8 percent of the vote, while the SPD received only 23 percent. The Christian Democrats formed a governing coalition with their preferred partner, the Free Democratic Party (FDP).

As shown in Table 7.1 in 2005 there are 73 articles that mention either Schröder or Merkel; Merkel is mentioned in 49 articles and Schröder in 47. For the 2009 election, the total number of articles that mention Merkel or Steinmeier is 56. Merkel is mentioned in 47 articles while Steinmeier is discussed in 34. Overall press coverage decreased in 2009 because the 2009 election was widely regarded as boring, partly because prior to the election, Merkel and Steinmeier's parties were governing together in a Grand Coalition with Merkel as Chancellor and Steinmeier as Foreign Minister and Vice Chancellor. The expectation throughout the campaign was that Merkel would be re-elected as Chancellor, and the only open question was which coalition partner. Furthermore, coverage of the 2005 election was likely more extensive both because the outcome was less certain and because of the novelty of Merkel's candidacy as the first woman and the first easterner to run for Chancellor.

Evidence from the existing scholarly literature presents mixed results on whether men and women receive different amounts of media coverage. Some research has found that male candidates receive more

Table 7.1 Total Press Coverage in *Der Spiegel* by Election and Candidate

	Total Articles Mentioning Either Candidate	Total Mentioning Merkel	Total Mentioning Her Opponent (Schröder in 2005; Steinmeier in 2009)
2005	73	49	47
2009	56	47	34

coverage than female candidates.[10] Other work has found that men and women receive closer to equal coverage.[11] For the elections under consideration here, Merkel received either equal or more coverage than either of her opponents, running both as challenger and incumbent. Clearly these results do not show the female candidate receiving less coverage as other scholars have found in some cases. Merkel received coverage approximately equal to Schröder's when she was the challenger and she received more coverage than her opponent when she was the incumbent.

GENDER STEREOTYPING

Traits

As discussed in the introductory chapter, the literature on gender stereotyping and voting reveals that voters perceive male and female candidates as having different personality traits, and stereotypical male personality traits are generally viewed as more compatible with executive office.[12] Analysis of the media coverage of the 2005 campaign reveals that Merkel disrupts this pattern. The media presented Merkel as having both male and female personality traits.[13] Merkel is seen as lacking the strength to lead. Her success is attributed not to her own ability but to widespread exhaustion with politics, to her eastern background keeping her out of the CDU's campaign finance scandal, and to her being a protégé of Helmut Kohl's.[14] When she is given credit for her own success, it is mostly because of her diligence, an attribute considered feminine.[15] Sometimes when she is presented positively, it is because of characteristics that are not in keeping with leadership, particularly with executive leadership. For example, her habit of giggling is viewed as charming, as is her tendency of shrugging her shoulders when she does not know the answer to something. In this way, the media presented Merkel as having typically female personality traits.[16]

On the other hand, Merkel is also presented as a "woman who wants to govern", as being goal-oriented and strong, and as being ambitious. She is frequently referred to as being especially rational, a trait that can be traced back to her training as a natural scientist. Linked to her rationality, she is almost never regarded as emotional, but rather is seen as cold, reserved, and aloof.[17]

Erfurt et al. argue that Merkel's candidacy presents a quandary for media and voters alike. On the one hand, the media were ready to present a more stereotypical view of Merkel's candidacy and success: Merkel as the beneficiary of luck and of assistance from others, particularly from

Helmut Kohl. On the other hand, that clearly did not accurately portray the entire story and Merkel's own ambition and ability were also reported, even though these traits did not fit expectations for a female candidate.[18]

Merkel's personal biography and her self-presentation have made it less likely that voters will affiliate her with feminine personality traits. According to a long-time observer, Merkel's training as a natural scientist has had an important effect on how she views politics.[19] She values rationality, competence, and knowledge, all of which are traditionally male personality traits. Furthermore, her eastern background makes it difficult for her to share her private emotions. This trait can make her seem distant rather than warm and compassionate.[20] Her leadership approach is sometimes viewed as passive—as waiting for others to make the decision, which she then ratifies. However, Helmut Kohl had a similar decision-making style and he was not generally regarded as passive (or feminine).[21]

Issues

The content analysis done here reveals that "female" issues simply were not a major part of the campaign, either in 2005 or 2009, at least not as the campaign was covered by *Der Spiegel*. Table 7.2 provides a list of what issues were mentioned and how frequently they were mentioned in connection with one of the candidates.

As this analysis reveals, the coverage of issues affiliated with each candidate was remarkably similar. For both Merkel and Schröder, the

Table 7.2   Issues in the 2005 National Campaign in Germany

	Absolute Number of Articles (Percentage of Total)
Angela Merkel	
Economics	14 (29)
Foreign Policy	5 (10)
Energy/Environment	4 (8)
Family Policy	2 (4)
Gerhard Schröder	
Economics	11 (23)
Foreign Policy	9 (19)
Energy/Environment	7 (15)
Science/Innovation	3 (6)
Education	1 (2)

economy was the top issue, followed closely by foreign policy, both issues on which men are usually considered more competent. Merkel received somewhat more coverage on economic issues. This difference is largely because of her controversial choice of Paul Kirchhof as her shadow Finance Minister. Kirchhof, a professor at the University of Heidelberg, advocated a flat tax among other far-reaching tax reforms. Kirchhof had many supporters and detractors and his selection as Finance Minister became a centerpiece of the campaign. Schröder received somewhat more coverage on foreign policy, not surprising since he was the sitting Chancellor. For both candidates, energy and the environment was the third most common issue covered. Two articles mentioned Merkel in connection to family policy, a more feminine issue area, but one article mentioned Schröder in conjunction with education, also a feminine issue area. However, these issues were not a dominant part of the campaign. Overall, the focus of the coverage was on issues perceived as masculine.

Press coverage of issues in the campaign was very similar in 2009. As is clear from Table 7.3, the most important issues of the campaign are foreign policy, the financial crisis, and the economy.[22]

Not only are these the top issues mentioned in connection with each candidate, the rankings are the same and the percentages of total articles about each candidate that discuss a particular issue are extremely close. Merkel, now the incumbent, is connected slightly more often to foreign policy, while Steinmeier is connected slightly more often to the financial crisis and economic issues. Foreign policy ranks so highly partly

Table 7.3   Issues in the 2009 National Campaign in Germany

	Absolute Number of Articles (Percentage of Total)
Angela Merkel	
Foreign Policy	14 (30)
Financial Crisis	9 (19)
Economics	5 (11)
Energy/Environment	3 (6)
Health	2 (4)
Family Policy	1 (2)
Crime	1 (2)
Religion	1 (2)
Frank-Walter Steinmeier	
Foreign Policy	9 (26)
Financial Crisis	9 (26)
Economics	6 (18)
Energy/Environment	1 (3)

because, from a German perspective, the financial crisis is often perceived as a foreign policy issue. The G20 summit in Pittsburgh occurred during this time period and both candidates attended, despite it taking place just days before the election. The German military presence in Afghanistan was also very much an issue, especially in the final weeks of the campaign. All three of the top issues should be considered "male" issues.[23]

The next most common issue for both candidates is once again energy and the environment. The environment is often categorized as a "female" issue.[24] In the articles under consideration here, the environment is almost always linked with energy policy because most of the articles concern the environmental consequences of particular energy policy decisions. The energy policy aspects under discussion frequently have to do with Germany's relationship with Russia, linking the environment (a "female" issue) with foreign policy (a "male" issue). In any case, energy and the environment are mentioned fairly equally in relationship to both candidates.

Merkel is connected with a broader array of issues than Steinmeier. The additional issues discussed in connection with Merkel—health, family policy, crime, and religion—could all be considered "female" issues, but obviously they are not considered as the most important topics of the campaign.

For the case of Germany, it does not appear that issue coverage presents any kind of bias against a female candidate for executive office. Indeed, the wider range of issues connected to Merkel might indicate that she is perceived as more able to act with authority on a broader range of topics than her opponent. More likely, however, is that Merkel received more press coverage because she is the incumbent. Schröder also received coverage on a slightly broader range of issues when he was the incumbent. When comparing Merkel's first campaign as a challenger to her second campaign as an incumbent, there is not a noticeable difference in issue coverage. There is also apparently no gender difference in issue coverage. For both campaigns, the major issues of the day were largely economic and foreign policy. This trend is to be expected as male issues are generally more strongly associated with executive office. However, the trend of male issues being associated with executive office does not appear to have had any negative repercussions for Merkel's candidacies.

MEDIA FRAMING

Previous scholarship has found that male candidates tend to get more issue coverage while female candidates get more horse-race coverage.[25]

This discrepancy on issue coverage also holds in Germany, even during the campaign when Merkel was an incumbent. For the 2005 election, 57 percent of the articles on Schröder contained issue coverage while only 45 percent of the articles on Merkel did. This gender difference continued in 2009 when 56 percent of the articles on Steinmeier included issue coverage with only 49 percent of Merkel's articles including issue coverage. In terms of horse-race coverage, it is especially negative horse-race coverage that is damaging. A female candidate who is expected to lose will be hit hardest by the lack of issue coverage. In Merkel's case, though, she was widely expected to win throughout both campaigns; the only open question was what the coalition arrangements would be. It is not likely that the minimal difference in issue coverage had a significant effect. The amount of coverage and the issue-orientation of coverage did not negatively affect Merkel's candidacy. The rest of this section examines a variety of gendered frames that are sometimes used by the media.

Appearance

Merkel's appearance has been the subject of an enormous amount of discussion since she first came on the political scene 20 years ago. She has also made very significant changes in her appearance over this time. In Merkel's case, though, the question of whether she looks sufficiently feminine has been inextricably linked with the question of whether she looks sufficiently western. As one of her biographers put it, Merkel "appeared as an 'Ossi-Frau' [Eastern woman] constantly hanging around the government moaning."[26] She was frequently referred to as a "grey mouse" and there were endless jokes about her hairstyle.[27] In her early days as Minister for Women and Youth, she sometimes wore long pleated skirts that were notably "eastern" in appearance. When Merkel updated her image—whether bobbing her hair, starting to wear pant suits, or putting on make-up and jewelry—these changes were perceived as both feminizing and westernizing. As Merkel herself put it (citing East German author Monika Maron): "We have hair, the West Germans have hair-dos."[28] To the extent that she was becoming more feminine, she may have been perceived as becoming less politically competent. However, to the extent that she was seen as becoming more western, she was perceived as becoming *more* competent. For Merkel, feminization overlapped directly with professionalization.

In 2005 Merkel and Schröder had their appearance mentioned in two articles each (4 percent of the total articles for each of them). During this election, then, gender does not seem to have played a role in how much appearance was a part of campaign coverage. In 2009, though, Merkel's appearance was discussed in *Der Spiegel* more often than her opponent's. Seven out of 47 articles about Merkel made some reference to her clothing, her hair, or some other element of her appearance (15%). For Steinmeier, only 3 out of 34 articles (9%) referenced his appearance. For Merkel, these articles frequently refer to her clothing. For example, in a story about the battle for the votes of senior citizens, the discussion of Merkel begins: "Angela Merkel has a sense for what older ladies like. For example, eggplant-colored blazers with brown buttons. 'She looks sharp' whispers a pensioner with her hair in a white permanent."[29]

Three of the seven articles referencing Merkel's appearance are reports about a particular campaign poster put together by CDU candidate Vera Lengsfeld. Lengsfeld is another woman from the former East Germany, fairly close to Merkel in age and somewhat similar in appearance. She brought international publicity to her campaign for the Bundestag through a poster that showed side-by-side pictures of Merkel and Lengsfeld in very low-cut dresses with the caption "We have more to offer." This poster and the response it provoked are probably worthy of their own article. On the one hand, this represents a very old-fashioned method of advertising with women's bodies. On the other hand, the poster was issued by a female candidate and advertises the sexuality of two middle-aged women. It was also clearly meant as at least partially humorous and humor is an important and positive trait in German politics. If the Lengsfeld articles are excluded, then Merkel's appearance was mentioned in four out of 47 articles in 2009 (9%), a very similar number as Steinmeier.

First Name

One common media frame is that female rather than male candidates are more frequently referred to by their first name (implying familiarity, but not authority) or by both first and last names (implying that female candidates are still unknown and require an introduction). For the data under consideration here, there are no significant differences in which combination of names is used to refer to the candidates.

As with issue coverage, the form of the name used to refer to the candidates is strikingly similar. As shown in Table 7.4 both candidates are most frequently referred to by both their first and last names, but also very frequently referred to by last name alone. Referencing a candidate by first name alone was exceptionally rare. This pattern holds across both elections under consideration. It is worth noting that *Der Spiegel* is a serious news magazine. The boulevard press might take a less formal approach when referring to candidates.[30]

Table 7.4 Articles Using First Name, Last Name, or Both in 2005 and 2009

2005	Absolute Number of Articles (Percentage of Total)
Angela Merkel	
First and Last Name	43 (88)
First Name Alone	2 (4)
Last Name Alone	33 (67)
Gerhard Schröder	
First and Last Name	40 (85)
First Name Alone	2 (4)
Last Name Alone	28 (60)

2009	Absolute Number of Articles (Percentage of Total)[1]
Angela Merkel	
First and Last Name	39 (83)
First Name Alone	0 (0)
Last Name Alone	30 (64)
Frank-Walter Steinmeier	
First and Last Name	27 (79)
First Name Alone	1 (3)
Last Name Alone	21 (62)

[1]Percentages total more than 100 percent because articles might refer to a candidate in a variety of ways.

"First Woman"

Merkel suffered somewhat under this frame during the 2005 election. The press developed the supposedly amusing question "Kann-di-dat?" This is a play on words. It is both an informal way of asking "Can she do that?" and the German word for candidate "Kandidat."[31] This phrase focuses on the novelty of a female candidate in a way that immediately casts doubt on her capability. By 2009, however, Merkel had been Chancellor for four years and was nearly assured of re-election. The "first woman" frame had vanished.

"Wife of"

Sometimes the media presents female candidates in their relationships to powerful men. Of course, this is most true of candidates who are related to well-known male politicians. Merkel is married, but her husband has remained absolutely private and is not part of her political career. He did not even appear in public with her when she accepted her victories in 2005 and 2009. He is rarely seen in public at all—usually only at a once a year outing to an opera festival. While political spouses are much less visible in Germany than in the United States, other candidates' spouses do sometimes campaign for them. Even the gay partner of the new Foreign Minister, Guido Westerwelle, appeared at the party on election night, whereas Merkel's husband did not.[32]

This arrangement is an interesting solution to the problem. On the one hand, Merkel's husband is as close to a political-non-entity as one can imagine. This arrangement means that no one could possibly view her as subservient to him politically. On the other hand, if political wives make positive contributions to their husbands' campaigns and careers, then Merkel is forced to get along without whatever benefit spouses might supply.

Emotions

Finally, sometimes female candidates are presented as overly-emotional, perhaps driven by their hormones rather than by their reason. Once again, Merkel has not been negatively affected by this gendered frame. She is rarely, if ever, portrayed as emotional at all. Instead, she is frequently seen as logical and rational, characteristics she supposedly draws from her training as a natural scientist. Indeed, part of the process of professionalization/westernization/feminization discussed above has included her being *more* emotional in public, particularly smiling more.

Merkel has largely been able to avoid the influence of gendered media frames. The effect of the most prominent frame, appearance, has been significantly moderated because of its largely positive interaction with the change from eastern to western standards of appearance.

DOUBLE BINDS

In addition to the gendered media frames discussed above, female candidates for executive office are frequently subject to a series of "double binds"—situations in which they are "damned if they do and damned if they don't." While some of these double binds have affected Merkel, she has also once again been able to avoid many of them, frequently because of her eastern background.

One double bind many female candidates face is that they are perceived as either too feminine or too masculine. Merkel has struggled with this issue, or perhaps to be more accurate, the media has struggled with how to present her. Merkel is occasionally presented as a man and the press has sometimes used the neuter form, calling her "das Merkel."[33] Scholars have argued that she had to become an "honorary man" in order to succeed.[34] However, as noted above, the East-West question has complicated and thereby ameliorated this double bind, as has the passing of time. As is discussed below, Merkel's success may begin to open the possibility of cultural constructs that combine femininity and competence.

Some double binds that troubled female candidates for executive office elsewhere have had little effect on Merkel. She has not suffered from being too young (and therefore seen as inexperienced) or too old (and therefore seen as grandmotherly). While her youth was an issue early in her career (generally a positive one), by the time she became Chancellor, Merkel had been involved with national level politics for fifteen years and therefore had experience. However, she was still the youngest person to become German Chancellor, a fact that is often overlooked because she was also the first woman.

Female candidates are often perceived as being agents of change, a stance which sacrifices their ability to emphasize their experience (and therefore, their competence). However, Merkel's status as an easterner (and therefore a CDU outsider) meant she could bring both change and experience to the table. Because she remained outside the center of her party, she was not tainted by the CDU's campaign finance scandal and she has benefited from her ability to bring change and renewal. On the other hand, by the time she broke with Helmut Kohl over the scandal, she already had eight years experience as a cabinet member and one year experience as General Secretary. Her status as a high-ranking party outsider—which derived both from being female and being from the east—meant she could represent both change and experience.

Some female politicians suffer under the double bind of being either connected or independent. Being connected to a prominent male politician (often through familial ties) is one of the few ways for female politicians to come to prominence themselves. However, this situation means that female politicians are consistently viewed in a dependent relationship. Merkel is not related to a well-known male politician, but she was widely regarded as a protégé of Helmut Kohl's and to some extent under his shadow. Once again, her break with him following the campaign finance scandal allowed her to use the connection to come to prominence, but then gain her independence as she left her former mentor behind.

Female politicians are frequently subjected to a series of double binds. For Merkel, however, being from the former East Germany often disrupted these double binds so that they did not apply to her in any serious way.

THE "MOMMY PROBLEM"

For Merkel, the "Mommy Problem" works in her favor. Women on the left may be perceived as "doubly" left—which puts them on the fringe of their parties and away from the moderate center. As a woman from the *right*, however, Merkel is perceived as being from the left wing of her own party; that position places her closer to the political center.[35] Voters who are unsure about the more conservative strains within the CDU may be still willing to vote for Merkel because she will moderate the party.[36] In this way, Merkel benefits from the "Mommy Problem."

Merkel has another kind of "Mommy Problem" as well; she is childless. She did marry her long-time partner, Joachim Sauer, in 1998, as her political career started to take off. Her husband almost never appears in public with her. But she has no children. This issue was raised by Doris Schröder-Kopf, Chancellor Gerhard Schröder's wife, in the 2005 election. Late in the campaign, Schröder-Kopf was quoted in *Die Zeit* as saying "With her biography, she does not embody the experiences of most women. German women are trying to combine children, family, and career. That isn't Merkel's world. Merkel's politics are partially responsible for the absence of children in Germany today".[37] This attack was both nuanced and multi-sided. First, it is notable that the SPD did not have a man deliver it, but instead the wife of the Chancellor. Particularly in 2005 with the ultra-macho Gerhard Schröder as its candidate, the SPD was wary that overly-vicious attacks on Merkel would seem un-gentlemanly.[38] Having a woman raise the issue avoided that problem.

The framing of the attack, however, highlights east-west differences in the challenge of combining work and family. *West* German women have struggled with how to reconcile children and career for decades. For *East* German women, though, the problem was non-existent. The East German government provided extensive child care and the majority of East German women both had children and worked full time.[39] Before the fall of the Berlin wall in 1989, 89 percent of East German women were in paid employment compared with only 55 percent of West German women.[40] Particularly since it was issued by a woman, Doris Schröder-Kopf's attack was much more likely to be seen as accusing Merkel of being insufficiently western rather than insufficiently female. Merkel's lack of children is much more unusual in the eastern context than in the western context. But what is clear from Schröder-Kopf's comments is that she is not sympathizing with Eastern German women whose access to daycare and jobs was dramatically curtailed by unification. Perhaps, she is angry that Merkel (and other easterners) managed to dodge the work-family reconciliation struggle that is so difficult for women in the west.

For the 2005 campaign, the Schröder-Kopf attack is the only reference to Merkel's motherhood in *Der Spiegel* for the time period under consideration. It would have been reasonable to expect that this issue would fade in importance. By 2009 the voters all knew that Merkel does not have children; perhaps motherhood would become simply irrelevant in Merkel's case. Rather than the issue of motherhood becoming unimportant, however, in the 2009 campaign Merkel was made into a metaphorical mother. On August 31, 2009, *Der Spiegel* ran a lengthy article on Merkel's cabinet meetings.[41] The first several paragraphs discuss how friendly and nice the meetings are, how various cabinet minister get their preferred variety of tea and bouquets on their birthdays. Several of Merkel's ministers compare her to "Mutter Beimer" —the kind, concerned mother from *Lindenstrasse*, Germany's longest running soap opera.

Another lengthy article analyzing the campaign includes the following passage:

> She is now the people's Chancellor, not just the partisan Chancellor. She is the worrier, the mother of all, the queen of Germany. When she talks about the SPD—you don't hear any malice, no triumph, rather just caring and the analytical perspective considering what a weak SPD would mean for the country. Merkel the mother hen takes the SPD-chick under her wing.[42]

In a third article, Merkel is referred to off-handedly as the "Landesmutter," the mother of the country.[43] Rather than Merkel's lack of biological motherhood disappearing with time, her relationship to motherhood has been transformed. Instead of being the target of criticism for her lack of biological children, Merkel is being made into the mother of all: the mother of the cabinet, the mother of Germany, even the mother of the SPD.

Surprisingly, the images presented here are largely positive. A mother is, after all, a female authority figure. Kohl was often referred to as the father of German unification; Merkel is now the mother of a united Germany. Instead of a stern, protective father, Merkel's image is presented as a caring, compassionate mother. Her image is becoming feminized without the sacrifice of her masculine attributes of competence, rationality, and seriousness. For a politician who has at times appeared cold and unfeeling, the addition of feminine traits without the loss of masculine ones may actually be advantageous.

In one of the articles that refers to Merkel as a mother, but also in two additional articles which do not, Merkel is put into the role of hostess.[44] In addition to arranging for the proper tea at cabinet meetings, she is described as making shopping lists, discussing what to serve at state banquets and distributing bouquets on cabinet members' birthdays. There are no references to either Gerhard Schröder or Frank-Walter Steinmeier acting as a host. The role of hostess is also largely a positive one and furthermore, often a quite powerful one.[45] In portraying Merkel as a mother and a hostess, the media may be developing new positive stereotypical images for powerful female leaders.

CONCLUSION

The analysis of *Der Spiegel's* press coverage for Angela Merkel's campaigns in 2005 and 2009 confirms some of the hypotheses about women running for executive office and challenges others. The press coverage reveals a surprising amount of gender equality in terms of the amount of coverage, the issues discussed in relationship with the candidates, and the names with which *Der Spiegel* refers to the candidates. In these ways, press coverage of Merkel and her male opponents was quite similar.

The hypothesis that the appearance of female candidates receives more coverage generates mixed results. On the one hand, Schröder and Merkel received approximately equal coverage in 2005. On the other hand, Merkel's appearance got more coverage than Steinmeier's in 2009 and historically the press has covered her appearance extensively. For this issue, though, Merkel's easternness disrupts traditional gender expectations. The changes in Merkel's appearance made her both more feminine (and possibly less competent) and more western (and definitely more professional). Similarly, the standard double binds that many female candidates are subjected to operated differently in Merkel's case because of her eastern background.

Finally, particularly Merkel's second campaign reveals an opening in the press to new powerful images of women: mother and hostess. It is likely that after four years in office, potential stereotypical images of powerless women simply made no sense in connection with Merkel and the press began to find other images with which to describe her campaign. The image of mother may be especially useful to a female candidate like Merkel without biological children, both because she does not have the real responsibility of her own children and because as a metaphorical mother she can be portrayed as having more in common with other mothers with whom voters may be familiar. The image of hostess as a feminine role, on the other hand, may be widely available to female candidates. The hostess role might allow female politicians to be both gracious and powerful, to be generous while controlling both the agenda and the decision-making process. Although Merkel's eastern background is not easily duplicated in other contexts, the empowered feminine roles of mother and hostess may be able to be used by female politicians elsewhere to good effect.

Acknowledgments

Thank you to my colleagues and students at Wesleyan who offered insightful questions and comments in various settings. Thank you also to my husband, Kevin, for both moral and technical support and to my children, Patrick and Geneva, for understanding that I sometimes needed to work when they would rather I had been available for play. Thank you to Rainbow Murray and Melody Rose. Their helpful feedback sharpened my writing and my thinking.

NOTES

1. Piper A. Hodson, "Routes to Power: An Examination of Political Change, Rulership, and Women's Access to Executive Office," in *The Other Elites: Women, Politics, and Power in the Executive Branch*, ed. MaryAnne Borrelli and Janet M. Martin (Boulder: Lynne Rienner, 1997); Michael A. Genovese, "Women as National Leaders: What Do We Know?," in *Women as National Leaders*, ed. Michael A. Genovese (London: Sage, 1993); Farida Jalalzai, "Women Rule: Shattering the Executive Glass Ceiling," *Politics and Gender* 4, no. 2 (2008).

2. Jalalzai, "Women Rule: Shattering the Executive Glass Ceiling."

3. Ibid.

4. Karlheinz Niclauss, *Kanzlerdemokratie: Regierungsführung von Konrad Adenauer bis Gerhard Schröder* (Paderborn: Schöningh, 2004).

5. Genovese, "Women as National Leaders: What Do We Know?" Jalalzai, "Women Rule: Shattering the Executive Glass Ceiling." Hodson, "Routes to Power: An Examination of Political Change, Rulership, and Women's Access to Executive Office."

6. Sarah Elise Wiliarty, "Chancellor Angela Merkel—a Sign of Hope or the Exception That Proves the Rule?," *Politics and Gender* 4, no. 3 (2008).

7. ———, "Angela Merkel's Path to Power: The Role of Internal Party Dynamics and Leadership," *German Politics* 17, no. 1 (2008); ———, *Bringing Women to the Party: The CDU and the Politics of Gender in Germany* (Cambridge: Cambridge University Press, forthcoming).

8. Myra Marx Ferree, "The Rise and Fall of 'Mommy Politics': Feminism and Unification in (East) Germany," *Feminist Studies* 19, no. 1 (1993); S. Meyer and E. Schulze, "After the Fall of the Wall: The Impact of the Transition on East German Women," *Political Psychology* 19, no. 1 (1998); Eileen Trzcinski, "Gender and German Unification," *Affilia-Journal of Women and Social Work* 13, no. 1 (1998); Brigitte Young, *Triumph of the Fatherland: German Unification and the Marginalization of Women* (Ann Arbor: University of Michigan Press, 1999); I. Miethe, "From 'Mother of the Revolution' to 'Fathers of Unification': Concepts of Politics among Women Activists Following German Unification," *Social Politics* 6, no. 1 (1999).

9. J. W. Koch, "Do Citizens Apply Gender Stereotypes to Infer Candidates' Ideological Orientations?," *Journal of Politics* 62, no. 2 (2000). On the tendency

of parties of the left to elect more women, see Miki Caul Kittilson, *Challenging Parties, Changing Parliaments: Women and Elected Office in Contemporary Western Europe* (Ohio State University Press, 2006). R. E. Matland, "Institutional Variables Affecting Female Representation in National Legislatures—the Case of Norway," *Journal of Politics* 55, no. 3 (1993).

10. K. F. Kahn, "The Distorted Mirror—Press Coverage of Women Candidates for Statewide Office," *Journal of Politics* 56, no. 1 (1994); Kim Fridkin Kahn, *The Political Consequences of Being a Woman: How Stereotypes Influence the Conduct and Consequences of Political Campaigns* (New York: Columbia University Press, 1996); Caroline Heldman, Susan J. Carroll and Stephanie Olson, "She Brought Only a Skirt: Print Media Coverage of Elizabeth Dole's Bid for the Republican Presidential Nomination," *Political Communication* 22, no. 3 (2005).

11. K. B. Smith, "When All's Fair: Signs of Parity in Media Coverage of Female Candidates," *Political Communication* 14, no. 1 (1997); Farida Jalalzai, "Women Candidates and the Media: 1992–2000 Elections," *Politics and Policy* 34, no. 3 (2006); Miki Caul Kittilson and Kim Fridkin, "Gender, Candidate Portrayals, and Election Campaigns: A Comparative Perspective," *Politics and Gender* 4, no. 3 (2008).

12. L. Huddy and N. Terkildsen, "Gender Stereotypes and the Perception of Male and Female Candidates," *American Journal of Political Science* 37, no. 1 (1993); Kathleen A. Dolan, *Voting for Women: How the Public Evaluates Women Candidates* (Westview Press, 2004).

13. Philine Erfurt, Anja Haase, and Julia Rosshart, "Mediale Geschlechterkonstruktionen im Bundestagswahlkampf 2005," in *"Kann die Das?" Angela Merkels Kampf um die Macht: Geschlechterbilder und Geschlechterpolitiken im Bundestagswahlkampf 2005*, ed. Sylka Schloz (Berlin: Karl Kietz Verlag, 2007), p. 30.

14. Ibid.

15. Ibid.

16. Ibid., p. 31.

17. Ibid., pp. 31–32.

18. Ibid.

19. Gerd Langguth, *Angela Merkel: Aufstieg zur Macht*, second ed. (Munich: Deutscher Taschenbuch Verlag GmbH & Co., 2008), p. 393.

20. Ibid., p. 401.

21. Wiliarty, "Angela Merkel's Path to Power: The Role of Internal Party Dynamics and Leadership," p. 85.

22. The coding "Economics" indicates an economic issue separate from the financial crisis.

23. D. Alexander and K. Andersen, "Gender as a Factor in the Attribution of Leadership Traits," *Political Research Quarterly* 46, no. 3 (1993); K. Dolan, "Do Women Candidates Play to Gender Stereotypes? Do Men Candidates Play to Women? Candidate Sex and Issues Priorities on Campaign Websites," *Political Research Quarterly* 58, no. 1 (2005).

24. Alexander and Andersen, "Gender as a Factor in the Attribution of Leadership Traits." Kahn, "The Distorted Mirror—Press Coverage of Women Candidates for Statewide Office." Jalalzai, "Women Candidates and the Media: 1992–2000 Elections."

25. Kahn, "The Distorted Mirror—Press Coverage of Women Candidates for Statewide Office"; ———, *The Political Consequences of Being a Woman: How Stereotypes Influence the Conduct and Consequences of Political Campaigns*; Pippa Norris, *Women, Media, and Politics* (Oxford University Press, 1997); Jalalzai, "Women Candidates and the Media: 1992–2000 Elections."

26. Nicole Schley, *Angela Merkel: Deutschlands Zukunft ist Weiblich* (Munich: Knaur Taschenbuch Verlag, 2005), p. 73.

27. Evelyn Roll, *Die Kanzlerin: Angela Merkels Weg zur Macht* (Ullstein TB-Verlag, 2009), p. 172.

28. Hugo Mueller-Vogg and Angela Merkel, *Mein Weg* (Hamburg: Hoffmann und Campe, 2004), p. 128. as cited in: Joyce Marie Mushaben, "Deconstructing Gender in German Politics: The Extreme Makeover of Angela Merkel," in *German Studies Association Annual Meeting* (Pittsburgh PA 2006).

29. Katrin Elger, Alexander Neubacher, and Michael Sauga, "Die alte Macht," *Der Spiegel*, September 7, 2009, p. 70.

30. Although Merkel was not often referred to by her first name in the press, her campaign made frequent use of a nickname, "Angie." In 2005, Merkel's campaign often played the Rolling Stones song "Angie" at campaign rallies. That practice ended both because the Rolling Stones threatened to sue and because CDU campaign staff realized that the song does not end well for the "Angie" of the title.

31. Erfurt, Haase, and Rosshart, "Mediale Geschlechterkonstruktionen im Bundestagswahlkampf 2005," p. 29.

32. Interestingly, Merkel has never been seriously accused of being a lesbian though childless women with husbands out of the public eye are often subject to that accusation in other countries.

33. Erfurt, Haase, and Rosshart, "Mediale Geschlechterkonstruktionen im Bundestagswahlkampf 2005," p. 29.

34. Ibid; Mushaben, "Deconstructing Gender in German Politics: The Extreme Makeover of Angela Merkel."

35. Koch, "Do Citizens Apply Gender Stereotypes to Infer Candidates' Ideological Orientations?"

36. It is certainly true that the two times the Christian Democrats ran a Chancellor candidate from the CSU—their more conservative sister party in Bavaria—they suffered a severe electoral loss. The CSU may have a "Daddy Problem."

37. As cited in: Markus Feldenkirchen et al., "Poltern und Pöbeln," *Der Spiegel*, September 5, 2005, p. 22.

38. Ibid.

39. There is a large literature on the differences between the experiences of women in East and West Germany both before and after unification. For some examples, see: Ferree, "The Rise and Fall of 'Mommy Politics': Feminism and Unification in (East) Germany." Meyer and Schulze, "After the Fall of the Wall: The Impact of the Transition on East German Women." Trzcinski, "Gender and German Unification." Miethe, "From 'Mother of the Revolution' to 'Fathers of Unification': Concepts of Politics among Women Activists Following German Unification." Young, *Triumph of the Fatherland: German Unification and the Marginalization of Women.*

40. Anna Matysiak and Stephanie Steinmetz, "Finding Their Way? Female Employment Patterns in West Germany, East Germany, and Poland,"*European Sociological Review 2008,* 24, no. 3 (2008).

41. Markus Feldenkirchen et al., "Das wäre die Höchststrafe," *Der Spiegel*, August 31 2009, p. 54.

42. Christoph Schwennicke, "Germanias Kampf um Berlin," Ibid., September 21, p. 38.

43. Elke Schmitter, "Angst und Biedersinn," Ibid., p. 148.

44. Markus Feldenkirchen et al., "Das wäre die Höchststrafe," Ibid., August 31, p. 54. Dirk Kurbjuweit, "Gegen die Gierigen," *Der Spiegel*, August 31, 2009, p. 25. Petra Bornhöft et al., "Im Zweifel links," *Der Spiegel*, September 7, 2009, p. 20.

45. Susan K. Harris, *The Cultural Work of the Late Nineteeth-Century Hostess: Annie Adams Fields and Mary Gladstone Drew* (Basingstoke and New York: Palgrave Macmillan, 2002).

CHAPTER EIGHT

Ma Ellen: Liberia's Iron Lady?

Melinda Adams

On November 8, 2005, Ellen Johnson Sirleaf won the second round of the Liberian presidential elections, becoming Africa's first female elected head of state. Sirleaf's campaign benefited from external factors, namely Liberia's post-conflict environment and the support of an active women's movement. Campaign choices were also critical to her success. Sirleaf strategically navigated the double binds that have presented obstacles for female candidates in other contexts. Her campaign effectively portrayed her as the candidate who best represented both experience *and* change and who embodied the mix of the masculine and feminine character traits needed in Liberia's post-conflict environment. Sirleaf's campaign depicted her as "Ma Ellen," the mother and grandmother who would care for Liberia's population by promoting peace, education, and development and as Liberia's "Iron Lady," a well educated, experienced politician with "zero tolerance" for corruption. Sirleaf was both the empathetic mother figure and a woman tough enough to stand up to former warlords and corrupt politicians. In sum, a combination of external factors, campaign choices, and personal characteristics contributed to Sirleaf's victory.

BACKGROUND

Liberia's 2005 presidential election was part of a broader political transition following decades of authoritarianism, political instability, and civil conflict. From Liberia's independence in 1847 until 1980, an Americo-Liberian elite, which comprised just 2.5 percent of the population, controlled the political system.[1] In 1980, Samuel Doe, an indigenous Liberian, launched a coup d'état that overthrew then-president William Tolbert and ended nearly one hundred years of domination by the True Whig Party. Doe's reign was dictatorial. It continued the politics of exclusion that characterized previous administrations; although under Doe, it was those of Krahn ethnicity—rather than the Americo-Liberians—who received the top military and political appointments. In 1985, Doe organized elections and claimed the presidency, though the elections were widely criticized as blatantly rigged. Charles Taylor, an Americo-Liberian who worked briefly in Doe's government, launched an insurgency in 1989 that led to the overthrow of Doe and pushed the country into a seven-year civil war. After a successful ceasefire was brokered in August 1996, special presidential elections were held in July 1997. Taylor won in a landslide with over 75 percent of the votes. Sirleaf came in a distant second with just 9.58 percent of the votes. Taylor's victory has been attributed to a variety of factors, including his control over the media, his extensive campaign funds, and voters' fears that his failure to win would lead to renewed violence.[2] Sirleaf's 1997 campaign emphasized her opposition to Doe and her non-involvement in the conflict; however, her links to the Tolbert administration, her association with the urban elite, and the fact that she had lived abroad during the civil war hurt her candidacy.[3] In 1999, Liberia spiraled into violence once again. A 2003 peace accord led to Taylor's exile to Nigeria, the appointment of a transitional government, and the organization of 2005 legislative and presidential elections.

The 2005 presidential elections stood out from previous elections in that they were not dominated by the Americo-Liberian elite, a political incumbent, or a warlord, creating an opening for the emergence of a new political leader.[4] Members of the transitional government were barred from running for the presidency. Though far from perfect, the 2005 elections were viewed by international election observers as relatively free and fair. Liberia has a presidential system with a bicameral legislature. To be elected, a candidate must receive a majority of the votes. If no candidate wins over 50 percent of the votes in the first round of elections, then the two candidates with the most votes participate in a second round.[5] Twenty-two candidates, including two women, participated in the first round, which was held on October 11th. After the votes were tallied, George Weah, the international soccer star, was on top with 28.3 percent and Sirleaf was in second place with 19.8 percent (the other female candidate, Margaret Tor-Thompson, came in 13th with 0.9% of the vote).[6] Since neither candidate received a majority of the votes, the two faced off in the second round on November 8th. The next section examines the role that gender stereotypes played in the runoff campaign.

GENDER STEREOTYPES

Traits

Scholars studying gender and politics have found that men and women are associated with different character traits. Women are generally associated with "warmth, expressiveness, gentleness, compassion, and emotion," while men tend to be viewed as "strong, competent, rational, aggressive, and knowledgeable."[7] Since the traits that are more commonly associated with men are also those that are considered essential for successful leaders, men are frequently viewed as better equipped for the job of leading a nation.[8] Women may be perceived as either possessing the wrong types of traits to be effective leaders or as being too masculine and, therefore, deviating from expected gender norms.

Throughout the campaign, Sirleaf was largely able to escape these criticisms by effectively portraying herself as someone who possessed both stereotypically masculine and feminine characteristics. Sirleaf presented herself as someone who could thrive in traditionally masculine arenas. She highlighted her Ivy-league education and past political and professional experience in areas traditionally dominated by men. She holds a Master's degree in Public Administration (MPA) from Harvard University. After completing her degree in 1971, she returned to Liberia and held several positions in Tolbert's administration, eventually becoming Minister of Finance. After two brief periods of imprisonment for political reasons in the 1980s, Sirleaf fled Liberia. While abroad, she held a series of high-level positions at Citibank, HSBC Equator Bank, the United Nations Development Program (UNDP), and the World Bank. Sirleaf drew on these experiences to make the case that she had the strength and toughness needed to succeed in male-dominated spheres and that she was an "Iron Lady," who could stand up to former warlords and corrupt politicians.

Sirleaf also made the case that her experience as a woman prepared her for the presidency. Throughout the campaign, Sirleaf called attention to the fact that she was a mother and a grandmother. Speaking to *The Perspective*, a U.S.-based news magazine published by the Liberian Democratic Future (LDF), Sirleaf stated, for example: "I believe that there are certain attributes in a woman that give her some advantages over a man. Women are usually more honest, more sensitive to issues and bring a stronger sense of commitment and dedication to what they do. Maybe because they were mothers, and being a mother you have that special attention for the family, for the young, for children."[9] In the documentary, *Iron Ladies of Liberia*, Sirleaf notes that Liberians often respond favorably to her "Old Ma" political style, in which she approached constituents as a mother who listened to them. Sirleaf's campaign implicitly argued that as a woman—and a mother—she would bring feminine leadership qualities, such as warmth and compassion, to the presidency. After years of corruption, mismanagement, and violence associated with Liberia's previous male leaders, Sirleaf's commitment to create a government that was more honest, open, and responsive to constituents resonated with Liberians.

Ideology

The literature on gender stereotypes in politics, which to date has been drawn primarily from studies of the American and European contexts, finds that voters tend to perceive women as being more liberal than men.[10] In 1997 and 2005, Sirleaf was the standard bearer for the Unity Party (UP), which has not been characterized by a strong ideological position but has been identified as the party that has traditionally appealed to businesspeople, technocrats, and the middle class.[11] In the Liberian context, ideology plays a very limited role in elections and Sirleaf was not closely identified with any specific ideological position. Political parties are generally associated with individuals and regional strongholds rather than with an ideology. Sawyer argues that "there are hardly any significant differences among Liberian political parties that can be discerned from their official pronouncements and declared programmes."[12] Since voters do not generally place parties or candidates on a left-right spectrum, this type of gender stereotype was not relevant in the 2005 Liberian presidential election.

Issues

Studies on gender stereotypes and elections have found that the media and the general public view women and men as having different areas of competence. Men are frequently viewed as having greater expertise in the areas of defense, foreign policy, and economics, while women are seen as stronger on the issues of poverty, health care, and education.[13] Some of these stereotypes may not hold in all contexts: Kahn, for example, suggests agricultural policy as an area where men hold an advantage, though this is not necessarily the case in much of Africa where women comprise the vast majority of subsistence farmers.[14] Nevertheless, most of these stereotypes do seem to travel to non-Western contexts. The fact that national elections tend to be defined around issues that are associated with men means that female candidates often fight an uphill battle in which they need to prove their knowledge in these areas. The 2005 Liberian election came at a critical moment in Liberian history as the country was transitioning from nearly two decades of conflict and unrest. Key issues during the campaign included conflict resolution, transitional justice, economic development, education, and corruption. Sirleaf's campaign not only highlighted her strengths in areas traditionally associated with women (e.g., education, anti-corruption, and conflict resolution), but was able to use her personal experience to make the case that she was the most qualified candidate in an area—the economy—generally associated with men. Claiming expertise in the economy was critical to Sirleaf's success. In a country facing unemployment rates as high as 90 percent with little working infrastructure (even the capital city, Monrovia, lacked electricity), the economy was the most important issue of the campaign.

Around the world in places like Israel, Sudan, Rwanda, Liberia, and elsewhere, women have organized to promote peace in their countries and regions,[15] leading to the perception that peace and conflict resolution are areas where women enjoy greater competence. In Liberia, both candidates made the case that they were the best placed to promote these goals. Sirleaf asserted that she would promote reconciliation through a truth commission and programs designed to integrate former combatants into society. Weah emphasized his lack of involvement in Liberia's past political troubles and argued that his clean hands allowed him to promote peace more effectively.

During Liberia's civil war, women were more often seen as peace makers than as perpetrators of violence. This general perception did not mean that individual women did not participate in the conflict, but rather that on the whole, men were more likely to be directly involved in violence. The Liberian women's movement played a critical role in the peace process. Women's groups—including the Liberian Women's Initiative (LWI), Women in Peace Building Network (WIPNET), the Association of Female Lawyers in Liberia (AFELL), and the Mano River Union Women Peace Network (MARWOPNET)—raised awareness about the conflict and its effects on civilians, pressured faction leaders to participate in peace talks, lobbied for the inclusion of women in official peace negotiations and for the appointment of Ruth Perry as the Head of Liberia's Council of State, and provided support to those displaced by violence.[16] Sirleaf's candidacy benefited from this general perception of women as peacemakers.

Sirleaf's reputation as a peace builder, though, was tainted slightly by her initial support of Charles Taylor's insurgency in the late 1980s. While Sirleaf's support for Taylor was short-lived, her critics played up her connection to Taylor. Weah sought to exploit this opening by positioning himself as the candidate with the cleanest hands. Unlike Sirleaf, Weah was not actively involved in Liberian politics in the 1980s and 1990s. He left Liberia in 1987 to play soccer for a Cameroonian club team.

In 1988, he left Cameroon to play in Europe, playing for teams in France, Italy, and England. In 1995, while Liberia's civil war raged, Weah was named FIFA's World Player of the Year, European Footballer of the Year, and African Footballer of the Year. His success on the soccer field led to his appointment by UNICEF as a Goodwill Ambassador in 1997. In this capacity, he traveled around the world promoting children's rights. Weah's position as a peace builder and as someone removed from past political struggles was compromised, however, by his supporters (much of support seemed to come from young male former combatants) and by endorsements from former warlords such as Alhaji Kromah and Prince Johnson. When preliminary second-round election results indicated that a Weah victory was unlikely, Weah's supporters chanted slogans such as "No Weah, No Peace" at political rallies, further weakening his claims that he was the candidate best able to promote lasting peace in the country.[17]

While the economy is traditionally viewed as a masculine issue,[18] Ellen Johnson Sirleaf's extensive experience in this area gave her the edge over Weah. Given Liberia's heavy reliance on international assistance, Sirleaf's international connections and her ability to inspire donors' confidence were important strengths. During the campaign, she was able to claim credibly that she was the only candidate who would be able to bring immediate relief to Liberia. Weah sought to compensate for his thin résumé and lack of formal education by highlighting his common sense. He criticized Sirleaf's choices as Minister of Finance and argued that common sense rather than an Ivy-League degree was the key to good leadership.

Education is often viewed as a women's issue,[19] and the Liberian election fit this pattern. Liberia's educational system was devastated during the war, and Liberia has one of the lowest literacy rates in the world. Given the differences in the candidates' levels of education, it is not surprising that Sirleaf held an edge in this issue. His campaign downplayed the importance of education, and a popular slogan at his rallies was: "you know book, you not know book, I will vote for you," which sought to minimize his lack of education. Ellen supporters, in contrast, promoted her high level of education, chanting slogans like "Who know book, Ellen knows book" at her campaign events.

Combating corruption is frequently viewed as a women's issue. Kahn notes that women are perceived as having greater competence in the area of maintaining honesty and integrity in government.[20] Dollar, Fisman, and Gatti find that higher levels of women in politics correlates with lower levels of corruption.[21] Swamy et al.'s study of gender and corruption finds that women are less likely to condone corruption than men, female managers are less likely to be involved in bribery, and states with higher percentages of women in government and the market have lower levels of corruption.[22] Other studies suggest that these findings are spurious[23]; nevertheless, voters' perceptions of women's and men's participation in corruption—rather than the reality of whether women are less corrupt than men—are key. If voters perceive women as less corrupt and as more likely to establish transparent policies, they may be more likely to vote for them.

Given Liberia's reputation for high levels of corruption, both Weah and Sirleaf took strong stands against it and sought to present themselves as the best placed to promote good governance. Sirleaf indicated that she would increase state salaries and pay salaries on time so that state employees would be less inclined to engage in corruption. She also stated that she would adopt a policy of "zero tolerance" and root out corrupt individuals in government. Weah argued that under his administration, those found guilty of graft would be fined and imprisoned, their assets would be confiscated, and they would be banned from working in the government in the future. The fact that Sirleaf is a woman may have given her an edge in this area since women in general were seen as less corrupt than men.

MEDIA FRAMING

Media coverage of the 2005 Liberian presidential election reinforced some, but not all, common gender stereotypes. The press frequently referred to Sirleaf solely by her first name, while it rarely did so for Weah. The Liberian press sometimes mentioned that, if successful, Sirleaf would become the first female elected president in Africa, though media sources did not dwell on Sirleaf's "first woman" status excessively, perhaps because famed soccer star Weah's rags-to-riches story was also compelling. Media coverage highlighted Sirleaf's potential to bring change to Liberia. Coverage of Weah also underscored his ability to serve as a change agent, emphasizing his clean hands and lack of connections with previous administrations. In contrast to coverage of female candidates in other contexts, the Liberian press did not focus on Sirleaf's appearance, discuss her (lack of) family connections, or portray her as highly emotional.

This section of the paper is based on an analysis of Liberian press coverage of Sirleaf and Weah between October 11 and November 12, 2005, the month between the first and second rounds of elections. The time period under review was extended a few days past the runoff election (November 8th) to include media coverage of election results. Since there were only two candidates (rather than 22)—and one woman and one man—during the runoff period, gender stereotypes were more pronounced. Also, the short time frame under study (one month) facilitated a closer analysis of all available Liberian media sources. Liberian newspaper articles were collected through LexisNexis searches. They included: *The Analyst*, *The Liberian Observer/Daily Observer*, *The News*, *The Inquirer*, and *FrontPageAfrica*, an online news source.

A variety of sources was consulted to minimize any imbalances found in individual publications. Using the framework identified in the introductory chapter, I identified a range of codes, such as "name," "appearance," "experience," and "change" and then coded the articles according to these parameters.

Overall, George Weah received slightly more media coverage than Ellen Johnson Sirleaf. The search yielded 538 articles that mentioned Weah in comparison with 470 articles that mentioned Sirleaf. Many of the articles discussed both of them, but overall there was slightly more print and online media coverage of Weah than Sirleaf during this critical election period, echoing the results of other studies. In a study of U.S. Senate candidates, Kahn found, for example, that female candidates consistently received less press coverage than male candidates.[24] After eliminating articles that were from foreign sources and ones that were repeated, I had a total of 278 articles.

Media coverage of the candidates emphasized their differences. In many ways, it was a campaign of opposites. Sirleaf was 66 years old during the campaign, while Weah was just 39. Their levels of education and amount of professional experience differed substantially. The candidates also drew support from very different constituencies. Young people, especially young men, were the primary base of support for the Weah campaign, while women of all ages played a key role in promoting Sirleaf's candidacy. While Sirleaf sought to present herself as someone who held strengths in both stereotypically masculine and feminine spheres, Weah, a former soccer star whose political rallies were packed with young men, was identified almost exclusively with masculine areas.

Descriptions of Weah highlighted his football prowess, describing him as "the former A.C. Milan player,"[25] "soccer star,"[26] "former soccer legend,"[27] and "famed international footballer of the year,"[28] and emphasized his rags-to-riches story. The *Liberian Observer*, for example, wrote: "Here's a man with world football celebrity status and unquestionable love of country. . . . Weah has risen from humble beginnings, gifted with uncommon skill to kick leather on the field and become hero to many, even to those who don't normally watch the game."[29] During the campaign, Weah disclosed a net worth of $3 million. Weah's wealth was generally viewed in a positive light. Having already made his fortune, he was seen as less likely to engage in corruption. Also, Weah had already invested some of his personal wealth in the national soccer team, so there was a sense that he would use his wealth to promote national unity and to benefit the country.

Media portrayals of Weah also highlighted his lack of political experience. Depending on the slant of the writer or interviewee, this lack of experience was couched in either positive or negative terms. Positive accounts focused on his "clean hands." Weah's lack of experience meant he was not tainted by the sins of previous administrations. Weah sought to capitalize on his lack of connections with discredited former politicians. Negative accounts portrayed him as a "political novice,"[30] a "political green horn,"[31] and as someone who was not ready to take on the tasks facing Liberia at such a critical moment. Some publications referred to him as "Ambassador Weah" based on his role as a UNICEF goodwill ambassador, perhaps as an attempt to give him some political gravitas.[32] In contrast to most elections, experience was as much a liability as strength in Liberia since it meant the candidate had connections with previous administrations that were linked to exclusivity, corruption, and violence. This context created an opening for Sirleaf since she did not face a male opponent in the second round with a high level of political experience. As a woman and as someone who had challenged earlier administrations even as she worked for them, she was able to highlight her experience without becoming discredited.

Descriptions of Sirleaf, in contrast, emphasized her education and economic and political experience. She was frequently described as a "Harvard-trained economist,"[33] a "former World Bank official,"[34] and as a "financial expert."[35] A *Liberian Observer* article stated: "Hardly any person in today's Liberia can boast of being a more qualified and experienced technocrat with the courage she has demonstrated and who is also a politician of high standing with proven democratic credentials like Sirleaf."[36] Experience, though, cut both ways and some media sources raised concerns about Sirleaf's participation in previous administrations. One article raised the question of how Sirleaf escaped execution in 1980 when nearly all ministers were killed by Doe and his cronies. The media also printed allegations that Sirleaf initially supported Taylor's invasion, before later becoming a vocal critic and a political opponent in the 1997 presidential elections.

Appearance

Media coverage of Sirleaf rarely mentioned her appearance. Her age—she was 66 at the time of the campaign—and a culture of respect for older, postmenopausal women in Liberia and Africa more generally may have contributed to the dearth of discussion of her physical appearance. Coverage of a younger female candidate may have paid greater attention to appearance. Nevertheless, Sirleaf was aware of the fact that her appearance would shape voters' perceptions of her. When taking pictures for her campaign posters, she experimented with Western and African clothing. On the advice of an American campaign adviser, Larry Gibson, Sirleaf decided to appear bareheaded in her official campaign photo. Not wearing the traditional Liberian head wrap signaled that like African male politicians she could "exercise the freedom to wear either African or Western clothes."[37]

First Name

Press coverage of Sirleaf frequently referred to her as "Ellen." Weah, in contrast, was rarely called "George." What was particularly striking in the media coverage of the two candidates was how commonly headlines from a variety of news sources juxtaposed "Ellen" and "Weah." A few examples include: "Weah or Ellen Presidency is History Making,"[38] "Morlu Throws His Weight Behind Ellen, VP in Weah's Corner,"[39] "Ellen Invites Weah to a Debate,"[40] "As NEC Releases Preliminary Results: Weah Leads, Korto, Ellen Follow,"[41] and "Ellen Still Leads As Weah Cries Foul."[42] Out of 278 headlines, 23.7 percent (66) used "Ellen," while only two headlines referred to her as "Ellen Johnson Sirleaf" and only one headline referred to her as "Johnson Sirleaf." In contrast, 20.9 percent (58) of the headlines used "Weah," including 7.9 percent (22) that juxtaposed "Ellen" and "Weah." Only three headlines referred to him as "George Weah" and none referred to him solely as "George."

As indicated in the introductory chapter of this book, the use of the first name of a female candidate can indicate familiarity and warmth rather than authority and gravitas. In addition, it can imply newness and lack of familiarity when used with a surname. In the Liberian context, the use of "Ellen" rather than "Johnson Sirleaf" or "Sirleaf" seemed to make her more approachable without significantly diminishing perceptions of authority. Unlike many female candidates, Sirleaf was portrayed by the media as the candidate with the most experience, education, and preparation for the presidency. Weah, not Sirleaf, was portrayed as the "green horn" and political lightweight. Sirleaf's nickname, "Liberia's Iron Lady," also negated any sense of softness or weakness. In the Liberian case, the use of the first name complemented other media portrayals of Sirleaf as the tough, competent, and experienced politician and technocrat, softening her image. The frequent use of "Ellen" in the media and by the campaign did not seem to weaken her candidacy, and, in fact, may have strengthened it by softening her and making her appear more approachable.

"First Woman"

While the Liberian media acknowledged the potentially path-breaking nature of Sirleaf's candidacy, Weah's compelling story line dominated press coverage. Bauer notes, for example:

> George Weah was the campaign's obvious Cinderella story; he had been raised in a Monrovia slum and grew up to become a world-class soccer star in Europe. Weah's stardom caused the media to ignore the other compelling story of the campaign: the potential for Africa to have its first elected female head of state.[43]

This is not to say that the media completed discounted the history-making potential of Sirleaf's candidacy. An editorial published by *FrontPageAfrica* acknowledged: "Even if you don't like Ellen, just imagine how close you women have come to the corridors of power for the first time in the 158-year history of our country."[44] Other publications similarly noted that a "win for Madam Ellen Johnson Sirleaf would go down in the annals of African history,"[45] even if it took a backseat to coverage of Weah's remarkable transition from soccer star to presidential aspirant.

Change

Both Weah and Sirleaf presented themselves as the candidate that represented change. Sirleaf's gender immediately identified her with change. She made the case that men were responsible for Liberia's political and economic problems and campaigned with the slogan, "All the men have failed, let's try a woman." Her deep résumé made it impossible for her to distance herself completely with Liberia's past problems. Her links to previous elite-dominated administrations and tainted political leaders meant that she was also associated with the status quo.

Weah's outsider status enabled him to make the case that he was the candidate who most embodied change. He argued:

> I am the new kid on the block. I represent hope. I represent development. I represent steadfast commitment to the country. Liberians also know that I am not a controversial figure, neither am I a divisive figure. I am brand new to the Liberian political arena. As I read it, the mood of the country is that they want someone neutral, someone new with extensive demonstrable commitment to this country that can unite and develop this country from the bottom-up. Many see me as that person.[46]

Having built his reputation on the soccer field rather than in government offices, Weah was also able to seize the change mantle. As a soccer star, he had broad name recognition and was viewed positively by the majority of the electorate. As a political amateur, he lacked ties to discredited politicians and was free from scrutiny of past political choices.

"Wife of"

One way that the Liberian case deviates from cases of women leaders in Latin America and Asia is that Sirleaf did not have any family connections to political leaders. Sirleaf was divorced; her ex-husband was deceased, and she had no strong familial connections to previous political leaders. While familial connections have been a key path to power for women in Latin America and Asia,[47] they have not played as important a role in Africa.

Emotions

Media coverage of Sirleaf did not portray her as highly emotional. In fact, it was more likely to characterize her as an "Iron Lady," who was tough, rational, and tenacious. A UN Integrated Regional Information Networks (IRIN) article indicated that Sirleaf gained her nickname because of her "no-nonsense political style."[48] One journalist who accompanied Sirleaf's campaign as it traveled across the country stated, "I always thought the nickname 'Iron Lady' referred to her indomitable state of mind. I had no idea that it also referred to her physical toughness. She never stops to eat or drink."[49] An *Analyst* article indicated that her political fans see her as "an icon of phenomenal achievements and the embodiment of strength, stoic commitment and integrity."[50]

DOUBLE BINDS

Too Masculine or Too Feminine

Journalist Michaela Wrong characterized Sirleaf as "not really a woman."[51] Rather than shy away from this characterization, her campaign embraced it, adopting the slogan, "Ellen, she's our man." Unlike other "Iron Ladies" such as Margaret Thatcher and Golda Meir, however, Sirleaf also embraced a softer image of "Ma Ellen," the mother and grandmother who would care for the Liberian nation. In an interview with *The Perspective*, a U.S.-based news magazine published by the Liberian Democratic Future, Sirleaf indicated, for example:

> I believe that there are certain attributes in a woman that give her some advantages over a man. Women are usually more honest, more sensitive to issues and bring a stronger sense of commitment and dedication to what they do. Maybe because they were mothers, and being a mother you have that special attention for the family, for the young, for children ... All in all I am glad I am a woman and I think in Liberia today, it is time for women to show what they can do.[52]

A campaign press release characterized Sirleaf "as a mother who cares deeply about the children and youth of this country."[53] By balancing these two personas, Sirleaf was able to avoid the trap of being perceived as either too masculine or too feminine; she was both.

Too Young or Too Old

Sirleaf's age facilitated her ability to present these dual personas. Though she was 66 at the time of the campaign, there was little discussion of her being too old to run the country. Age was identified with wisdom and experience and juxtaposed with Weah's relative youth and lack of political experience. Traditionally in many African communities, older, post-menopausal women are respected and wield significant power. This respect for older women seemed to help Sirleaf's campaign. In addition, her age lessened fears of an imperial presidency, a real threat in a country with a history of single-party rule and leaders who have held on to power for decades. During the campaign, Sirleaf indicated that she would only run for one six-year term. Faced with questions about her commitment to a single term—since few African leaders have willingly left power after such a short turn in office—Sirleaf's campaign representatives emphasized that she would be 72 in 2011 and had no reason to lie. While her age would not preclude her from running again in 2011—Liberia does not have an age restriction on presidential candidates like Benin does—it did seem to reassure the electorate that she did not plan to hold on to power forever.

Experience or Change

As discussed above, Sirleaf's gender enabled her to present herself as a break from previous leaders. Given that women are seen as having different leadership styles and areas of competence, the election of the country's first female president was associated with change. Her vast political experience and her participation in previous administrations, however, tempered this image, allowing her to be the candidate of both experience and change. A campaign poster sought to capitalize on her ability to do both these things, juxtaposing an image from 1986 of her coming out of jail with her fist in the air with a recent photo of her in the same pose. Describing the poster, Sirleaf said: "It aligned with the part of our strategy that called for emphasizing my deep experience, bringing attention both to the fact that I had been in government service for many years, going back to the days of the Tolbert administration, and to the fact that, at the same time, I had consistently challenged the government when I thought it was wrong."[54]

Sirleaf's social background (e.g., the fact that she was more closely linked to the Americo-Liberian elite than Weah) meant that she was also viewed as the status quo candidate. One of the cleavages that remains relevant in Liberian politics is between Americo-Liberians (or Congos) and indigenous Liberians. After having experienced decades of Americo-Liberian control of political and economic power, many indigenous Liberians do not want another "Congo" leader to emerge. Despite the fact that Sirleaf emphasized her Gola and Kru indigenous background throughout the campaign, she was perceived by many Liberians as part of the Americo-Liberian elite. Weah, in contrast, was viewed by the electorate as an authentic indigenous African, which led to support for him among what Sawyer dubbed the "heritage movement," a group of Liberians united only by the fact that they wanted to prevent the emergence of an Americo-Liberian president."[55]

EXTERNAL FACTORS

Existing scholarship suggests that women are more likely to win executive positions if they are seeking to be a prime minister rather than a president, when the position has little power, when the candidate is the wife or daughter of a prominent politician, and when a country is in the midst of an economic or political crisis. The Liberian case does not confirm the first three hypotheses, though it does suggest that women are more likely to succeed in crisis environments. The failure of past political leaders in Liberia created an opening for Sirleaf. Liberia's economic crisis also benefited Sirleaf since her educational background, professional experience, and international reputation reassured the electorate that she would be ready to take on Liberia's economic problems from day one and would enjoy the support of the international community, a critical factor given Liberia's heavy reliance on foreign aid. Throughout the campaign, she played up her experience, juxtaposing it with Weah's thin résumé in the areas of economics and politics.

The study of Sirleaf's campaign sheds light on why women have won executive elections in some countries but not others. It suggests that external factors are important and that women are more likely to find success in countries that have recently experienced conflict or a political crisis. Liberia's post-conflict environment created an opening for a female candidate. No incumbents competed in the 2005 presidential election, creating a relatively level playing field among candidates—a rarity in African presidential elections. There was a perception among the electorate that women were less responsible for Liberia's troubles and less likely to engage in corruption.

Support from Liberian women, which crossed ethnic and class lines, seemed to play an important role in her victory. The Ministry of Gender and Development undertook a voter registration drive that increased the percentage of registered voters who were women from under 30 percent to over 50 percent in less than a month.[56] Literate females boasted the highest turnout figures (77.1% in October and 69.9% in November) of any groups in Liberia.[57] A number of women's organizations, including the Liberian Women Initiative (LWI), endorsed Sirleaf. In a review of civil societal activity by various groups during the election period, Jacqui Bauer finds that women's groups sustained a similar level of activity throughout the entire campaign period (first and second rounds), while other groups experienced a drop in activity from anywhere between 37 percent and 70 percent during the second round.[58] In her inaugural address, Sirleaf acknowledged the important role that women played in her election, stating: "During the period of our elections, Liberian women were galvanized—and demonstrated unmatched passion, enthusiasm, and support for my candidacy. They stood with me; they defended me; they worked with me; they prayed for me."[59]

Sirleaf seized on these openings. Her campaign highlighted her achievements in traditionally masculine areas (especially economics and finance); however, it also emphasized how her experiences as a woman enabled her to bring special skills to the job that were critical in Liberia's post-conflict environment. She was able to draw on her education, previous political positions, and experience in multilateral organizations to demonstrate that she had the experience to lead Liberia. At the same time, she was able to promote herself as a source of positive change. The fact that she is a woman made it clear that her election would not be politics as usual. Her gender facilitated a strategic positioning as the candidate who embodied both masculine and feminine leadership traits and represented continuity *and* change.

Acknowledgments

I would like to thank John Scherpereel, Gwynn Thomas, and Rainbow Murray for their valuable and helpful comments on this project.

NOTES

1. John Akokpari and Elisabete Azevedo, "Post-Conflict Elections in Africa: Liberia and Guinea-Bissau in Comparative Perspective," *African Journal of International Affairs* 10, no. 1–2 (2007): 73–92.

2. Jacqui Bauer, "Women and the 2005 Election in Liberia," *Journal of Modern African Studies* 47, no. 2 (2009): 193–211; David Harris, "From 'Warlord' to 'Democratic' President: How Charles Taylor Won the 1997 Liberian Elections," *Journal of Modern African Studies* 37, no. 3 (1999): 431–455; Terrence Lyons, *Voting for Peace: Postconflict Elections in Liberia* (Washington: Brookings Institution Press, 1999); Mary H. Moran and M. Anne Pitcher, "The 'Basket Case' and the 'Poster Child': Explaining the End of Civil Conflicts in Liberia and Mozambique," *Third World Quarterly* 25, no.3 (2004): 501–519.

3. Harris, "From 'Warlord' ".

4. David Harris, "Liberia 2005: An Unusual African Post-Conflict Election," *Journal of Modern African Studies* 44, no. 3 (2006): 375–395; Amos Sawyer, "Emerging Patterns in Liberia's Post-Conflict Politics: Observations from the 2005 Elections," *African Affairs* 107, 427 (2008): 177–199.

5. Republic of Liberia, *2004 Electoral Reform Law* (Monrovia: NEC), http://www.necliberia.org/content/legaldocs/laws/elereformlaw.pdf, accessed August 28, 2009.

6. National Elections Commission, Republic of Liberia, *Turnout for the 11 October and 8 November 2005 Elections* (Monrovia: NEC), http://necliberia.org/results/PDFs/2005ElectionsTurnout.pdf, accessed August 28, 2009.

7. Kathleen Dolan, *Voting for Women: How the Public Evaluates Women Candidates* (Boulder: Westview Press, 2004), p. 60.

8. Leonie Huddy and Nayda Terkildsen, "The Consequences of Gender Stereotypes for Women Candidates at Different Levels and Types of Office," *Political Research Quarterly* 46 (1993): 503–525.

9. Abdoulaye Dukulé, "Ellen Johnson Sirleaf Speaks on Governance, Elections, and Other Issues (Interview)," *The Perspective*, May 6, 2005, http://www.theperspective.org/articles/0506200502.html (February 25, 2007).

10. Deborah Alexander and Kristi Andersen, "Gender as a Factor in the Attribution of Leadership Traits," *Political Research Quarterly* 46, no. 3 (1993): 527–545; Leonie Huddy and Nayda Terkildsen, "Gender Stereotypes and the Perception of Male and Female Candidates," *American Journal of Political Science* 37, no. 1 (1993): 119–147.

11. Sawyer, "Emerging Patterns," p. 183.

12. Ibid., pp. 6–7.

13. Kim Fridkin Kahn, *The Political Consequences of Being a Woman: How Stereotypes Influence the Conduct and Consequences of Political Campaigns* (New York: Columbia University Press, 1996); Jennifer Lawless, "Women, War, and Winning Elections: Gender Stereotyping in the Post-September 11th Era," *Political Research Quarterly* 57, no. 3 (2004): 479–490.

14. Kahn, *Political Consequences*, p. 9.

15. Elisabeth Rehn and Ellen Johnson Sirleaf, *Women, War, and Peace: The Independent Experts' Assessment on the Impact of Armed Conflict and Women's Role in Peace-building* (New York: United Nations Development Fund for Women (UNIFEM), 2002).

16. African Women and Peace Support Group (AWPSG), *Liberian Women Peacemakers* (Trenton, NJ: African World Press, 2004).

17. "Will He? While His Opponent Claims Victory, Weah Faces Daunting Task," *FrontPageAfrica*, November 11, 2005.

18. Kahn, *Political Consequences*; Lawless, "Women, War, Winning Elections."

19. Ibid.

20. Kahn, *Political Consequences*, p. 9.

21. David Dollar, Raymond Fisman, and Roberta Gatti, "Are Women Really the 'Fairer' Sex? Corruption and Women in Government," Policy Research Report on Gender and Development (Working Paper Series, No. 4, 1999).

22. Anand Swamy, Stephen Knack, Young Lee, and Omar Azfar, "Gender and Corruption," in Stephen Knack ed. *Democracy, Governance, & Gender* (Ann Arbor: University of Michigan Press, 2003).

23. For example, Hung-En Sung, "Fairer Sex or Fairer System? Gender and Corruption Revisited," *Social Forces* 82, no. 2 (2003): 703–723.

24. Kahn, *Political Consequences*, p. 45.

25. "Runoff Election Certain," *Liberian Observer*, October 17, 2005.

26. "Runoff Election: Tribal Divide Resonates, as Liberians Head to the Polls," *FrontPageAfrica*, November 6, 2005.

27. "Snags of Runoff Rivalry," *The Analyst*, October 19, 2005.

28. "Runoff Election Certain," *Liberian Observer*, October 17, 2005.

29. "Liberians Vote—Subregion Waits with Bated Breath," *Liberian Observer*, November 7, 2005.

30. "Runoff Elections Underway in Liberia," *FrontPageAfrica*, November 8, 2005.

31. "Meet the Runoff 2005 Candidates," *The Analyst*, October 31, 2005.

32. *FrontPageAfrica*, November 8, 2005.

33. "Runoff Election: Tribal Divide Resonates, as Liberians Head to the Polls," *FrontPageAfrica*, November 6, 2005.

34. "Meet the Runoff 2005 Candidates," *The Analyst*, October 31, 2005.

35. "Runoff Election Certain," *Liberian Observer*, October 17, 2005.

36. "Liberians Vote—Subregion Waits with Bated Breath," *Liberian Observer*, November 7, 2005.

37. Ellen Johnson Sirleaf, *This Child Will be Great: Memoir of a Remarkable Life by Africa's First Woman President* (New York: HarperCollins, 2009), p. 252.

38. *The Analyst*, October 18, 2005.

39. *FrontPageAfrica*, November 1, 2005.

40. *The Analyst*, October 28, 2005.

41. *The Inquirer*, October 13, 2005.

42. *Liberian Observer*, November 10, 2005.

43. Bauer, "Women," pp. 196–197.

44. "A Memo to Fellow Liberians—It's about our Country's Future," *FrontPageAfrica*, November 6, 2005.

45. *The Analyst*, October 18, 2005.

46. "'I Will Win' Weah Says, Gives Reasons Why," *The Analyst*, November 5, 2005.

47. Farida Jalalzai, "Women Rule: Shattering the Executive Glass Ceiling," *Politics & Gender* 4, no. 2 (2008): 205–231.

48. "'King George' Squares Up for Election Runoff with 'Iron Lady,'" UN IRIN, October 17, 2005.

49. "Weah and Sirleaf Close Out Campaigning," *allAfrica*, November 7, 2005.

50. "Ellen Johnson Sirleaf, The Candidate at the Verge of Making History," *The Analyst*, November 1, 2005.

51. Wrong, Michaela, *New Statesman*, November 28, 2005, p. 27.

52. Dukulé, "Johnson Sirleaf Speaks."

53. "Ellen Receives Nationwide Support" 2005.

54. Johnson Sirleaf, *This Child*, p. 252.

55. Sawyer, "Emerging Patterns," p. 11.

56. National Elections Commission, Republic of Liberia, 2005 Voter Registration Statistics (Monrovia: NEC), http://necliberia.org/Statistics_Maps/dstatistics 10september2005.pdf, accessed August 28, 2009.

57. National Elections Commission, "Turnout."

58. Bauer, "Women."

59. Ellen Johnson Sirleaf, "Inaugural Address of H. E. Ellen Johnson Sirleaf," 2006, http://www.emansion.gov.lr/doc/inaugural_add_1.pdf, accessed August 29, 2009.

CHAPTER NINE

Renegotiating Political Leadership: Michelle Bachelet's Rise to the Chilean Presidency

Susan Franceschet and Gwynn Thomas

T he election of Michelle Bachelet, socialist, single mother, and admitted agnostic, as Chile's president in January 2006 seems to contradict Chile's reputation as one of Latin America's most socially conservative countries. This apparent paradox was a prominent media frame in much of the English-language press coverage of Bachelet's election.[1] But Bachelet's election is also surprising when examined in light of the scholarly literature on women's election to executive office. In one of the few cross-national studies of women's access to executive positions, Farida Jalalzai finds that women are more likely to achieve the highest office when the office itself has relatively few powers, and in situations of political instability or crisis. She also finds that in Latin America, no female president has risen to the presidency without familial ties to male politicians.[2] Bachelet's election challenges each one of these factors: Chile's presidency is among the most powerful in Latin America, and the country is the envy of most of its neighbors for its political stability and economic success. Bachelet is neither a wife, widow, nor daughter of past or current male political elites. Moreover, although hailing from the coalition that had governed Chile for sixteen years, Bachelet was a relative newcomer to politics, having never previously held elected office. Instead, her political rise occurred through executive appointment. She held two cabinet portfolios in the administration of Ricardo Lagos (2000–2006), but remained outside of the inner elite circle of the coalition.

Of the three aspects of this book's theoretical framework gender ster eotyping, media framing, and external factors—our analysis of Bachelet's election highlights the importance of external factors. Our main argument is that gender stereotypes and the discourses of various actors (political opponents, the media, and the candidate and her supporters) who frame female candidates must be interpreted contextually. Precisely because gender is socially constructed, and its meaning often contested, the significance of the gender stereotypes that emerge during a presidential campaign can only be understood in reference to the contextual factors that shape the political environment. This means that the impact of media framing is dependent on existing public perceptions of the candidate. Yet even these perceptions are filtered through various features of the socio-political context.

In this chapter, we show that the 2005 presidential campaign was contested in a context highly favorable to Bachelet, allowing her to increase the specific advantages associated with her gender while mitigating a number of disadvantages women face as presidential candidates. A confluence of long-term social processes and shorter- to medium-term political and economic trends created the necessary space for a progressive female candidate from outside of the country's traditional political class to successfully compete for the presidency. Long-term processes include transformations in social understandings of appropriate gender roles. Medium- or short-term processes are political and economic trends that create specific opportunities for candidates from particular parties with a particular set of campaign issues. In the Chilean case, the 1990 transition to democracy, and the role played by feminist and women's movements within that process, ushered in a slow yet undeniable process of social change which altered social attitudes toward women's public roles. The center-left Concertación de los Partidos por la Democracia (Coalition of Parties for Democracy) has successfully contested every set of elections, from the local level to the presidency, since 1990 when it helped usher in the return to democracy. During this time, Chile's economy and political system have been among the most stable in Latin America. While a favorable political context was crucial to Bachelet's election, her personal charisma, enormous popularity with citizens (especially women), and her ability to successfully counter her competitors' attempts to depict her gender in a negative manner were also decisive. This context, described in more detail below, meant that Bachelet's election did not conform to the hypothesis set out in the book's introduction, that is, that women from left parties face greater hurdles to election. Instead, Bachelet benefited from public perceptions that she hailed from her party's more progressive wing and that she was deeply concerned with social issues.

This chapter has two main sections. The first provides a brief overview of Chile's political and electoral system and the role that women have played in it. The second outlines the three main factors that explain

Bachelet's success: a favorable political context; her enormous popularity with Chileans; and her ability to manage the gender issues that arose during her campaign, namely, the gendered assumptions about her lack of capacity for executive office. Given the embedded and contextual nature of gender ideology, we employed a qualitative analysis based on a process of inductive analysis of visual and textual sources of Chile's presidential election.[3] We analyzed how the candidates' incorporated and/or challenged Chile's broader gendered ideologies of men and women's respective personal characteristics, leadership styles, issue interests, and political strengths in electoral materials.

The central source for this chapter was a complete set of the television advertisements, called *franja*, for all presidential candidates during both the first and the second round of the campaign. Chile strictly regulates television propaganda, providing the same amount of airtime on all national television stations to presidential candidates in both the first and second rounds of the election. Candidates are not allowed to purchase more television airtime and the *franja*—instead of being shown throughout the day—are grouped in two showings, once in the morning and once in the evening. This means that the candidates television propaganda are watched back-to-back, easily compared, and heavily debated in other forms of media (in the newspapers, on radio, and television news and entertainment shows that dominate Chilean television), thus increasing their importance and influence in defining the issues and debates of the electoral campaign. The *franja* therefore represent an ideal source for analyzing and comparing the role of gender beliefs in each candidate's campaigns. Additional sources included media reports, public statements, pamphlets, campaign slogans, and proposed programs. Both authors drew on extensive field research experience in Chile around issues of gender and women's political participation. One author, Thomas, engaged in participant observation and interviews in Santiago, Chile during the 2005–2006 presidential campaign.

SETTING THE CONTEXT: DEMOCRATIC POLITICS AND GENDER RELATIONS IN CHILE, 1990–2005

The 2005 presidential campaign occurred in an environment characterized by a unique set of historical legacies and institutional features that emerged out of Chile's transition to democracy in 1990. Most important, the electoral system compels the center and left parties to compete in a coalition. Keeping the coalition together, however, has led to a series of informal political arrangements that began to attract increased criticism. Three main criticisms stand out as relevant in defining the context for the 2005 elections. First, internal disagreements within the coalition and the need to bargain with the conservative opposition led successive Concertación governments to act timidly on a range of pressing, but controversial issues, including the country's high levels of socio-economic inequality, addressing the human rights abuses under the Pinochet dictatorship, and gender discrimination. Second, there was a growing sense that political elites were increasingly distant from and even disinterested in the concerns of ordinary Chileans and that key decisions were reached through intra-elite bargaining rather than through public debate.[4] Third, high rates of incumbency in congress and the same group of leaders receiving cabinet posts led to growing criticisms about the absence of new faces in the governing coalition.

Chile's model of politics meant that a number of social groups had unmet political and economic demands and were growing increasingly frustrated by the slow pace of change. Women represented one such group, and, as we discuss, Bachelet clearly targeted the unrealized demands of female voters. Organized women had played a key role in the seventeen-year struggle against the dictatorship, and had lobbied the newly elected democratic government to address the numerous sources of gender inequality in society, the economy, politics, and the law. The government response to women's equality demands was to create a women's policy agency, the National Women's Service (SERNAM), charged with designing public policies to address the problems women confronted. The parties of the right, along with segments of the Christian Democratic party, were deeply conservative on social issues, however, accounting for the uneven progress on women's rights issues. Given the need for coalition unity and the essential veto power that the right had in the legislative arena, a number of issues that feminist activists had lobbied for—namely, a more equitable marital property law, expanded reproductive rights, and quotas for women in politics—remained absent from the government agenda. No gains were made in the area of reproductive rights, women's representation, or the gendered inequities in the pension system. Bachelet promised change in all of these areas.

In Chile, as elsewhere, gender inequality is not only rooted in formal institutions such as family law, but also in societal attitudes towards women's appropriate roles. On some measures, public attitudes towards women's roles have changed since 1990, yet for other measures, Chilean society retains fairly traditional values about gender roles. A national public opinion survey undertaken in 1995 reveals fairly conservative attitudes about women's appropriate roles in politics and the workforce. While agreeing that it is acceptable for married women to work (89%), more than half of the respondents (54%) also believed that women who stay home with their children are better mothers.[5] Only 33 percent of respondents believed both sexes equally capable of serving as president of the country.[6] While public opinion surveys continue to reveal consistently traditional attitudes towards women's primary roles as mothers and home-makers, both men and women in Chile hold fairly liberal attitudes on a range of moral issues, ranging from divorce and sexuality to the acceptability of cohabitation without marriage. In 2002, Centro de Estudios Públicos (CEP) took a composite of five questions on moral issues and concluded that 77 percent of the population is either liberal or mostly liberal.[7] Palacios and Martinez argue Chilean women adhere to a "conservative liberalism."[8] Women's attitudes on certain issues, namely the priority given to motherhood and caring roles, lean toward conservatism, but on most other issues, such as women's access to politics, divorce, and even abortion, the majority of women are somewhat more liberal. A 2004 Latinbarometer survey found that Chileans were substantially less discriminating against women political leaders in 2004 than in 1995, with only 26 percent strongly agreeing that "men make better political leaders than women."[9] Survey data thus reveal highly complex and even contradictory attitudes about men and women's social roles. There remains a strong association between womanhood and motherhood, yet there is substantial tolerance of women's autonomy in other areas (e.g., decisions about marriage), and endorsement of the need to promote women's participation in public life and politics.

Growing tolerance for women's political participation, however, does not mean that women and men are perceived as possessing the same political strengths and capabilities. Similar to other countries in this study, women and men are often seen as having different styles of participation and leadership. Women are viewed as more honest, less corrupt, more interested in the common good and self-sacrificing, and less likely to be motivated by personal ambition, which parallels how many voters viewed Bachelet's strengths.[10] Local and informal politics are often seen as more appropriate for women's strengths and interests given that this type of politics centers around "issues that directly affect their families and their communities."[11] Formal politics, heavily dominated by men, on the other hand, is seen as more in-line with masculine character traits, including firmness and decisiveness. Women's relative exclusion from formal politics is also maintained by the resistance of male party leaders to incorporating women. Women from all parties have noted that women remain on the margins of power in the parties, and leaders have resisted, or failed, to implement quotas to increase the number of women nominated for elected office.[12] Women's exclusion helps to perpetuate a distinctly masculine style of political leadership that women must navigate. In terms of gender relations, Chile changed a great deal between 1990 and 2005. Yet, as noted, both in political-institutional terms and societal attitudes, the goal of gender equality remained elusive. As we show in the next section, Bachelet undertook a highly gendered campaign, speaking directly to many of the unrealized goals of women.

GENDER AND THE 2005–2006 PRESIDENTIAL CAMPAIGN: CONTINUITY AND CHANGE

The 2005 elections were the first since 1989 in which the rightist coalition (the Alianza) failed to agree on a single candidate, forcing Bachelet to compete against two conservative candidates. Joaquín Lavín represented the Independent Democratic Union, a traditional and deeply conservative party, and Sebastian Piñera was the candidate of the National Renovation Party, a more modern and moderate right party. The electoral campaign that brought Bachelet to the presidency was marked by the seemingly contradictory themes of "continuity and change." When examined more closely, however, the goals of continuity and change were not in competition. The specific types of continuity and change desired by voters operated on two different (and uniquely gendered) levels. On one level, Chileans were eager to continue electing Concertación governments because the coalition had provided a return to democracy, political stability, economic growth, and a substantial reduction in poverty. But on another level, many citizens felt a growing distance between themselves and the political class. Chileans, therefore wanted change, but crucially, a change in the *style*, not necessarily the *content*, of politics. In this context, Bachelet's sex became an advantage, because it was a very obvious change. The "change" frame was thus an opportunity. But, as noted in the introductory chapter of this book, the change frame, along with the "first woman" frame, carries risks as well as opportunities. Gendered stereotypes and assumptions about political strengths and the capacities needed for executive leadership became key to the campaign itself as Bachelet's competitors sought to discredit her. Bachelet's success owes not simply to a favorable political and economic context, but also to her own popularity and her ability to counter the negative gender stereotypes her opponents sought to plant in the minds of voters. This section covers each of these three factors.

External Factors: Balancing Continuity and Change

The main reason for the resonance of a "continuity" frame was the successes of Bachelet's predecessors, particularly the government of Ricardo Lagos, elected in 2000 and leaving office with a 71 percent approval rating.[13] His popularity derives from a number of accomplishments including an economic growth rate of 6.2 percent, a drop in unemployment and inflation, an increase in per capita GDP, and a 29 percent increase in the minimum wage.[14] Most important, the socio-economic policies of the three successive Concertación governments had produced a sizable drop in Chile's poverty rate, from 45 percent in 1987 to just

18.8 percent in 2003.[15] These economic indicators produced considerable optimism among Chileans about their country's future prospects.[16]

The favorable economic indicators do not tell the whole story, however. Although Concertación governments have been effective at achieving economic growth and poverty reduction, they have not succeeded in reducing the gap between the wealthy and the poor, thereby creating an opportunity for a candidate prioritizing social equality. Polls revealed that Chileans were deeply concerned about social issues. From early on in the campaign, Bachelet was perceived as better equipped to handle health care, poverty, and education, all issues traditionally associated with parties on the left. Only on fighting crime and generating employment did her two opponents receive higher rankings than Bachelet.[17] Moreover, being a woman, combined with her background as a medical doctor, allowed her to position herself as both knowledgeable about and interested in health care, education, and poverty reduction, all issues often stereotyped in Chile and other countries as particularly related to women's political interests and strengths. Her focus on social issues did not produce a "Mommy Problem" because the context was one in which previous governments had failed to resolve pressing social issues.

A campaign focusing on a change in style also found broad appeal in an electorate that was fed up with the overarching style of Concertación politics. In some countries, the kinds of external factors that create opportunities for female candidates take the form of economic collapse or political crisis. In Chile, it was precisely the opposite: the political and institutional stability provided by the Concertación coalition, combined with solid economic progress, provided an opportunity for a female candidate from the governing coalition. In an interview with a leading national newspaper, outgoing president Ricardo Lagos noted that Michelle Bachelet represented both continuity and change: continuity in terms of government policy, and change in terms of having a female leader. He noted that a woman leader represented "warmth and affection."[18] These qualities were desirable precisely because the economic and political successes of the three previous Concertación governments had been achieved through a model of politics that "increasingly [struck] the public as distant at best and self-serving and exclusionary at worst."[19]

In addition to frustration with a technocratic model of politics, the Concertación was also hit by a series of corruption scandals in 2004–2005. This made it advantageous for Bachelet to remind voters of her outsider status. When releasing her program for government, she prefaced it by stating, "I do not belong to the traditional elite. My name is not one of the names of the founders of Chile." More important, she noted that her nomination "did not emerge from negotiations behind closed doors or from a party conclave."[20] In addition to Bachelet's sex, which provided an automatic signal of change, her leadership style was also very different from that of both her predecessors and her opponents. As we discuss in the next sections, having a female candidate, and particularly a candidate with the type of qualities that Bachelet possessed, produced a campaign where the (gendered) meanings of leadership had to be renegotiated.

While Chileans wanted change in terms of style, they also clearly desired continuity with the policies that yielded economic success and political stability. During the campaign for the first round, Bachelet did not emphasize her continuity with the policies of the Lagos administration, despite the overwhelming popularity of the outgoing president, focusing instead on change.[21] It was only after her relatively poor performance in the first round where she personally received fewer votes than the Concertación's winning congressional candidates that her campaign strategy shifted and the theme of continuity was given more prominence. This shift involved giving more visibility in the campaign to key political figures from the coalition. Hence, the electoral advantages of Bachelet's "outsider" status should not be over-emphasized.[22]

The "Citizens' Candidate": Opinion Polls and Bachelet's Surging Popularity

While external factors provided a propitious climate for a woman candidate, Bachelet's success in securing the Concertación's nomination had not been a foregone conclusion. Bachelet not only had to position herself against male party elites, but her main opponent for the nomination was also a woman, Soledad Alvear, the official candidate of the more centrist Christian Democratic Party. Politically accomplished, Alvear had been the first woman to serve as Minister of Foreign Affairs under President Lagos after serving as Minister of Justice under President Frei and as the first director of SERNAM under President Aylwin. As a woman, Alvear also benefited from the desire for change and the generally favorable environment for a candidate from the governing coalition. In opinion polls asking people to name the five political figures (excluding the President) with the best future, Alvear was the Concertación figure with the highest numbers from May of 2000 to September of 2004, when she was overtaken by Bachelet.[23] Alvear withdrew her candidacy in the open primary because of her inability to compete with Bachelet in the polls. Indeed, Bachelet's dominance in a series of public opinion polls about who Chileans wanted to see as the next president, and not the strength of her support by party elites, is widely credited for her success in securing the nomination as the single candidate for the Concertación.[24]

Alvear's inability to challenge Bachelet successfully highlights the importance of Bachelet's own personal charisma, charm, and leadership style. Bachelet's growing support directly correlated with the greater public exposure that she garnered after her appointment as the Minister of Defense in 2002. In addition to being the first woman in Chile and Latin America to serve in this post, Bachelet's personal biography fascinated the media. Bachelet's father, a general in the air force, had been killed by the dictatorship due to his support for toppled president Salvador Allende. Bachelet and her mother were also detained, tortured, and exiled. This background, in addition to her commitment to promoting both human rights and reconciliation between the military and the larger society, captured Chile's attention, especially during the 30th anniversary of the coup in 2003.[25]

Media exposure, while necessary, is not sufficient to explain Bachelet's popularity. As Chileans got to know Bachelet through her media exposure, they were charmed by her personal charisma and ability to connect to Chileans from all walks of life. To launch her campaign for the nomination, Bachelet conducted what she called a "listening tour" where she toured Chile, meeting people in informal meetings to "listen" to their concerns and learn about what issues they considered most pressing. This tour not only introduced her to voters throughout Chile, but also cemented her image as non-elitist and down-to-earth. Bachelet's easy manner and approachability set her apart from the more formal, technocratic, and distant style of other Chilean politicians. Her ability to laugh at her own foibles and to make jokes helped her appear down-to-earth and fun, a welcome change from President Lagos, who while generally admired, was seen as possessing a very authoritative style of governing and tended to come across as pedantic. The widespread use of Bachelet's first name was seen mostly as a reflection of her approachability and warmth, although there was some discussion about why her male opponents were not similarly named.[26] The idea that popular support rather than party negotiating drove Bachelet's candidacy was picked up by Bachelet's supporters who began to depict her as the citizens' candidate. The gendered stereotypes about leadership and the capacities needed to govern a country must be interpreted in light of the images and popularity of Bachelet described above.

A President without a Tie? Renegotiating Political Leadership

Bachelet's candidacy brought to the fore previously implicit connections between men, masculinity, and political leadership and presented her with specific challenges not faced by her male opponents. Public perceptions of Bachelet as a candidate reveal the gendered understandings of the different leadership capacities of men and women. When the campaign began in November 2005, CEP published a poll detailing the character traits possessed by the candidates and needed by a president. The poll revealed that Bachelet's strongest traits were her honesty (40%), concern for the real problems of the country (41%), and common sentiment (41%). She polled less strongly on her capacity to make difficult decisions (36%) and firmness in confronting pressures (35%).[27] Public opinion in Chile thus fits broader patterns in which women political leaders are associated with stereotypically feminine qualities (compassion, warmth, kindness, and selflessness) while men are perceived as possessing leadership traits most associated with executive office (strength, competency, rationality, aggressiveness). [28]

In all presidential elections, personal qualities are often central to how campaigns seek to persuade voters to support a particular candidate. This tendency was strengthened in Chile's 2005 election because of Bachelet's position as the candidate for the politically stronger Concertación and her dominance of important social issues.[29] Bachelet's few weaknesses were related to her style of political leadership. For example, political analyst Patricio Navia argued that "while the Concertación provided effective government, doubts abound with respect to the candidate of the coalition . . . If Bachelet does not win it will be because the problem can be found in her personal credibility" and her inability to convince Chileans that she "has the weight [*da el ancho*] to govern."[30] These criticisms reveal the gendered assumptions about leadership that confront female candidates. Like the other women candidates examined in this book, Bachelet had to negotiate the double-bind of femininity/competency and to counter lingering doubts about the ability of a woman to assume an office previously held only by men. These doubts were part of both the campaign strategies of her opponents and how she was framed by the Chilean media.

The media framing of the three candidates' character traits confirms findings elsewhere that women candidates are subjected to more negative framings about their leadership. A content analysis of Chile's three largest newspapers in terms of circulation (*El Mercurio, La Tercera*, and *Las Últimas Noticias*) conducted by communication scholars Valenzuela and Correa reveals that press coverage of coded personal attributes (charisma/compassion, honesty, leadership, aggressiveness, and competency) of the presidential candidates was rarely neutral, but instead most often framed positively or negatively.[31] The gendered differences between the candidates are striking. While 84 percent of the stories framed Bachelet's charisma/compassion as positive (and only 6% as negative), only 41 percent of the coverage presented her leadership as positive and 31 percent as negative. Out of the five categories, only in competency did the percentage of negative framing greatly exceed the positive for Bachelet. Fifty-four percent of the coverage of competency was negative, compared to 29 percent as positive. Lavín and Piñera fared much better in terms of positive media framing of competency (40 and 61%, respectively) and leadership (44 and 45%, respectively).[32] This type of framing can be seen in a report by *La Tercera*, a leading national newspaper, about the themes dominating the presidential election. The report singled out the phrase *no da el ancho* (she's a lightweight) to capture the criticisms against Bachelet's leadership capacity, claiming that while the phrase was used publicly by the opposition only, it was also voiced by some members of the Concertación who had doubts about her ability to govern.[33]

As the campaign developed, it also became clear that her opponents perceived her leadership style as a potential weakness. Throughout the campaign, the opposition attempted to position Bachelet as trustworthy but not capable, as very likable, but not a disciplined and take-charge leader who could successfully govern.[34] Piñera, the candidate for the RN, was particularly direct in his attacks, asking whether warmth and approachability were really what was needed by a president. In an interview, he first praised Bachelet as likable, empathetic, and capable, but went on to argue, "to be President, much more is required. It requires leadership, strength, knowledge, the capacity to organize teams, the capacity to captain a boat so that it arrives at a good port. In my opinion, when she was the Minister of Health and Defense she did not demonstrate these capabilities."[35]

More subtly, Piñera framed himself as clearly possessing the leadership qualities that Bachelet lacked. For example, Piñera described his leadership abilities in a *franja*, in the following way:

> Honestly, I feel prepared, because being a good President requires much more than good intentions, it requires leadership, courage, will. I feel that I have prepared all of my life for this challenge, from when I was a school student in engineering and economy, as a father, as a university professor for more than 20 years, as a businessman that started from nothing and that with much force and dedication succeeded in creating businesses, generating jobs, as a Senator.[36]

In this spot, Piñera highlights both his type of political leadership (force, will, dedication) and his range of past experience, often in fields seen as more masculine (engineering, economics, business, politics). While Bachelet has "good intentions," she is not up to the task. In another *franja* spot, Piñera explicitly draws on his past as a business leader: "to lead the great company that is called Chile, it requires leadership, courage, will, knowledge, experience. I have achieved successes in life; I know what needs to be done. I know how to do it. For these reasons I am asking for the opportunity to lead." Lavín, the candidate from UDI, differentiated his leadership style from Bachelet's by highlighting his law and order credentials. A prominent slogan in his campaign was *mano dura* (firm hand)

and his *franja* were filled with spots of Lavín promising to protect Chileans from crime and to make sure criminals were punished. Implicitly, this conveys the sense that Bachelet's more feminine style would be "softer" on criminals and thus fail to provide order and security.

In addition to openly questioning her abilities, Piñera and Lavín indirectly questioned Bachelet's fitness for the presidency by presenting themselves as embodying the idealized masculine image of the Chilean presidency. Masculine perceptions of presidential capacity are promoted not only through linking of the presidency with specific character traits and issues more associated with men and masculinity, but also through the cultural icons, images, and metaphors associated with the office. In Chile, the presidency is heavily associated with idealized understandings of men's roles as husbands and fathers (Power 2002; Thomas, forthcoming).[37] As a supporter of Lavín argued in a television commercial, "[Lavín] is a man of his word, a family man, and that is what is needed now for our country."[38] Piñera's and Lavín's campaign materials heavily featured images of both men as devoted fathers surrounded by their wives and children. In his first television spot, Piñera introduced himself by talking about his love for his wife of 32 years, his children, and how the birth of his first grandchild strengthened his determination to run for the presidency.[39] Both candidate's wives also appeared numerous time in campaign material to testify to their husband's commitment to protecting women, children, and the family.

Not only did this strategy frame the two male candidates as embodying idealized paternal images of past (male) presidents, but it also highlighted the enormous disparity between Bachelet and Chile's previous presidents. Not only was Bachelet a woman, but she was also divorced, had born her third child out of wedlock, and was not currently involved in a long-term relationship. Focusing on their own positions in idealized heterosexual families (married, with multiple children, never divorced) helped Lavín and Piñera present themselves as "presidential" in a way that was denied to Bachelet, because of her gender and her family life. Interestingly, unlike other women without husbands that have sometimes been labeled as lesbians by their critics, this charge was never made against Bachelet. Bachelet's true "Mommy Problem" in the 2005–2006 campaign centered not around her leftist ideologies, but her challenge to the particularly paternal cultural resonance of the Chilean presidency. Cultural standards that considered personal attacks as outside the bounds of the politically acceptable prevented Lavín and Piñera from explicitly attacking Bachelet's personal life. Moreover, they might have been worried that such a strategy would backfire with women voters because of the high rates of single-female heads-of-households, particularly among lower-working class women. As an important constituency for the Chilean right,[40] neither Lavín nor Piñera could afford to alienate lower working-class women by launching attacks against Bachelet's personal life. Additionally, Bachelet was making a concerted effort to court this group of voters.

Bachelet and her campaign were clearly cognizant of the need to respond to overt critiques and the more subtle lingering doubts of her leadership abilities. Throughout the campaign, she pursued two major strategies. First, she actively worked to present her qualifications to the voters, particularly in terms of her career training and political experience. Second, she sought to reframe the debate over her personal qualifications by arguing that doubts about her political leadership were based in sexism and were part of a larger pattern of cultural resistance to women's inclusion in politics. She defended her style of political leadership and argued that it would deepen Chile's democracy by bringing in the views and perspectives of excluded groups. This strategy was particularly apparent in the second round of the campaign when she competed directly with Piñera.

Throughout the campaign, Bachelet had to confront one of the most pernicious gender stereotypes in politics: "that women are assumed to be less qualified to hold public office then men, even when they have more experience and stronger credentials."[41] Chilean sociologist Clarisa Hardy notes that this type of sexism is very strong in Chile and is evident in the lack of "belief in the abilities of women and the questioning women face in terms of the type of their leadership. There are questions because women have never filled these roles like men, and at the least, are scrutinized as something unknown."[42] To counter this tendency, Bachelet's campaign worked hard to present Bachelet as having the preparation and background needed to assume the presidency.[43] In particular, Bachelet repeatedly referred to her past political positions (Minister of Health, Minister of Defense) and her medical training. In the *franja* spot where she introduces herself and her qualifications, Bachelet neatly invoked all three to describe her personal biography, stating, "I am a medical professional ... I know how to heal hurts ... in the Ministry of Health I took on the mission of protecting all the citizens of Chile internally and when ... I went to the Ministry of Defense, I knew that I could do much more than protect all the citizens from the outside, I had in my hands the possibility of collaborating to heal the most profound wound that had divided my country."[44] Bachelet both reminds Chileans of her training and political experience, and uses very confident and forceful language ("I know," "I took on the mission") to describe her abilities. However, she also manages to deftly avoid appearing too masculine by highlighting her concern for her fellow citizens and her ability to heal real and symbolic wounds. In the second round, her campaign responded to concerns over her political leadership with a spot that highlighted her knowledge of international issues and fluency in multiple languages.

In the ad, Bachelet is shown surrounded by members of the press asking her questions in French, German, and English, as well as Spanish about issues such as international trade, and tensions between Chile and Bolivia. She is shown as poised and calm, easily switching between the different languages in her response.[45] She is cool and composed under pressure and prepared to assume leadership on the world stage where she will be able to speak to other leaders in their own language.

Bachelet particularly turned to her successful tenure as Minister of Defense (perhaps the most masculine of cabinet positions) to combat the perception that she was too "soft" to be president. Nothing captures this strategy better than her use of her past experience to frame her position on crime. Crime had emerged as a major issue in the campaign, and according to polls, Bachelet was perceived as weaker than her male opponents, particularly Lavín.[46] In outlining her ability to deal effectively with crime, Bachelet stated, "I was Minister of Defense, I know that it is necessary to create a unified command that will coordinate a firm hand (*mano dura*) with an intelligent hand."[47] Bachelet's campaign also featured numerous images of Bachelet as Minster of Defense, particularly those showing her inspecting troops, riding in a tank, being saluted by military officers, and striding in front of the top generals of Chile's four main military branches (air force, navy, army, and police). These images were undoubtedly meant to assuage doubts about her ability to firmly lead the state, and assume even the most masculine responsibilities of the president as the commander-in-chief of the armed forces.

Bachelet's campaign also confronted the charge that she did not possess the right type of political leadership. Often, women politicians have positioned themselves as capable executive leaders by adopting a masculine leadership style. The classic example of this strategy is the "Iron Lady" style promoted by Margaret Thatcher. In her recent presidential campaign in the United States, Hillary Clinton sought to prove her toughness and competency and her supporters portrayed her leadership style in explicitly masculine metaphors ("testicular fortitude").[48] As noted in the introduction, this places women in the unenviable position of seeking to prove they are "masculine" enough for the presidency, without losing their "femininity" and being regarded as not a proper woman. When women pursue this strategy, however, they can also reinforce perceptions that masculine character traits are those most needed for executive office, thus reinforcing the linkage among men, masculinity, and the presidency.

Bachelet departed from this pattern. Instead, she explicitly recognized the gendered connotation of political leadership and crafted campaign strategies that framed her own leadership as feminine. Moreover, she depicted this as a positive change from the past dominance of a masculine style based too much on authoritative command and the imposition of one's will over others. Bachelet claimed her leadership style was about working for consensus and inclusion, listening to all points of view and then creating a common goal, and about leading teams. She explicitly labeled this as "feminine leadership" in order to differentiate it from the political leadership assumed by male politicians. In the first *franja* of the second round, Bachelet drew a clear line between her leadership and Piñera's, arguing that "[d]irecting a country is not the same as directing a business, you must know the people, listen to them, talk with them to understand what they feel and need." She claimed to bring "a different leadership with the sensibility of one that looks at things from another angle."[49] This spot framed her perceived strengths—approachability, consensus-building, openness—as the characteristics most needed by a good leader. In crafting this strategy, Bachelet and her campaign deftly linked her leadership style to the other dominant themes of her campaign: her promise to bring about change, to promote gender equality, and to promote the inclusion of marginalized groups.[50] Bachelet's campaign associated her more feminine style of leadership as part of ongoing efforts to overcome the patterns of political marginalization inherited from the military dictatorships.

Bachelet was also forthright in labeling as sexist criticisms about her character, leadership, and abilities. She argued that such criticisms were evidence of the widespread sexism that women faced when they attempted to compete with men for jobs traditionally dominated by men, appealing to voters to recognize her own and women's general abilities. In an interview, Bachelet characterized these criticisms as "tremendously *machista*" and noted that they were part of broader "electoral strategies."[51] This strategy resonated with female voters, many of whom had probably experienced similar treatment in their jobs or broader lives. This type of direct challenge was more apparent in the second round of the election and responded to the voting patterns that emerged in the first round. Although the traditional gender gap in Chile was for women to favor conservative candidates, Bachelet reversed this. Unlike previous Concertación presidential candidates, Bachelet won more votes from women (47%) than men (44.8%). This showed two things: that Bachelet's appeals to women were effective and that some male voters may have held doubts about her leadership capacities.

In the second round, Bachelet's campaign had to maintain her support among women—particularly by trying to capture more of the lower working-class women who had voted for Lavín—as well as appeal to male voters more explicitly by increasing the presence of male political heavyweights associated with Lagos. Directly confronting the critiques of her leadership style and capacity worked for both groups. This more direct approach was easily seen in Bachelet's first spot in the second round *franja*, which she began by looking directly into the camera, and addressing male members of the audience by saying, "I want to speak to those [Chileans] that did not vote for me because I am a woman." She continued, "every family is a kingdom, in which the father rules but the mother governs. Your wife, your girlfriend, your daughter, and your mother can do it [govern]—they demonstrate it every day of their lives."[52] This spot directly confronted possible concerns about her leadership style, arguing that to doubt her abilities because she is a woman is to doubt the abilities of the women in the lives of the viewer. This spot was shown more than any other spot produced in the second round. Bachelet also began to conclude her ads with the slogan "Word of a Woman," reminding voters of her honesty and dedication.

Labeling attacks against her leadership style and capabilities "sexist" was successful in putting Piñera on the defensive and potentially damaging his attempt to win over the lower-working class women who had supported Lavín in the first round. In an interview, Piñera was asked if his criticisms against Bachelet reflected a sexist attitude. He answered by saying, "In generic terms a woman is absolutely and perfectly prepared to be president of the Republic, but one has to have the qualities that this charge requires and demand."[53] However, Bachelet was fairly effective in making the distinction between women in the abstract and herself as the woman candidate harder to draw.

In the end, Bachelet's success in responding to critiques about her leadership and competence is evident in the final vote share. Bachelet handily won the second round run-off vote with 53.5 percent of the vote and was elected president. She managed to maintain her appeal to women voters (53.3%) and to re-establish the traditional dominance of the Concertación among men, receiving 53.7 percent of men's votes. The size of her victory compared to the much closer 2000 election of Lagos—when he defeated Lavín by a little-less than 3 percent of the vote (51.3% to 48.6%)—was almost entirely based on her support among women voters, particularly among young women and working-class women.

CONCLUSION

In this chapter, we have highlighted the ways in which Michelle Bachelet's election both mirrors yet departs significantly from patterns seen in other countries when women contest executive office. All of the common gender stereotypes in which masculine attributes are more closely associated with leadership and competence in governing were present in Chile. Bachelet's opponents and the media framed her as not possessing the weight (*no da el ancho*) to govern the country. Likewise, her personal qualities, namely her approachability, joviality, and concern for social issues, were linked to her gender and explicitly cast by her opponents as lacking significance for the challenge of governing. While these stereotypes harmed candidates elsewhere, they were not sufficient to outweigh other factors that account for Bachelet's success. As the candidate of the governing coalition, Bachelet also benefited from the desire for continuity with the coalition's record of political stability and economic growth. We have argued here that external factors, combined with Bachelet's charisma and early popularity with citizens, created a context that minimized the impact of negative gender stereotypes and media framing. Bachelet's ability to portray a more "feminine style" of political leadership in a positive light depended on a larger context where many Chileans were worried about the limitations of their current democratic system. Chile's political history, particularly the importance of feminist and women's movements in the struggle for democracy and a widespread perception that women were not yet sufficiently incorporated into political life, provided Bachelet with advantages not shared across all the cases. Above all, Bachelet embodied precisely the kind of "change" that Chileans wanted: someone who emphasized a bottom-up democratic process and a real concern for social justice.

NOTES

1. The Chilean press, however, paid much less attention to Bachelet's status as a single mother, focusing instead on other personal attributes such as leadership style and governance capacities.
2. Farida Jalalzai, "Women Rule: Shattering the Executive Glass Ceiling," *Politics and Gender* 4, no. 2 (2008): 205–231.
3. Anselm C. Strauss and Juliet Corbin, *Basics of Qualitative Research: Techniques and Procedures for Developing Grounded Theory*, 2nd ed. (Thousand Oaks: Sage, 1998).
4. Silvia Borzutzky and Gregory B. Weeks, "Introduction," in Borzutzky and Weeks, eds., *The Bachelet Government* (Gainesville: University of Florida Press, 2010).
5. Carla Lehmann, "La Mujer Chilena Hoy: Trabajo, Familia y Valores," *Estudios Públicos* 60 (Spring 1995): 159–202.
6. Ibid., p. 176.
7. Centro de Estudios Públicos, "Estudio Nacional de Opinión Pública: Mujer, Trabajo, Familia y Valores," (Santiago, Chile, 2002).
8. Margarita Palacios and Javier Martínez, "Liberalism and Conservatism in Chile: Attitudes and Opinions of Chilean Women at the Start of the Twenty-first Century," *Journal of Latin American Studies* 38, no. 1 (2006), pp. 18–19.
9. The figure in Chile was substantially lower than many other Latin American countries.
10. Marcela Ríos Tobar, "Seizing a Window of Opportunity? The Election of President Bachelet in Chile," *Politics and Gender* 4, no. 3 (2008): 509–519.
11. Susan Franceschet, *Women and Politics in Chile* (Boulder: Lynne Rienner Publishers, 2005); Elsa Chaney, *Supermadre: Women and Politics in Latin America* (Austin: University of Texas Press, 1979).

12. Franceschet, *Women and Politics in Chile*; Fiona Macaulay, *Gender Politics in Brazil and Chile: The Role of Parties in National and Local Policymaking* (New York: Palgrave Macmillan, 2006).

13. Chile's Constitution does not permit consecutive re-election.

14. Alan Angell and Cristobal Reig, "Change or Continuity? The Chilean Elections of 2005–2006," *Bulletin of Latin American Research* 25, no. 4 (2006): 481–502; Mauricio Morales Quiroga, "La Primera Mujer Presidenta de Chile: ¿Qué Explicó el Triunfo de Michelle Bachelet en las Elecciones de 2005–2006?" *Latin American Research Review* 43, no. 1 (2008): 7–32.

15. Angell and Reig, "Change or Continuity?," p. 483.

16. Quiroga, "La Primera Mujer Presidenta," p. 19.

17. Centro de Estudios Públicos, "Estudio National de Opinión Pública No. 23, Octubre-Noviembre," 2005, accessed at www.cepchile.cl on June 25, 2009, Santiago, Chile. Lavín, the far-right candidate, was ranked higher in terms of combating crime, and Piñera was perceived as more capable of generating employment.

18. *La Tercera*, May 30, 2005.

19. Arturo Valenzuela and Lucía Dammert, "Problems of Success in Chile," *Journal of Democracy* 17, no. 4 (2006): 65–79, p.73.

20. "Estoy Contigo: Michelle Bachelet's Programa del Gobierno." October 18, 2005.

21. In this round, Bachelet received 45.9 percent, Piñera received 25.4 percent, and Lavín got 23.3 percent of the vote. Chile's electoral law requires that presidents achieve a majority of the popular vote. When no candidate receives a majority, a second round is held between the two candidates receiving the highest vote shares.

22. Angell and Reig, "Change or Continuity?"; Ricardo Gamboa and Carolina Segovia, "Las Elecciones Presidenciales y Parlamentarias en Chile, Diciembre 2005–Enero 2006," *Revista de Ciencia Política* 26, no. 1 (2006): 84–113.

23. Carlos Huneeus and Alejandra López, "Las Encuestas en Las Elecciones Presidencialies del 2005," in Carlos Huneeus, Fabiola Berríos, and Ricardo Gamboa, eds., *Las Elecciones Chilenas de 2005: Partidos, coaliciones y votantes en transición* (Santiago: Catalonia, 2007), p. 238. At this time, opposition candidate Joaquín Lavín was the dominant political figure, having almost defeated Lagos in 2000. Many pundits predicted that Lavín would be the next president.

24. Quiroga, "La Primera Mujer Presidenta"; Gwynn Thomas, "What No Tie? Political Campaigns, Gender, and Redefining Political Leadership in Chile," presented at the *Latin American Studies Association's International Conference*, Montreal, Canada, 2007.

25. Huneeus and Lopez, "Las Encuestas," pp. 238–239.

26. Sebatián Valenzuela and Teresa Correa, "Press Coverage and Public Opinion on Women Candidates: The Case of Chile's Michelle Bachelet," International Communication Gazette 71, no. 3 (2009): 203–223.

27. Centro de Estudios Públicos, 2005.

28. Kathleen Dolan, *Voting for Women: How the Public Evaluates Women Candidates* (Boulder: Westview Press, 2004), p. 60; Leonie Huddy and Nayda Terkildsen, "Gender Stereotypes and the Perception of Male and Female Candidates," *American Journal of Political Science* 37, no.1 (1993): 119–147.

29. Alan Angell, "Cambio o Continuidad? Las Elecciones Chilenas de 2005–2006," in Huneeus and Gamboa, eds., *Las Elecciones Chilenas de 2005*.

30. Navia, Patricio, "¿Da el ancho?" *La Tercera*, December 18, 2005.

31. Valenzuela and Correa, "Press Coverage and Public Opinion."

32. Ibid., p. 214.

33. *La Tercera*, "Las ideas, eslónganes y los trucos que marcaron la campana 2005," January 15, 2006, (accessed January 15, 2006).

34. Thomas, "What No Tie?"

35. *Ercilla*, 2 January, 2006, no. 3.284, p. 13.

36. *Franja*, November 25, 2005.

37. Margaret Power, *Right-Wing Women in Chile: Feminine Power and the Struggle against Allende, 1964–1973* (University Park: Pennsylvania State University Press, 2002); Gwynn Thomas, *It's a Family Affair: Mobilizing Citizens, Claiming Leadership and Contesting Legitimacy in Chilean Politics*. It is still forthcoming with Penn State University Press.

38. *Franja*, November 12, 2005.

39. *Franja*, November 13, 2005.

40. Power, *Right-Wing Women in Chile*.

41. Susan J. Carroll, "Reflections on Gender and Hillary Clinton's Presidential Campaign: The Good, the Bad, and the Misogynic," *Politics and Gender* 5, no.1 (2009): 1–20, p. 6.

42. Paz Lagos, María, "Luces y sombras del liderazgo feminine" *Ya, La Revista de El Mercurio*, December 27, 2005, no. 1162, p. 29.

43. Gwynn Thomas and Melinda Adams, "Breaking the Final Glass Ceiling: The Influence of Gender in the Election of Ellen Johnson-Sirleaf and Michelle Bachelet," *Journal of Women, Politics, and Policy* 31, no. 2 (2010): 105–131.

44. *Franja*, November 11, 2005. The "wound" refers to the political repression and human rights abuses committed by the military under the military dictatorship.

45. *Franja*, January 9, 2006.

46. Centro de Estudios Públicos, 2005.

47. *Franja*, November 13, 2005.

48. Quoted in Carroll, "Hillary Clinton's Presidential Campaign," p. 8.

49. *Franja*, January 1, 2006.

50. Thomas, "What No Tie?"

51. Jorge Marirrodriga, "Bachelet anuncia que la mitad de su Gabinete estará formado por mujeres" *El Pais*, January 14, 2006, www.elpais.com (accessed August 13, 2006). For a similar discussion, see also, *La Tercera*, "Las ideas, eslónganes y los trucos que marcaron la campaña 2005, January 15, 2006, (accessed January 15, 2006).

52. *Franja*, January 1, 2006.

53. *Ercilla*, January 2, 2006, no. 3.284, p. 13.

CHAPTER TEN

Primera Dama, Prima Donna? Media Constructions of Cristina Fernández de Kirchner in Argentina

Jennifer M. Piscopo

INTRODUCTION

This chapter discusses the case of Cristina Fernández de Kirchner, who made a successful bid for the presidency of Argentina in 2007. The press coverage of the Fernández campaign shows that, even when the woman appears as the likely winner, journalists' gender bias still works to undermine the credibility and credentials of female candidates. Even Cristina Fernández, a two-term senator, party leader, and noted jurist, faced criticisms that focused on her femininity rather than her policy, her marriage rather than her career.

At the time of the campaign, Fernández and her husband, then-president Néstor Kirchner, formed a political power couple whose presence and popularity dominated both the executive and legislative branches of Argentina's presidential system. A key leader in the Senate during her husband's presidency, Fernández represented the legislative arm of a policy agenda known as *Kirchnerismo*: an aggressive, left-leaning program of using state resources to deepen social reforms and challenge the business sector. These programmatic goals of *Los K* ["The Ks"] were highly polarizing: the couple triggered a rupture within their Peronist Party, forming their own wing known as *Frente para la Victoria* (Victory Front). Observers either praised *Los K* as defiantly populist or vilified them as deeply clientelistic. Fernández was thus a prominent and controversial public figure, both as senator and as first lady. Overall, the sheer dominance of the "Kirchnerista" machine foreclosed upon the possibility that credible challengers to

Los K would emerge in the 2007 executive race. These features explained Fernández's easy victory, as well as shaped much of the media treatment Fernández received during the campaign.

To explore this media treatment, I analyze 127 feature and opinion articles from the three main, national, daily newspapers in Argentina: *Página 12*, *Clarín*, and *La Nación*.[1] The three newspapers are located at different points along the political spectrum. *La Nación* is the most right-leaning and offered the most criticism of the populist elements that characterized the Néstor Kirchner presidency. The articles in *Clarín* trend towards the center, and the articles in *Página 12* trend toward the left. While both *Clarín* and *Página 12* generally sympathize with underserved and marginalized populations—those sectors that most supported the Kirchners—these newspapers' feature articles remained neutral in their coverage of the Fernández campaign. The newspaper articles cover a fourteen-week period, from July 14, 2007 to October 30, 2007; these dates mark one day prior to the launch of the Fernández candidacy and two days after her electoral victory, respectively. Articles were read for qualitative content, such as mentions of Fernández's appearance, as well as coded for quantitative data, namely the number of times journalists employed different configurations of Fernández's first name and surname, and the number of times she was referenced as either senator or first lady.[2]

Taken together, the data show a lack of systematic bias in terms of the labels (first name versus surname, and senator versus first lady) used to describe Fernández. The data do reveal, however, a predominant media frame of "wife of" and an overarching preoccupation with the "dual condition" of the candidate as senator and first lady. The dominant question of the campaign was thus whether Fernández represented continuity or change, her husband or herself. This double bind structured a narrative of Fernández's campaign as a *transfer of power from husband to wife*. These stories followed Fernández relentlessly. To illustrate this argument, the chapter proceeds as follows. First, I discuss how the specific features of the Argentine case explain both the Fernández victory and the patterns in media coverage. Then, I provide an in-depth discussion of these patterns, looking at the "type" of person the media portrayed Fernández to be, as well as the framing and double binds created by media attention to Fernández's dual condition. I argue that Fernández's *own* ambiguity about her dual status exacerbated the media's preoccupation with this issue, creating a negative feedback loop between the candidate and journalists. Finally, I discuss the domestic and international coverage of Fernández's visits to Europe and North America, the clearest instances in which the press discussed Fernández not as simply a candidate, but as a *woman* candidate.

THE ARGENTINE CONTEXT: WOMEN'S VISIBILITY AND A NON-COMPETITIVE RACE

This section discusses two features which made the Argentine case unique. First, female politicians in Argentina had made extraordinary leadership gains *prior to* Fernández's bid for the presidency. Second, the Kirchners' political dominance gave Fernández an open opportunity for contesting—and winning—the presidency.

Female Politicians as Commonplace

Cristina Fernández ran for president in a country already accustomed to women holding positions of political authority. In 1991, Argentina became the first country in the world to pass a gender quota law for legislative elections. The law requires that political parties nominate 30 percent of women to closed candidate lists. The quota law contains a strong placement mandate—demanding that parties locate women's name in *electable* spots on the candidate lists—and is vigorously enforced. These features have ensured the numerical success of the quota: women's presence climbed in the chamber of deputies from 6 percent before the quota law to an average of 25 percent during the 1990s, reaching 30 percent by 2001, and 35 percent at the time of Fernández's campaign launch in July 2007.[3] The quota was extended to the Senate in 2001, with similar effects: women's presence jumped 5 percent before the quota to 33 percent after the quota, and was at 43 percent in July 2007.[4] While the political parties often resist the quota by claiming there are "no women" to nominate, the numbers suggest that female leaders are no longer a novelty in Argentina.

Indeed, the early 2000s in Argentina were marked by widespread, and well-publicized, gains for women's political leadership. First, was the diffusion of the quota law, both to the national Senate and to the provincial legislatures; by 2007, 23 of Argentina's 24 provincial governments applied a quota law for local elections. Second, was President Néstor Kirchner's well-publicized appointment of "first women": Kirchner selected two female judges for the Supreme Court, a female defense minister, and a female minister of the economy. Third, was that female parliamentarians made progress in gaining leadership positions on the more prestigious legislative commissions, and both the lower chamber (*Cámara de Diputados*) and the upper chamber (*Senado*) had women as their second-vice presidents by 2007.

Certainly, female politicians in Argentina continue to confront numerous socio-cultural obstacles in their exercise of power. In the parliament, these obstacles include entrenched gender beliefs that marginalize most women to the less-prestigious committees, as well as conservative resistance that brands female legislators' efforts to liberalize reproductive rights or criminalize sexual harassment as "feminist" and therefore "crazy."[5] Nonetheless, women's presence in the Argentine legislative, executive, and judicial branches means that neither the media nor citizens can discuss politics *without* mentioning a woman's role or contribution. The presence of women in power is no longer regarded as extraordinary, but as routine.

Cristina Fernández thus launched her presidential bid in an environment which, if not entirely gender neutral, was at least habituated to the presence of female leaders. In 2007, before the official campaign launch, but when Fernández's candidacy was certain, *Página 12* surveyed 400 residents of greater Buenos Aires about their views on women in power. Eighty percent signaled women's political presence as a "positive new development" for the Argentinean government. Eighty-nine percent rejected the statement that women were inherently weaker politicians than men, instead attributing weakness to individual variation rather than gender difference. While survey respondents recognized that *machismo* (sexism) had not disappeared—many acknowledged that a female president's decision-making would suffer greater scrutiny than a male president's decision-making—the respondents also regarded a female president as a viable "new alternative" for Argentine politics.[6] Overall, the respondents manifested no discernible voter bias against a female executive candidate.

The Boring and Predictable Election

While the expectation that associates a female executive with renovation and renewal is gendered, the expectation was framed theoretically and is not necessarily applicable to Fernández herself. Fernández was neither a neophyte nor an outsider. She first entered politics as a law student, and she met her husband, Néstor Kirchner, through their shared activism in the student wing of the Peronist party. Elected to the Senate in 1995, and reelected in 2001, she was serving her third term at the time of her presidential bid. She was president of the Senate's influential Constitutional Affairs committee, and member of the equally important Commissions on International Relations, Budget, and Defense. Her husband's election to the presidency in 2003 further augmented her leadership profile, both in the Senate chamber and within the Peronist Party.

The Kirchners' *Frente para la Victoria* was enormously popular among constituents. As president, Néstor Kirchner had expanded social services for the poor voters who formed the majority of the Peronist party's base. He had taken the courageous step of bringing military generals to trial for human rights abuses committed during the 1976–1983 dictatorship, and overseen a period of economic growth and recovery. The opposition, while decrying the Kirchners' alleged clientelism and corruption, was—according to one journalist—"the most divided opposition in Argentine history."[7] While Argentina has been a competitive, multi-party system, the various "anti-K" factions both inside and outside the Peronist party were, in 2007, beset by crippling personality conflicts. The opposition could not coordinate on a single leader.

Thus, the overwhelming fact that explains Fernández's victory was the absence of serious competition. A journalist summarized the presidential campaign as follows: "This race is shockingly boring. It's a result by default. The opposition is divided and has no personality. The people are uninvolved and unengaged. . . . Cristina is Coca-Cola, or the product that is very clear what it's about."[8] Foreign correspondents echoed this sentiment, with a British journalist noting, "There is neither a serious campaign from the government nor the opposition. Cristina Kirchner presents herself as the winner, and all the remaining candidates accept it."[9] Indeed, Néstor Kirchner's 2008 budget, sent to Congress in September 2007—in the middle of the campaign—was known as "Cristina's budget."[10] In the beginning of October 2007, three weeks *prior* to the election date, the media began covering Cristina Fernández's cabinet picks.[11]

The context of a non-competitive race and women's visibility as political leaders has implications for analyzing the media treatment of Cristina Fernández during the campaign. First, the 2007 presidential

Table 10.1 The Parallel Political Careers of Cristina and Néstor Kirchner

Cristina Fernández de Kirchner	Néstor Kirchner
1989–1995: Provincial Legislator in Province of Santa Cruz	1987–1991: Mayor of Rio Gallegos, Province of Santa Cruz
1994: Assembly Member for the National Constitutional Convention	1991–2003: Governor of Province of Santa Cruz
1995–1997: National Senator for Santa Cruz	
1997–2001: National Diputada (lower-house representative) for Santa Cruz	
2001–2005: National Senator for Santa Cruz	2003–2007: President of Argentina
2005: National Senator for the Province of Buenos Aires	
2007: President of Argentina	

Source: Elaboration by Author.

campaign in Argentina was *not* an issue campaign: the opposition failed to offer a coherent alternative to *Kirchnerismo* and there was scant substantive material which journalists and pundits could use to compare the candidates on the issues. Of the 127 news stories and editorials analyzed, only 42 (or 33%) referenced an ideological position or actual claim made by Cristina Fernández. The vast majority of the articles and editorials—77 percent—simply described and summarized campaign acts or events.

Second, the closest (but still distant) challenger to Cristina Fernández was also a woman. The competitor, Elisa Carrió, was similar to Cristina Fernández in terms of legislative experience and party leadership: Carrió had served two-and-a-half terms in the *Cámara de Diputados* (1995–1999, 1999–2003, and 2005–2007), and was founder of her own left-leaning political party. Carrió's and Fernández's parties both occupied the left of the political spectrum; yet, whereas Fernández's audience was poor and underserved voters, Carrió's "social justice without clientelism" arguments appealed to the educated intellectuals of the middle classes. As such, Carrió was a regular on the Argentine political scene. She had contested Néstor Kirchner in the 2003 presidential elections, placing fourth. While some favored her social democratic agenda, others regarded her tendency to build electoral alliances with competitors (especially those from the neoliberal right) as disappointingly opportunistic. That she became the strongest challenger to Fernández speaks mostly to her role as the "perennial candidate"—Carrió was Pepsi to Fernández's Coca-Cola, or the other household name in the race.

Thus, some standard analyses of gender bias in media coverage do not apply in the Argentine case. The top two contenders were women. The campaign itself was "empty of ideas, debates, and proposals."[12] One cannot compare the issue coverage between male and female candidates, nor the viability or horse race coverage between male and female candidates.[13] While the media paid some attention to the traits of female candidates, referring to Carrió as *la gorda* or *la gordita* ("the fat one") and Fernández as *flamante* (attention-grabbing) and *volcánica* (fiery), the predominant media attention focused on Cristina Fernández in her dual roles as first lady and senator.[14]

Gender thus surfaced in the campaign not in the contrast between male and female contenders, but in relation to Cristina Fernández's own personal style and professional profile. Most notably, gendered commentary appeared as the media grappled with Fernández's dual status. Carrió responded by highlighting her own independence, making frequent references to not being anyone's wife. Fernández's response—proclaiming her presidency as either perpetuating the good times of *Kirchnerismo* or bringing about a new *Cristinismo*—was ambiguous. As discussed more fully below, Fernández wanted to be perceived both as continuing her husband's successful policies *and* as introducing an independent agenda.

These idiosyncrasies specific to the Argentine case—two women contenders, a female-friendly, non-competitive race, and a frontrunner with an ambiguous message—explain why the gender bias of the media, though present, was not as prejudicial as the theory predicts.

GENDER STEREOTYPES AND CRISTINA FERNÁNDEZ'S "TYPE"

The transfer of power narrative that unfolded during Fernández's campaign first depended on the "type" of politician Cristina Fernández appeared to be: a strong-willed militant who pushed the executive branch's Peronist agenda in the Senate. In analyzing Fernández's victory speech, at the close of the campaign, one journalist summarized Fernández as "a woman capable of doing politics, militant and smart at the same time." The journalist also suggested that Fernández introduced "the feminine" into the acceptance speech; the journalist mentioned Fernández's flowered dress, affectionate greeting of children, and call for her "fellow sisters" to celebrate a woman's ascendency to the executive.[15] This journalist's positive evaluation of Fernández's political capacities and feminine identity is, however, unique among the 127 articles surveyed. During the campaign, and in the days following the election, the majority of the media criticized Fernández's *lack* of these very attributes. Gender expectations about "the feminine" in politics led the media to portray Cristina Fernández, who *violated* these expectations, as authoritarian, aloof, vain, and self-centered.

One of the most widespread images of the campaign launch was a photo showing only Fernández's foot, encased in a high heel and firmly planted on a stage. The image of the shoe is out of focus, but in focus appears a group of men, seated below the stage, looking attentively at the shoe. The men are members of Néstor Kirchner's cabinet. This image transforms Fernández into a cipher of control and strength, a female dominator of male politicians. The media frequently mentioned Fernández's confrontational manner, referencing, for instance, her "vehement style" and her "hard and argumentative speech."[16] In one reported incident, she snapped furiously at her husband—in what she apparently thought was *sotte voce*—for confusing the order of speakers at a campaign event.[17] The overall image of Cristina Fernández was authoritarian.[18]

While strength and forcefulness are often perceived as positive traits for male candidates, the attribution of these traits to Fernández activated a negative association of abrasiveness and coldness. One commentator observed that Fernández did not want to "mix with the people"; in fact, the impression was that Cristina Fernández felt repulsed by the common crowds.[19] Halfway through the campaign, the media gleefully reported that the Fernández team had hired image consultants to *sensibilizar* (sensitize) the candidate—essentially, to make her more warm, friendly, and approachable.[20] Another journalist noted that the campaign acts which featured poses of "Cristina smiling, Cristina with misty eyes, Cristina bringing her hands to the heart" were calculated appeals to emotion, efforts "to create a more human feel" and overcome the "distance and frigidness" that had thus far characterized Fernández's career.[21] The portrayal of Fernández as lofty and inaccessible was exacerbated by the campaign's preference to eschew interviews with the domestic press. This refusal perhaps increased the media's tendency to view Fernández as cold, particularly when Fernández told a CNN en Español reporter that "the world did not pass through the press."[22] Whereas female candidates are often perceived as too maternal and too soft, the problem for Cristina Fernández was the perception that she lacked any nurturing or friendly instincts at all.

Cristina Fernández's femininity was not questioned, however, when it came to the media's coverage of her appearance. Her preference for bright colors, designer labels, and elaborate coiffeur generated commentaries on her vanity. When it came to appearance, Fernández shifted from not being feminine enough to being *too* feminine. In other words, Fernández was not casually or effortlessly beautiful; she was insecure and trying too hard. A poorly conceived joke made by Fernández, in which she said "she painted herself with makeup as if she were a door," quickly became one of the media's favorite catchphrases.[23] One journalist described Fernández's age as "fifty-four flirtatious, well-preserved years."[24] Another noted that "her style of dress has become more flamboyant, and her makeup more heavy, with her age."[25] The media attention on Fernández's appearance was more than a gendered news frame for covering Fernández's campaign acts; the attention reinforced the stereotype about her candidate "type." Not merely was she frigid and distant, but she was also self-promoting and self-obsessed.

The media gave much attention to Fernández's weakness for shopping, mentioning her Louis Vuitton handbags, her expensive face creams, and her colorful outfits. While her clothing was certainly described, in that Fernández was wearing a "blue suit" or was "dressed in clear tones," the larger focus was on the glamour of the dress itself. One article, for instance, noted how her "coquettishness" appeared in "her designer clothing, personal expenses, and certain eccentricities." The eccentricity in question was Fernández's preference to only drink mineral water of a certain brand, which (according to the article) her aides always provided.[26] One male challenger described Fernández as "a woman with a pleasing physique, elegant, and well put together" with whom he looked forward to debating.[27]

This focus on Fernández's extravagance was twinned with speculation about how often (not if) she had undergone cosmetic surgery. Indeed, a journalist interviewing Fernández for a local radio program asked her about her plastic surgeries—*before* he asked her opinion on campaign issues such as the economy and abortion. *Página 12* reported midway through the campaign that Fernández's image advisors wished the candidate would look "more natural," for everyone knew "the passion the senator has for her appearance . . . and the time her team must dedicate to cultivating her image."[28] The implication in these stories was that Fernández's artifice and artificiality were becoming a liability.

Evidence of her extravagance-as-liability comes from the image of Cristina Fernández that encapsulates how the press and the public perceived her: as "Queen Cristina."[29] This moniker was repeated over and over in the press. During a campaign act, for instance, Queen Cristina "threw kisses, mixed with the crowd, and adopted an oriental style of greeting, a small inclination forward with hands on her chest."[30] Underscoring this image further was the media attention to the luxuriousness of Fernández's hotel accommodations and private transport arrangements.[31] Further constructions of Fernández-as-royalty came from the incessant comparisons between Fernández and Eva Perón, the famous 1930s starlet who married General Juan Domingo Perón and became Argentina's most glamorous, most revered, most iconic, and most beloved first lady.

The domestic media's repetition of the foreign press's comments about Fernández's appearance—rather than about the substance of her campaign—further enforced the image of Fernández as royal beauty queen. The German press described Fernández as "attractive, unconventional, and with much self-esteem"; this description formed the opening sentence of the *La Nación* article covering Fernández's German tour. This same *La Nación* article mentioned Fernández's "glamour," and her brilliance in comparison to the female German Chancellor's drabness.[32] The Argentine press also repeated *The New York Times*'s references to "Queen Cristina," as well as the observation that Fernández's obsession with her appearance had transformed her presidential campaign into a "coronation."[33] The French press commented, in a remark much-repeated in Argentina, that Fernández sought to "inherit" the presidency.[34] The media also reported Ecuadorian President Rafael Correa's statement that Cristina Fernández symbolized "the beauty of Argentine women."[35] These quotes reveal more than gender stereotyping by the domestic and foreign press. Discussions of Cristina Fernández's appearance were used to portray her candidate *type*: she was an elitist, entitled snob who put her stardom before her professionalism. Instead of being constructed as a charismatic, strong (male) leader, she was viewed as a vain, self-aggrandizing (female) celebrity.

The construction of Cristina Fernández as both aggressive and authoritarian (and therefore too masculine), as well as self-obsessed and vain (and therefore not effortlessly feminine) also appeared on the Argentine variety show, *El Gran Cuñado* ("The Big Brother-in-Law"). While Hillary Clinton and Sarah Palin were mimicked by Amy Poehler and Tina Fey on *Saturday Night Live*, Cristina Fernández's character on the Argentine equivalent was—and still is—acted by a transvestite. The portrayal of Fernández by a transvestite perfectly captures how her persona, then as candidate and now as president, violates gendered expectations about female politicians' naturalness. The media viewed Cristina Fernández as a masculine diva.

Overall, however, the articles that referenced Fernández's dictatorial tendencies, her calculated softening, her plastic surgeries, or her appearance composed only 11 percent of the studied sample.[36] While the literature would suggest that this finding means that 11 percent *less* coverage was thus devoted to the substantive questions of the campaign,[37] the Argentine media did not, as previously noted, pay much attention to the substantive proposals of *any* candidate in the 2007 campaign. As discussed below, the media paid more systematic attention to Cristina Fernández's dual role of senator and first lady, and whether her presidential bid signaled the deepening of policies began by Néstor Kirchner or a shift to new policies conceived by Cristina Fernández.

MEDIA FRAMING AND DOUBLE BINDS: THE CAMPAIGN AS A TRANSFER OF POWER

This section analyzes how two media frames common in female candidates' executive campaigns—the "first name" and "wife of"—appeared in the Argentine case. These frames personalized Fernández and allowed journalists to indulge in comparisons between Fernández and other presidential spouses who had aspired to follow in their husbands' footsteps. When combined together, these frames created the *transfer of power* narrative that dominated much of the coverage of the Fernández campaign.

"First Name" and "Wife of"

Most women in Argentina do not take their husbands' names, retaining their family name throughout their careers. If an Argentine woman does take her husband's name, the formal name becomes her unmarried name *plus* her husband's name, as in the following construction: Cristina Fernández de Kirchner. In this construction—which is, in fact, the construction chosen by this politician—the appropriate shorthand is *Fernández*. Yet, in the media articles surveyed, only 11 (8.6%) referred to Fernández either as "Cristina Fernández" or as "Cristina Fernández de Kirchner." The vast majority of the articles referred to the candidate as "Cristina Kirchner" or just "Cristina." The use of Fernández's first name was pervasive, followed by the combined use of her first name and married surname. Of the 121 articles that invoked her name, 41 (33.8%) called her "Cristina" and 40 (33%) alternated references between "Cristina" or "Cristina Kirchner," for a combined total of 81 (67%) articles that used the familiar address. The pattern appears even more strongly when examining the headlines: 77 of 94 headlines (82%) called her "Cristina" or "Cristina Kirchner." Specifically, 43 headlines (45.7%) referred to her simply as "Cristina." In all, few headlines and few articles referenced the candidate by her full and complete name. Perhaps surprisingly, the paper using Fernández's name correctly most often—referring to her as "Cristina Fernández" or "Cristina Fernández de Kirchner"— was *La Nación*, the most conservative of the three newspapers in the sample and the most opposed to the Peronist policy agenda.

The references to "Cristina" appear in contrast to the references to "Kirchner," for when the surname appears alone in the articles, the allusion is to Néstor Kirchner. For instance, "Kirchner and Cristina campaigned together [in the city of] Formosa" and "Kirchner and Cristina are in [the city of] Río Negro."[38] Moreover, in nearly every reference to Fernández in relation to a male politician, her first name is used: on a visit to Spain, for example, "Cristina" visits the Spanish prime minister, "Zapatero."[39] On the one hand, the Fernández campaign encouraged the identification of their candidate as simply Cristina. For instance, once Julio Cobos agreed to abandon his post in the opposition party and become Fernández's running-mate, the official campaign slogan was *Cristina, Cobos y vos* ("Cristina, Cobos, and you"). On the other hand, Fernández preferred her full, formal name, telling CNN en Español's Carmen Aristeguí that "[It's] Cristina Fernández de Kirchner, for when you have been alongside a man for more than 30 years, have two children, and share a strong political career [. . .] there is a permanent interaction, and the result is that I am, after 32 years joined with him, Cristina Fernández de Kirchner, all together."[40] With this statement, Fernández clearly wishes for dual recognition, both as someone who shares her husband's political project and as someone who carries her own identity.

The ambiguity in Fernández's name—was she Cristina, Cristina Kirchner, Cristina Fernández, or Cristina Fernández de Kirchner—thus reflects the larger ambiguity about whether this candidate was a first lady or a senator, connected or independent. In the famous CNN interview, when Fernández was asked whether she was a "wife of, a senator, or a candidate," she responded, "Cristina Fernández is an Argentine woman, an active, longtime militant in politics, who is married to another longtime, active militant. It's that simple."[41] And note that, in this response, she referred to herself simply as "Cristina Fernández." The media, however, did not view Fernández's multiple roles as quite "that simple." While theories of media framing might suppose that the media focused *excessively* on Fernández as the *primera dama* (first lady), the data actually show a random, and equal distribution of references to Fernández as either a senator or a first lady.

In the sample of articles studied, the total number of references to Fernández as either *primera dama* or *senadora* (senator) was essentially identical: 142 mentions of Fernández as *senadora* and 149 mentions of Fernández as *primera dama* were spread evenly across 111 articles, and without noticeable clustering. Only a handful of articles referred to Fernández as first lady (13) without mentioning her role as senator, and a corresponding handful (14) referred to Fernández as a senator without noting her role as first lady. In other words, the vast majority of articles from all the newspapers referred to Fernández as *both* first lady and senator. The tendency did not vary across newspapers. Of course, the question also arises of which mention appears first—whether the articles identified Fernández *primarily* as senator or first lady. Yet again, there appears no pattern. Journalists were as likely to modify their first mention of Fernández with the descriptor of "senator" as they were likely to modify their first mention with the descriptor "first lady"; there was no statistical significance between the groups, nor was there a statistically significant difference based on the source. The media paid systematic attention to Fernández's dual roles, but did not emphasize one status over the other.

The lack of statistically-measurable bias in referring to Fernández as first lady or senator does not mean, however, that the media *accepted* Fernández's dual status. Attention to her role as first lady was particularly high during the weeks surrounding the campaign launch. For instance, one article's headline read, "The plan to launch the first lady's campaign in the country's interior."[42] This attention during the campaign's initial phase paralleled salacious attention to Néstor Kirchner's part in the process, and heralded the appearance of the continuity versus change double bind. One article described the scene of the campaign launch as Romeo and Juliet in reverse: "Kirchner" stood on the balcony of the theater, observing, as "Cristina" stood on the stage, declaring her love and affection for him. This love and affection became a campaign platform, as "Cristina Fernández reasserted the benefits of Néstor Kirchner's presidency, and promised to give institutional structure to the changes he had implemented." In addition, Fernández added that "The Argentines won't forget him, but I hope they won't miss him too much," suggesting, according to the journalist who reproduced the quotes, that Fernández would both extend and improve her *husband's* policies.[43]

The "wife of" frame became particularly thorny for Fernández given common knowledge that she was chosen to run by Kirchner—rather than selected in an openly competitive primary. The day of the campaign launch, one journalist printed that "It was Néstor Kirchner who decided, via *el dedo* (finger-pointing), that Cristina would be the presidential candidate."[44] The fact that Fernández was selected via *el dedo* became a handicap for the campaign for two reasons. First, Kirchner's decision to not seek reelection became interpreted as Fernández's vicious ability to seize the spotlight for her own self-promotion (rather than as Kirchner's gracious desire to extend an opportunity to a deserving co-partisan). Second, critics used *el dedo* to decry the insularity and corruption of the *Kirchneristas*—despite the fact that the vast majority of Argentina's executive and legislative candidates are chosen via appointment by the party boss.[45] Also grating was that Kirchner campaigned extensively on Fernández's behalf. Reporters followed Néstor Kirchner in the initial weeks of the campaign, noting that he often campaigned without his wife, or that she merely accompanied him. One journalist commented dryly that Kirchner would speak and "Cristina will just occupy the best position for the photo."[46] The latter comment also echoes the media's tendency to portray Fernández as vain and attention-seeking.

The media also enjoyed making the "wife of" comparisons between Fernández and other famous first ladies, such as Marta Sahagún of Mexico and Hillary Clinton of the United States. Sahagún, an activist in Mexico's conservative PAN party, married President Vicente Fox (also of the PAN) during his term in office. Sahagún had made previous, unsuccessful bids for local-level office, and her marriage to President Fox and her charitable foundation work fueled speculation that she would run for president when her husband's term ended in 2006. A series of corruption scandals related to Sahagún's foundations, however, ended her presidential pretensions. Sahagún was accused by the Mexican press of holding ambitions disproportionate to her qualifications. An Argentine journalist drew parallels between Fernández and Sahagún, who "tried to impose her candidacy on absolutely everyone in her party." While the journalist acknowledged that a "huge difference" existed between Sahagún, a pharmacist, and Fernández, a senator, the article clearly disparages both women as ambitious, corrupt wives. The largest parallel between the two, according to the journalist, was their ability to use their husbands' positions to access the executive and partisan resources necessary for a presidential campaign.[47]

Comparisons between Hillary Clinton and Cristina Fernández were equally unfavorable to Fernández. The Argentine candidate was called the "Hillary of Buenos Aires."[48] Like Clinton, Fernández was frequently accused of using her husband's position to launch her own political career. The vast majority of articles failed to note that Fernández—and

Clinton—had begun their political careers as activists *alongside* their husbands. The articles also failed to mention that Fernández—unlike Clinton—had been a senator *prior* to her husband's ascendancy to the executive. The one article acknowledging this difference still argued that Clinton surpassed Fernández in terms of political credentials: unlike Fernández, the journalist argued, Clinton was competing in an honest, direct, and open primary. The implication was that Fernández's candidacy, based on her husband's selection via *el dedo*, was less legitimate than that of Clinton. This same journalist also praised Clinton for launching her presidential bid "by herself, via the Internet" and "never once mentioning, not a single time, either her husband or his presidency." She further praised Bill Clinton because, while campaigning on behalf of his wife, "he made a great effort. . . . to make it clear that his wife, should she win, would be the one making the decisions."[49]

During one interview, Fernández expressed both appreciation for and frustration with the comparisons to Hillary Clinton. On the one hand, she admitted that she both liked and admired Clinton. On the other hand, she said, "I don't participate in politics because I am the president's wife." She then asked why no one complained about familial transfers of power in the United States, citing the passage of the presidency from Bush Senior to Bush Junior, and the possible passage of the office from Bill Clinton to Hillary Clinton. Fernández commented that it was important to avoid the hypocrisy associated with criticizing practices in Argentina while ignoring these practices in other countries.[50] Yet, in another interview, Fernández welcomed the comparison with Clinton: when faced with choosing between resembling Eva Perón or resembling Hillary Clinton, Fernández preferred to identify herself with a woman who became a politician (Clinton), rather than a woman who remained simply a first lady (Perón).[51] Indeed, Fernández repeatedly insisted that she mimicked neither Sahagún nor Perón.

These comments from Fernández suggest that she approached her own "dual condition" with both clarity and ambiguity. First, she clearly desired that the domestic and foreign press see her as a credible, independent politician who simply happened to be married to the president. The media's insistence on comparing Fernández to other first ladies, however, made Fernández's ability to articulate this self-image difficult. Fernández became forced to portray herself as similar to Clinton, especially when the alternatives were being like Sahagún or Perón. Moreover, the most sensible campaign strategy for Fernández *was* to run on her husband's and her party's past performance, given how enormously popular *Kirchernismo* was with voters. This decision compelled her to embrace her connectedness to Néstor Kirchner, thus landing her squarely within the continuity versus change double bind.

Continuity and Change: The Transfer of Power

Given the enormous popularity of the Kirchners' political project, which had antagonized the middle class but had enthused the popular sectors, Fernández's most sensible strategy was promising ideological and programmatic continuity. One journalist commented that Fernández's 2007 campaign speeches used the same language as Kirchner's orations four years earlier: "CFK used the same argument that her husband has been using since 2003, the necessity for an energetic integration of ideology and policy."[52] Another referred to her victory as a *reelection*, and not an election. Fernández herself made direct references to a seamless changeover.[53] For instance, she announced at a campaign stop that "We are not here with empty promises; we are here with the testimony and the evidence of what has been done." She claimed she would follow Kirchner's programs for "we do not know any other recipe"; she stressed that the transitional period between the October election and the December inauguration would be smooth, without shocks and crises.[54] At the same time, she stressed that the Kirchner project was incomplete, and that her presidency was required to consolidate the economic and social transformation that Argentina needed.[55]

Any candidate from the Kirchners' wing of the Peronist Party, *Frente para la Victoria*, would have run on a continuity platform. Yet, Fernández's status as first lady led the media to interpret this platform as a marital conspiracy rather than a reasonable strategy. For instance, one journalist commented: "The vote for Cristina is fundamentally a vote for the leadership and the project of Néstor Kirchner. For this reason, her leadership is not confirmed and the possibility that her husband will govern instead is generating ill will."[56] Had Fernández and Kirchner simply been co-partisans, rather than husband and wife, the comment would have ended with the observation that voting for Fernández meant supporting the programmatic goals of the *Frente para la Victoria*. Instead, the comment suggested that Kirchner, and not Fernández, would govern. Other journalists went farther, daring to ask Fernández questions such as "Are these your ideas or your husband's?" and "What will Néstor do if you win?"[57]

The tension between continuity and change meant that Fernández was truly trapped. Observers wanted her to simultaneously continue Kirchner's policies, and thus perpetuate good times, and diverge from Kirchner's policies, and thus show her independence. Yet, if she continued developing the "Agenda K," she was assumed to be too incompetent to govern on her own. And if she diverged too much from the *Frente para la Victoria* program, she was assumed to be too unilateral in her decision-making (which echoed the common understanding of her "type" as authoritarian).

For instance, one columnist noted that "if Kirchner's wife was a leader clearly independent and different from her husband, someone might reasonably believe that the government's current agenda would change."[58] Yet, given that voters were choosing Fernández in order to deepen the economic transformation initiated by her husband—and because the opposition offered no credible alternative—why *would not* Fernández maintain the current agenda? Even her supporters contradicted themselves on this point. For instance, the chief of Argentina's largest labor union described his position as follows: "We support Cristina Kirchner. We know Néstor Kirchner. Regarding Cristina, we have some doubts. But [Néstor] Kirchner brought us out of the economic crisis."[59] The paradox is quite evident: either Fernández was too connected and would not bring *enough* change, or she was too unpredictable, and would bring too *much* change. Or, as one commentator described the paradox: either Fernández needed to be controlled, so Kirchner *had* to govern behind the scenes, or Fernández wasn't controlling *enough*, so Kirchner would be *able* to wrestle control away from her. Argentines both hoped and feared that Kirchner would become Fernández's Rasputin.[60]

Fernández clearly wished to navigate this double bind, and portray herself as both sharing her husband's programmatic goals as well as possessing her own ideas. She responded to the question "are these your ideas or your husband's" by saying, "If you wish to know my husband's opinions, please ask him."[61] The limited media coverage of the issues was thus focused on instances where Fernández clearly differed from Kirchner. In the Argentine case, this issue coverage (though uncommon generally) focused less on simply stereotyping the candidate and more on attempting to determine where she ideologically diverged from the president.

The "change" half of the double bind thus appeared in the one area where Fernández indeed differed from Kirchner: making overtures to the business community. The media's focus on Fernández's rapprochement with the financial and industrial sectors was also infused with gendered commentary, as one journalist noted that "it will be a week of business with the smell of a woman's perfume."[62] Another reported that Fernández entered the meeting room and calmly took her place at the table "with all the men."[63] The reporters covering the series of sessions between Fernández and the business leaders also noted how pleased the *businessmen* were at Fernández's command of the issues and willingness to dialogue.[64] One journalist noted how an industrialist praised Fernández's ability to "understand these issues very well."[65]

The fanfare resulting from Fernández's courting of the business community was the only substantive effort by the media to identify precisely *how* Fernández would differ from Kirchner. As shown, the majority of speculation about her ability to bring about change centered on assumptions that her marriage reduced her independence, or on vague claims about her lack of trustworthiness rather than concrete evidence about her character or her platforms. Fernández herself also seemed unable to offer an alternative portrayal of her intentions.

BEING FEMALE AND THE *PRIMERA DAMA'S* INTERNATIONAL TOURS

Explicit references to Cristina Fernández de Kirchner as a woman were made infrequently by either the candidate herself or by the media. Fernández stressed that she would be the feminine *presidenta*—as opposed to the masculine *presidente*—yet she rarely invoked her gender beyond the necessities of grammatical correctness. She also used grammar strategically, asking her *compañeras de género* (female sisters) for the vote, rather than simply asking for the votes of her *compañeros* (brothers and sisters).[66] Such linguistic tweaks hardly manifest a deep commitment to gender solidarity. Yet Fernández confined herself to the world of grammar, and almost never referenced her status as a woman.[67] She referred to being female only when attending a women-specific campaign event, such as the opening of a "Women's Park" or the inauguration of a women's shelter. Yet, even in these instances, she referenced only her pride in Argentine women's advancement, and offered no substantive commitment to specific policies or programs that would promote such advancement.

Likewise, the media made few comments about Fernández's campaign as important for Argentine women, and even fewer comments that supposed Fernández would take political actions because of her gender. Several news stories discussed a group of female legislators and ministers who, as self-identified Fernández and Kirchner supporters, were known as *Las Generales K* (The "K" Female Generals). Journalists suggested that these women identified with *Kirchnerismo* and with Fernández, but there was *no* suggestion that *las generales* would assist Fernández with developing a female-centered policy agenda.[68] Indeed, *las generales* themselves explained that their label did not invoke any gender militancy; rather, they frequently met at a bar named "The General."[69] While some of *las generales* had independent reputations for being feminist advocates, their support for Fernández and Kirchner was based on shared party goals rather than shared feminist visions.

The major exception to the lack of attention to Fernández as a female candidate appeared in the press coverage of Fernández's visits to Europe and the United States. First, Fernández was widely criticized for spending much of the campaign period abroad in Germany, Austria, France, Spain, and the United States. This criticism originated because the press viewed

Fernández's foreign travel either as tourist jaunts undertaken by a first lady or as publicity trips taken by a candidate; these trips were not viewed as state visits made by a sitting senator and party leader. For instance, a *Clarín* article criticized the German Chancellor's decision to receive Fernández, for "the agenda of [Angela] Merkel includes neither first ladies nor presidential candidates."[70] Likewise, when Fernández and Kirchner traveled to Mexico, and Fernández met with the Mexican President as well as Mexican business leaders, the press noted "what stood out was how her activity was outside what was expected from a first lady." The reporter could then not resist adding that, "then again, much of what Cristina has done as first lady has not been typical."[71] The notion that Fernández had legitimate political business to carry out in Germany and in Mexico was in doubt. For instance, when Fernández spoke with German leaders about Argentina's debt to the Paris Club[72], journalists saw this intervention as a *first lady* delivering her husband's message, and not as a senator—who was seated on the international relations and finance committees—undertaking a legitimate diplomatic mission.[73]

Second, and more important, Fernández's meetings with prominent female leaders were described as girl power chats rather than substantive political discussions. Beyond failing to acknowledge that Merkel might receive Fernández in her capacity as senator, the German and Argentine press also noted that Fernández and Merkel spent "a good part of their meeting talking about what it was like to be a woman in power."[74] Likewise, when Fernández met the female president of the Austrian parliament and the female vice president of Spain, the press reported that they talked about their mutual understanding of being female leaders.[75] When Fernández met Cecilia Sarkozy, the wife of the French President, the media reported on their shared penchant "to go shopping."[76] When Fernández met Sègoléne Royal, who had recently been unsuccessful in her attempt to defeat Sarkozy for the French presidency, the media reported that Fernández's main reaction to Royal was that "we are truly in the Century of the Women." When Fernández had met Royal on a previous visit to France—before Royal lost her presidential bid—the media had then reported that the two "well-attired" women "met to have tea" and exchange electoral "good luck charms."[77] That these female leaders could—and *did*—discuss actual policy issues received scant media attention.

CONCLUSION

This chapter assessed gender bias in the media treatment of Cristina Fernández de Kirchner's executive campaign by looking at both quantitative patterns and qualitative descriptions across news articles from three major newspapers. While the quantitative analysis showed no statistically significant differences in journalists' tendency to label Fernández as either a first lady or a senator, this "dual condition" did provide structure to the qualitative coverage of the campaign. Less attention was paid to the fact that Fernández was running *as a woman*, mostly because Argentina was well-acclimated to the presence of female legislators, ministers, and judges, and because Fernández herself consciously avoided labeling herself as a *female* candidate. These factors meant that the "first woman" frame was largely absent. Nonetheless, the Argentine case shows that, even when women's political leadership is commonplace, gender bias in campaign coverage appears.

The Fernández campaign thus conforms to several expectations sketched out in the introductory chapter to this book. First, gendered media coverage meant that Fernández was not treated as a competent professional. Rather, she was portrayed as a spotlight-hungry starlet. This image was reinforced as Fernández found her femininity attacked by the press: she was constructed as artificial, cold, and aloof rather than natural, warm, and open. The media penalized her for violating traditional expectations about women as gentle and soft. Second, the media focused on Fernández's personal life to such an extent that her credibility and competency were further undermined. The media treated her marriage as a liability, viewing her as either a willful wife who overstepped her role or as an ideological puppet subject to her husband's backroom machinations. To reinforce this double bind—where Fernández was either too independent or too connected—the media paid scant attention to her legitimate political credentials. Thus, whereas some female executive candidates might find their political resumes overly-scrutinized, Fernández found her credentials downplayed and her celebrity highlighted.

The end result of this media treatment, as in other cases, was constructing Fernández as *not a serious politician*. The media could not attack her chances of winning, but they did attack the hubris that she had chosen to run at all. Fernández was construed as a strong-willed, vainglorious personality who would lead Argentina on the already-determined path of *Kirchnerismo*.

Acknowledgments

The author wishes to thank the following individuals for offering their assistance, and for sharing their thoughts and observations of the Cristina Fernández de Kirchner campaign: Mariana Caminotti, Jane Christie, Carlos Gervasoni, Natalia Gherardi, Yanilda González, Silvina Molina, Luis María Otero, Marcelo Pereyra, and Pate Palero. The author also extends a special thanks to Susan Franceschet for sharing her data.

NOTES

1. During the campaign, a research assistant was asked to gather any articles mentioning "Cristina Fernández/Cristina Kirchner/Cristina Fernández de Kirchner" from the three main newspapers. Upon assembling the data, the author checked to ensure that the gathered articles were evenly distributed across the time frame of the campaign, and that all newspapers were equally represented. To fill in any gaps or to repair any unevenness in the sample, the author searched the archives of the newspaper for the desired date(s), again using the variations on Fernández's name as the search term(s).

2. All quotations and headlines have been translated into English. Any errors in the translation are the author's own.

3. The failure to reach 30 percent of women in the Congress in the 1990s had to do with isolated cases of parties' non-compliance, and ambiguity about the placement mandate when parties were contesting only one or two seats.

4. Author's data. Also, see the Inter Parliamentary Union's "Women in Parliaments Database": http://www.ipu.org/wmn-e/classif-arc.htm.

5. Cf Jennifer M. Piscopo, "Engineering Quotas in Latin America," CILAS Working Paper Series, #23. San Diego, Center for Iberian and Latin American Studies, University of California, 2006; Susan Franceschet and Jennifer M. Piscopo, "Quotas and Women's Substantive Representation: Lessons from Argentina," *Politics & Gender* 4, no. 3 (2008): 393–425.

6. Raúl Kollman, "Is it Better to be a Female or Male Candidate?" *Página 12*, July 8, 2007.

7. Raúl Kollman, "In the Final Reckoning," *Página 12*, September 30, 2007.

8. Kollman, "In the Final Reckoning."

9. Lucas Colonna, "The Foreign Press Notes a Campaign without Debate or Ideas," *La Nación*, October 15, 2007.

10. Roberto Navarro, "The Numbers for 'Cristina's Budget,'" *Página 12*, September 12, 2007.

11. Diego Schurman, "Twenty Days from the Elections: Postcards from the Campaign," *Página 12*, October 7, 2007.

12. Colonna, "The Foreign Press."

13. Cf. Kim Fridkin Khan, "Does Being Male Help? An Investigation of the Effects of Candidate Gender and Campaign Coverage on Evaluations of U.S. Senate Candidates," *Journal of Politics* 54, no. 2 (1992): 497–517; Kim Fridkin Kahn, "The Distorted Mirror: Press Coverage of Women Candidates for Statewide Office," *Journal of Politics* 56, no. 1 (1994): 154–173.

14. *La gorda* and *La gordita* are common references to Elisa Carró. Cristina Fernández was called *flamante* by Oscar Guisoni ("Today Begins the Tour and Business Meetings in Spain," *Página 12*, July 22, 2007), and *volcánica* by Walter Curia ("Cristina, Against a Sparse Background and with a Conceptual Discourse," *Clarín*, July 20, 2007).

15. Silvina Premat, "A Modern Discourse and Without Spontaneity: The Semiologists Analyze the Words of Cristina Kirchner," *La Nación*, October 30, 2007.

16. Premat, "A Modern Discourse."

17. "The Inauguration of Public Works in the Township of Merlo," *Clarín*, September 21, 2007.

18. Sandra Russo, "Heels," *Página 12*, September 11, 2007.

19. Consultation with Argentine political expert, June 2007.

20. Mariana Verón, "Cristina Kirchner Has an Advisor to Become More Approachable to People," *La Nación*, October 1, 2007.

21. Schurman, "Twenty Days from the Elections."

22. Cristina Fernández de Kirchner, interview with Carmen Arísteguí, August 2, 2007.

23. In 2006, journalist Olga Wornat published an authorized biography of Cristina Fernández called *Reina Cristina (Queen Cristina)*. The comment from Fernández was taken from an interview in the book, and was echoed constantly throughout the campaign.

24. Fernando Gualdoni and Luis Prados, "Interview with Cristina Fernández de Kirchner in Spain," *Página 12*, July 27, 2007.

25. "A Life with Much Political Change and Attachment to her Husband," *La Nación*, September 26, 2007.

26. Araceli Viceconte, "The Experts Predict a Stronger Bilateral Relation: The German Press Compares Cristina and Hillary Clinton," *La Nación*, September 10, 2007.

27. "Ironies and Critiques from the Opposition," *Clarín*, July 20, 2007.

28. "Cristina de Kirchner and Julio Cobos Present Themselves," *Página 12*, August 14, 2007.

29. The origins of "Queen Cristina" may well be the title of Wornat's 2006 book of the same name.

30. Ibid., note 13.

31. Marcelo Pereyra, "El poder político, las mujeres y los medios en la Argentina (Political Power, Women, and the Media in Argentina)," paper presented at the Biennial Iberian-American Conference of Communication, Córdoba, Argentina, 2007.

32. Viceconte, "Experts Predict a Stronger Bilateral Relation."

33. "Cristina in the United States Press," *La Nación*, September 25, 2007.

34. Marcelo Pereyra, "Cristina Fernández: Señora de alguien con poder (Wife of Someone With Power)," *Artemisia*, October 24, 2007.

35. Miguel Jorquera, "Agreements and Campaign in the Visit of the President of Ecuador," *Página 12*, September 12, 2007.

36. Not counted in this statistic were the comparisons between Cristina Fernández and Eva Perón.

37. Cf Murray, this book.

38. "Act of the President and the Candidate of the Governing Party. Kirchner and Cristina campaign together in Formosa," *Clarín*, August 29, 2007.

39. Oscar Guisoni, "Cristina Fernández Met Yesterday with Rodríguez Zapatero in La Moncloa," *Página 12*, July 25, 2007.

40. Cristina Fernández de Kirchner, interview with Carmen Arísteguí, August 2, 2007.

41. Ibid.

42. Eulate, Mariano Pérez, "The Plan to Install the Candidacy of the First Lady in the Interior," *Clarín*, August 4, 2007.

43. Diego Schurman, "Cristina Fernández Was the Only Speaker in her Campaign Launch," *Página 12*, July 20, 2007.

44. Ana Barón, "Parallel Lives for the Wives of Kirchner and Clinton," *Clarín*, July 20, 2007.

45. Miguel de Luca, Miguel, Mark P. Jones, and María Inés Tula, "Back Rooms or Ballot Boxes? Candidate Nomination in Argentina," *Comparative Political Studies* 35, no. 4 (2002): 413–436.

46. Atilio Bleta, "The President Looks to Support the Candidacy of Cristina," *Clarín*, September 17, 2007.

47. Gerardo Alba de Albarrán, "Cristina, not Marta," *Página 12*, October 28, 2007.

48. "The Angel on High," *La Nación*, September 10, 2007.

49. Barón, "Parallel Lives for the Wives."

50. Fernando Gualdoni and Luis Prados, "Interview with Cristina Fernández de Kirchner in Spain," *Página 12*, July 27, 2007.

51. "Cristina in the American Press," *La Nación*, September 25, 2007.

52. "Lula Received Senator Cristina Kirchner 25 Days before the Elections," *Página 12*, October 4, 2007.

53. Mariano Grondona, "On Sunday, Was There an Election or a Reelection?" *La Nación*, October 30, 2007.

54. Eduardo van der Kooy, "Cristina Wants Gradual Changes," *Clarín*, September 9, 2007.

55. Mariana Verón, "The Changes that Remain Are Deep," *La Nación*, October 26, 2007.

56. Raúl Kollman, "In the Home Straight," *Página 12*, September 30, 2007.

57. Joaquín Morales Solá, "Néstor and Cristina Kirchner Are Similar but not the Same," *La Nación*, October 10, 2007, and Fernando Gualdoni and Luis Prados, "Interview with Cristina Fernández de Kirchner in Spain," *Página 12*, July 27, 2007.

58. Grondona, "An Election or a Reelection?"

59. Silva Naishtat. *Clarín*, "The Leader of the CGT Anticipates Difficulty with the Future Government," August 29, 2007.

60. Pereyra, "El poder político, las mujeres y los medios en la Argentina."

61. Morales Solá, "Néstor and Cristina Kirchner."

62. Alejandra Gallo, "Matrixes with Respect to the Relationship Between the Candidate and the Businessmen," *Clarin*, September 2, 2007.

63. Alejandra Gallo, "Definitions of the Senator and Candidate During the Lunch of Ideas," *Clarín*, September 5, 2007.

64. Mariana Verón, "Cristina Kirchner Endorsed the Business Sector," *La Nación*, September 5, 2007.

65. Silvia Naishtat, "An Encounter with Economic Definitions," *Clarín*, September 5, 2007.

66. Mariano Obarrio, "Kirchner Goes Out Looking for the Urban Vote," *La Nación*, October 20, 2007.

67. The author thanks Yanilda González for sharing her preliminary findings on the gender content of Fernández's speeches.

68. Diego Schurman, "The Female Generals K," *Página 12*, July 12, 2005.

69. Pereyra, "El poder político."

70. Martín Rodríguez Yerba "Vienna: Another Step in the Transformation of Cristina Kirchner," *La Nación*, September 13, 2007.

71. Fernando Cibeira, "The President Spoke of a New Institutionality; a New Mission for the Female President," *Página 12*, August 2, 2007.

72. The Paris Club is an informal group of 19 creditor countries from the developed world. Through the Paris Club, the creditors look for "coordinated and sustainable solutions to the payment difficulties experienced by debtor countries" (http://www.clubdeparis.org/).

73. Martín Rodríguez Yerba, "Political Gesture from Merkel to Cristina Kirchner," *La Nación*, September 12, 2007.

74. Rodríguez Yerba, "Viena: Another Step."

75. Oscar Guisoni, "Cristina Fernández Met Yesterday with Rodríguez Zapatero in the Moncloa," *Página 12*, July 25, 2007.

76. "The Angel on High," *La Nación*, September 10, 2007.

77. Pereya, "El Poder Politico."

PART 4

Conclusion

CHAPTER ELEVEN

Conclusion: A New Comparative Framework

Rainbow Murray

Over the nine case studies explored throughout this book, a recurring set of themes has emerged, based on the theoretical framework outlined in the introductory chapter. This concluding chapter revisits these themes, drawing together insights from across the range of case studies. Doing so allows us to evaluate the utility of lessons from the existing literature when applied to executive elections around the world. We discover that some of the stereotypes about gender are universal, and have common applicability throughout our study. At the same time, some of the expectations generated by the literature are not met when applied to executive (rather than legislative or subnational) office, and many of our expectations were confounded when faced with the different cultural norms present outside the United States.

We begin by summarizing the findings of the book across each aspect of our framework. We then consider ways in which the expectations of the literature need to be expanded and/or revised in order to account for the diversity of comparative case studies and the intensity of executive office. We conclude by pondering why some women candidates were successful when others were not, and what this can tell us for future women executive candidates around the world.

REVISITING THE FRAMEWORK

Our framework explored three key elements of gendered media coverage: gender stereotypes, media framing, and double binds. Within each of these broad areas we explored a range of sub-topics. Not every theme was applicable to every case study, so certain aspects of the framework are absent in some chapters. However, if some themes are frequently inaccurate or irrelevant, this becomes an important finding when re-appraising current wisdom. Hence, each aspect of gendered media coverage is discussed in terms of its overall usefulness and accuracy in depicting the challenges faced by different women candidates. We also examine the factors identified by Jalalzai as facilitating the election of women executives,[1] and consider whether the victorious women candidates studied in this book can attribute their victory to these factors, or whether other dimensions needed to be added to the analysis.

GENDER STEREOTYPES

We anticipated that gender stereotypes, at least in some form or other, would be present around the world. It is perhaps surprising, then, that there is a relative absence of the gender stereotypes predicted in the literature. The majority of women candidates did not experience significant issue or ideological stereotyping, and even trait stereotyping was not universal.

Traits

Some of the candidates who were more overtly feminine in their appearance were also attributed stereotypical traits. Ségolène Royal was frequently associated with feminine traits, both positive and negative, such as warmth, compassion, indecision, irrationality, and incompetence. Sarah Palin was cast in a mixed light, with some stereotypical trait attribution such as warmth, maternal instincts, and incompetence, alongside rather masculine traits such as aggression. Irene Sáez and Michelle Bachelet were also tarred with the brush of presumed incompetence, and this proved to be the most common and pernicious of gender stereotypes. However, Bachelet also benefited from some positive stereotypes, such as the compassion of a doctor, and the ability to heal the nation. Her warmth, humor, and willingness to listen were also viewed in a positive light.

For the remaining candidates, the expected stereotypical traits were either not a big issue (Ellen Johnson Sirleaf, Angela Merkel) or were even conspicuous by their absence (Hillary Rodham Clinton, Helen Clark, Cristina Fernández). As we discuss below, the absence of marked feminine traits in Clinton and Clark proved to be a source of disadvantage.

However, they did also benefit from association with the masculine traits of competence and intelligence. Fernández's "masculine" ambition sat uncomfortably alongside her more feminine traits, resulting in a public persona that was viewed as cold, vain, and self-promoting.[2]

We argued in the introductory chapter that it is masculine traits such as competence, intelligence, and rationality that are viewed most favorably in association with executive office, and candidates who strayed too far from this masculine norm found it difficult to establish their credibility. Of the four candidates portrayed in a feminized manner, only Bachelet succeeded in winning her election, both through positive coverage of her feminine traits and through other factors considered below and in Chapter 9. For the other successful candidates, a delicate balancing act was achieved of displaying the required masculine traits, without entirely ceding the positive associations of certain feminine traits. This balancing act is considered in greater detail in the section on double binds. What is clear is that the associations of executive office with masculine traits do not yet appear to have eroded. Women candidates have benefited from feminine traits only when they have been used to offset a perception of being too masculine; feminine traits alone are not considered sufficient qualification for executive office.

Ideology

We hypothesized in the introductory chapter, based on prior research,[3] that women would be considered more liberal and left-leaning than men. To our surprise, this stereotype was largely absent from our case studies. Merkel alone may have benefited slightly from her status as a woman on the right by being viewed as more close to the median voter. Clark may have experienced some negative ideological stereotyping in 2008, when she was portrayed as "Aunty Helen." Yet the absence of this categorization in the four previous elections in which Clark was a candidate casts doubt over the broader applicability of ideological stereotyping. Royal and Clinton encompassed a range of ideological standpoints on different issues, including a number of policies that placed them to the right of their parties. Palin was firmly oriented towards the right-wing of her party, and as knowledge of the candidate's issue stances became more widespread, any ideological stereotyping was quickly dispelled. Indeed, ideological stereotyping may not be applicable in executive elections precisely because voters have more opportunity to familiarize themselves with candidates' issue stances. The expectations of ideological stereotyping emerge from studies of elections below the national executive level, where stereotyping may play a greater role due to inferior knowledge about the individual candidate. Our study suggests that this hypothesis may not be appropriate for executive elections.

In addition, ideology plays a different role in some countries than others. In Liberia, for example, ideology was not a central aspect of the campaign. In Chile, women are viewed as *more* conservative than men. Unlike some other countries, where women have moved from the right to the left of men,[4] Chilean women have continued to vote to the right of men, and Bachelet's victory in 2005 was the first election where the gender gap disappeared.[5] For all these reasons, ideological stereotyping is not a reliable variable when making comparisons across countries at the executive level.

Issues

Our expectations of issue stereotyping were that women would be more strongly associated with "feminine" issues such as education and health care, while men would be more strongly associated with the more presidential issues of defense, security, and the economy. Again, our hypotheses were largely rejected. In a few case studies, issue stereotypes were present. For example, Royal was heavily associated with domestic and social policies, and struggled to gain any credibility within more masculine policy domains. Bachelet was also associated with feminized policy areas such as health care, although for Bachelet this association was positive, due to her training as a doctor. Bachelet also benefited from her experience as defense minister to gain credibility within this masculinized domain. Palin's issue coverage was mostly neutral, although the sex of the reporter did appear to influence the choice of issues covered.

For the most part, however, issue coverage did not appear to be strongly gendered. Some candidates, such as Clinton and Merkel, were effective in establishing their strength within traditionally masculine domains. Elections were also heavily driven by the issues of the day, and this varied from one election to another. In the United States in 2008, defense and the economy were foremost in voters' minds, with two wars and a burgeoning economic crisis. By contrast, in Liberia, issues such as education were an important aspect of the election. In the Argentinean election, issues barely permeated the agenda. Hence, issue stereotyping does not have a consistent impact across different countries.

The centrality of national issues in executive campaigns insures that executive candidates will be forced to address similar issues and to assert their competence on the key issues of the day. When "masculine" policy areas dominate the agenda, this may work against women

Table 11.1   Gender Stereotypes across the Different Case Studies

	Gender Stereotypes		
	Traits	Ideology	Issues
Irene Sáez	Somewhat	No	No
Ségolène Royal	Yes	No	Yes
Hillary Rodham Clinton	Mostly no	No	No
Sarah Palin	Yes	No	No, but depends on reporter's gender
Helen Clark	No	Only in 2008	No
Angela Merkel	No	Somewhat	No
Ellen Johnson Sirleaf	No	n/a	No
Michelle Bachelet	Yes	n/a (Chilean women seen as more to the right)	Yes (beneficial)
Cristina Fernández	No	No	n/a (not an issue campaign)

candidates, but most of the women candidates studied in this book were careful to demonstrate their competence in masculine domains. Sirleaf is a trained economist, Clinton used her service as First Lady and then as a Senator to boost her foreign policy credentials, while Merkel and Bachelet both have strong scientific backgrounds. Strength in masculine issues and/or the absence of such issues from the agenda appear to have favored women candidates. Conversely, Sáez, Royal, and Palin did not have sufficient expertise in masculine issues to be able to overcome this stereotype.

Overall, the use of different forms of gender stereotyping appears to have been less prevalent than we had expected. This is due both to the ability of some women candidates to tackle these stereotypes by playing to traditional male strengths, and to the limited applicability of some forms of stereotyping at the comparative executive level. Where the stereotypes did apply, they were often very costly to the candidates concerned, especially where the women candidates were not able to balance these stereotypes with a mixture of feminine and masculine attributes. Our findings are summarized in Table 11.1.

MEDIA FRAMING

While general gender stereotypes were less prevalent than we had expected, gendered media framing was a common occurrence across our case studies. We found that certain frames in particular, such as emphasis on appearance or use of first name, were widespread in their application. The use of these frames is a subtle but powerful way of undermining the authority of women candidates. We also noted that gendered media frames, which we had anticipated to be negative in their impact, were not always detrimental to women's campaigns. The use of the "first woman" frame, for example, was sometimes celebratory rather than demeaning. In most cases, however, gendered framing appears to have worked to the disadvantage of women candidates.

Appearance

Focus on the woman candidate's appearance was reported in almost every case study, the only exceptions being those of Sirleaf and Bachelet. In Sirleaf's case, the respect accorded to senior women within Liberian culture made such a frame inappropriate. Valenzuela and Correa found only 4 percent of stories that mentioned Bachelet's appearance, although there was some speculation about future romances due to Bachelet's single status.[6] For all the other candidates, there was an excessive focus on appearance. The cost of this focus was dual: it reinforced sexual and maternal frames in ways that were degrading to the candidates concerned, and it detracted from more substantive issue-based content. Palin and Sáez both received a strong focus on their status as former beauty queens, and along with Royal, they exemplified the "smart/attractive dichotomy," whereby beauty detracts from perceptions of intelligence.[7] Even when coverage of appearance did not focus on the woman's attractiveness, it was distracting and often degrading. Coverage of Fernández speculated on the amount of plastic surgery undergone by the candidate, and used this frame to reinforce the presentation of Fernández as vain, superficial, and extravagant. Merkel and Clinton were also cast in a relatively unfavorable light, with an emphasis on their age and their lack of glamour, although this was mitigated in the case of Merkel by a more positive emphasis on her transition from eastern to western styles. Overall, coverage of appearance was widespread, and its effects were mostly negative.

First name

The use of women candidates' first name was also widespread, affecting six of the nine women studied. The warmth and familiarity associated with the use of a first name are of limited benefit in a presidential contest, where gravitas and leadership are more valued traits. It is of note that several candidates contributed to the use of their first name in media coverage through their own emphasis on their first name. Clinton, perhaps in an attempt to distinguish herself from her husband (former President Bill Clinton), and/or to soften her hard public persona, made very frequent use of "Hillary" throughout her campaign.[8] Sáez created a political party around herself whose initials formed an acronym based on her first name, Irene. Meanwhile, Royal at least partially embraced the use of her first name, Ségolène, and the nickname "Ségo" that was juxtaposed with Nicolas Sarkozy's "Sarko." For example, her website was named the "Ségosphere." In all these cases, we cannot lay the blame for use of a woman candidate's first name entirely at the feet of the media, as the candidates embraced and even encouraged such behavior. Their reasons for doing so were varied; Clinton's motivations are more easily understandable, while Sáez and Royal might have been naïve to adopt a frame that ultimately worked to their disadvantage.

While several candidates contributed to the use of their first name in media coverage, the frame persisted even when it was neither welcomed nor encouraged by the candidate. Fernández, Bachelet, and Sirleaf were also subjected to excessive use of their first name. This usage did not prevent the election of these three candidates, but nor did it challenge the gendered usage of names, where men are more likely to be referred to deferentially by their surname and/or their title. Only three candidates succeeded in escaping the first name frame. Palin may have benefited from a very common first name and a more interesting surname. The period of her campaign was also relatively short, and she was not well known on the national stage before being added to the Republican ticket, so the use of both names was a reflection of the need to introduce her to the electorate. Clark, by contrast, benefited from a media culture that is careful to treat all politicians in a formal and courteous way, without distinction between men and women. Merkel made some limited use of her first name through playing the song "Angie" at campaign rallies, but media coverage did not over-emphasize this frame.

"First Woman"

The "first woman" frame has been depicted as a negative form of gendered framing by the literature; for example, Jamieson argues that this frame forces women constantly to reinvent the wheel by ignoring the progress made by previous generations of women.[9] We found that the "first woman" frame was present in almost every country other than Argentina, where women's well-established presence in politics,

Fernández's established place on the political stage, and the presence of women in the roles both of front-runner and challenger all served to disturb the use of this label. In numerous instances, the frame was both a blessing and a curse; it contributed to the hype and excitement surrounding women candidates, at the same time that it emphasized their novelty and brought into question their viability. Royal and Sáez are clear examples of the double-edged sword that the frame provided.

However, two additional factors were of note in the use of the "first woman" frame. While the frame was applied in countries where women had previously stood without success, such as in France or the United States, the frame was abandoned once a woman had succeeded in winning executive office. For instance, both Clark and Merkel were labeled as "first women" when initially seeking office, but the frame disappeared entirely once they were running again as the incumbent. This is a logical expectation, and suggests that the "first woman" narrative will endure only as long as women are excluded from executive office. A second, and more unexpected, finding is that women may have suffered when they distanced themselves from depictions as the first woman running for president. This was particularly the case both for Clinton and Sirleaf where their opponent also had symbolic or novelty value that could be used to steal the limelight. Clinton downplayed the significance of gender in her campaign, thus ceding the "first" frame to Barack Obama, whose symbolism as the first potential president of color was more effective in capturing the public imagination.[10] Likewise, the novelty of Sirleaf's opponent, George Weah, as a young footballer untainted by association with the country's violent conflict, threatened to undermine the importance of Sirleaf's campaign to be the first woman president not only of Liberia, but of any Africa country.

The issue of historical firsts is therefore a thorny one. There is undoubtedly some benefit to be had from this label, but being seen as a newcomer also risks detracting from a candidate's viability. Downplaying the frame without avoiding it altogether might be the best strategy. Once women have held executive office, the need to negotiate this question is thankfully removed.

Change

The framing of women candidates as representatives of change was largely absent from our case studies. In a few instances (Royal, Sirleaf, and Bachelet), being a woman was positively associated with political renewal. As predicted in the introductory chapter, this framing was also harmful for Royal, as the association with newness also suggested inexperience and lack of preparation. Sirleaf and Bachelet were not as negatively affected; Bachelet was able to use "change" as a way of providing renewal within the party that had been governing for fifteen years, while Sirleaf used this association to distance herself from Liberia's troubled past.

"Wife of"

The "wife of" frame was limited to those candidates with a prominent male partner, and three women in our studies (Clinton, Royal, and Fernández) were in this position. While all three women had considerable accomplishments within their own political trajectory that established their authority independent of their partners, media coverage often suggested that they owed their success to men. Clinton was accused by MSNBC commentator Chris Matthews of owing her entire political career to the sympathy generated by her husband's infidelity.[11] Fernández, who was married to a current rather than former president, was depicted as the First Lady rather than emphasizing her many independent political accomplishments, including her role as Senator. Royal, whose partner (François Hollande) was the party leader and a presumptive candidate for the presidency, was resented by those who would have preferred to see Hollande as the party's candidate. All three women had to fend off suggestions that their partner would be the one really governing while they would be nothing more than the public face of the presidency. While Bill Clinton had been able to make a virtue of his wife's talents, claiming that voters would get "two for one" when they elected him, Hillary Clinton was obliged to downplay the role that her husband would play in any future administration. Fernández was also viewed as being a continuation of her husband's policies, with the underlying suspicion that he would continue to be a president in all but name. Royal was deliberately vague about the role that Hollande might play in a future administration, stating simply that "all talents would be used;"[12] unbeknown to the public, she and Hollande had separated during her campaign.

The costs of having a prominent political partner are distinctly gendered; an influential wife might be seen as an asset, while a powerful husband might be seen as a liability, or as the true person seeking election. Women also risk emasculating their husbands if they are publicly more powerful than their male partner. The role of male partners who were not themselves politicians was much less of an issue; Merkel's husband maintained a very low profile, while Bachelet was single. Yet Palin was also treated with suspicion due to the visibility of her husband on the campaign trail. It would seem that a woman politician cannot benefit from marriage the way a man can; a male partner may be a liability unless he can be removed entirely from the public eye.

Emotions

Women were portrayed as emotional less often than might have been expected; in some instances, the candidate's *lack* of emotion was the bigger story. Royal was framed as emotional, especially after a public display of compassion towards a disabled man where Royal was visibly moved. As the public did not know about her separation from her partner, she was not given credit for concealing the distress this caused her. Like Royal, Clinton was the focus of great attention when she displayed emotions, such as when she welled up in Portsmouth during the New Hampshire primary.[13] However, the attention paid to Clinton's teary moment was amplified by the fact that it contradicted her public persona as hard and unfeeling. Women candidates are expected to demonstrate toughness in order to compete with men on the masculine turf of leadership, and this leaves little room for public displays of emotion. Clark and Fernández were also portrayed as cold and unfeeling, while Palin's self-presentation as a "hockey Mom" did not endear her to many voters. Merkel had to be encouraged to smile more and demonstrate greater warmth. Only Bachelet appears to have benefited from her image as warm and compassionate, perhaps because these are traits that sit comfortably alongside rationality and competence in someone with a medical background.

Perhaps a bigger factor than emotions is the issue of "likeability" in presidential elections. Women candidates are counseled by the literature on gender and politics against being too emotional in public, as this plays to public stereotypes of women who are irrational and even hysterical. At the same time, the strong emphases on toughness, competence, and rationality run counter to public expectations of women, and may make it harder for women who fulfill these criteria to be sufficiently likeable and appealing. This is an issue touched on briefly by Lawrence and Rose in their study of Clinton,[14] but our study suggests that this issue has wider applicability and should be incorporated into a comparative framework for studying women executive candidates. The notion of "likeability" cannot be considered an example of media framing, so much as a consequence of the gendered games that women candidates are forced to play. As such, it might usefully be incorporated into discussions of the masculinity/femininity double bind.

Volume of Coverage

Some of the chapters considered the volume of coverage of women and men candidates within their analysis, following earlier research which suggested that women might receive less coverage overall, and less substantive coverage in particular, than men.[15] No consistent patterns emerge here. Sáez and Clark enjoyed more coverage while they were the frontrunners, and less coverage as their popularity declined (during the campaign for Sáez, and in later campaigns for Clark). Clinton enjoyed as much coverage as her male opponents, although the tone was found to be more negative. Palin actually received far more coverage than Democratic vice-presidential nominee Joe Biden, perhaps as a result of her novelty status as a woman candidate and her controversial ideas. Unlike Clark, Merkel's coverage increased as a result of being the incumbent, but perhaps this was because her victory was widely anticipated, so she retained frontrunner status. Fernández also received widespread coverage in line with her position as the clear frontrunner. It seems that the biggest issue, for women as for men, is the candidate's position in the horse-race. A candidate who appears to be leading or catching up will generate more coverage than a candidate who has slipped behind or fallen out of contention.

Collectively, the various gendered frames used to cover women executive candidates appear to have been more damaging than trait or issue stereotyping. In particular, gender was prominent in the coverage of women candidates' appearance, their status as the potential "first woman" president or prime minister, and the widespread use of women's first names rather than their surnames. Women were also held to different standards than men concerning their freedom to show their feelings or their partners in public. The one area in which gendered media coverage might have worked to women's advantage was in the association of women with change, although this frame could also be a liability if associated with novelty, inexperience, or questions of viability. A summary of our findings is presented in Table 11.2.

DOUBLE BINDS

The combined effect of gender stereotyping and gendered media frames is best illustrated through the double binds facing women candidates. These binds were definitely felt by the majority of the candidates studied; Sirleaf was unique in being unaffected by any of the catch-22s that damaged the other candidates. It is illuminating that the candidates most hurt by double binds were the same four candidates who did not win their elections. While it is not possible to conclude with certainty that there is a causal relationship between the presence of double binds and the defeat of a candidate, the pattern is still striking.

Table 11.2 Media Framing across the Different Case Studies

	Media Framing						
	Appearance	First Name	First Woman	Change	"Wife of"	Emotions	Volume of Coverage
Irene Sáez	Yes	Yes	Yes	No	No	No	More, then equal, then less; less issue coverage
Ségolène Royal	Yes	Yes	Yes	Yes, initially	Yes	Yes	n/a[1]
Hillary Rodham Clinton	Yes	Yes	Limited	No	Yes	No	Equal, but more negative
Sarah Palin	Yes	No	Yes	No	No, but family emphasized	No	More
Helen Clark	Only in 1996	No	Only in 1996 and 1999	No	No	Only in 2002	More (1996–2002), less (2005-8)
Angela Merkel	Somewhat	No	Only in 2005	No	No	No	Equal (2005), more (2009) (but less issue coverage)
Ellen Johnson Sirleaf	No	Yes	Limited	Yes	No	No	Less
Michelle Bachelet	No	Yes	Yes	Yes (+ continuity)	No	Somewhat	n/a[1]
Cristina Fernández	Yes	Yes	No	No (continuity)	Yes	No	Normal[2]

[1]N/a indicates that data was not collected on this question.

[2]This is based on chapter author's perception of the campaign and Fernández's status as the frontrunner.

Too Masculine or Too Feminine

The bind of being too masculine or too feminine appeared to be the ultimate challenge of gender for women candidates. The obligation to meet up to the masculine expectations surrounding executive office placed women candidates in a position where they might then violate societal expectations of femininity. If women did try to remain within feminine roles, however, they suffered from a loss of credibility, with question marks raised over their viability and competence. With the exception of Sirleaf, every candidate was caught in this trap. Clinton, Clark, and Merkel all played on their strengths of competence, experience, intelligence, and toughness, although these traits unsettled gender expectations and raised questions of likeability. Clinton became categorized as a bitch, Clark as a lesbian, and Merkel as cold and aloof. Meanwhile, Sáez, Royal, Palin, and Bachelet had more feminine personas, yet all were subjected to doubts about their competence, experience, and viability. Fernández offered a different approach, combining a very feminine appearance with masculine traits, as Margaret Thatcher had done while prime minister of the United Kingdom. Only Sirleaf managed to combine warmth with authority, in a way that reflected her status as both a highly educated woman and a grandmother figure in an African country.

Too Young or Too Old

The double bind of "too young or too old" is based on the assumption that women of child-bearing age will be expected to sacrifice their careers for their children (or will be viewed with suspicion if childless), while older women will be unpalatable to an electorate that does not value seniority in women. To some extent, these expectations were met in the western countries studied. Royal (who had four children) and Palin (five children) were both questioned on who would take care of their children if they were elected, despite the presence of their male partners. Clark and Merkel were both criticized for their childlessness, while Clinton received humiliating comments from journalist Rush Limbaugh regarding her age.[16]

However, this double bind is less applicable in the other countries studied. Comments on Fernández's age were more limited to remarks about her attempts to preserve her looks, in keeping with evaluations of her as vain. Sáez also received unfavorable comments about her ageing looks (despite her relative youth), alongside speculation about her future maternity, although neither of these frames was dominant in the media coverage of her campaign. In Chile, there is a much broader range of people that represent age and attractiveness on television than in the United States. In addition, caring for children would be seen as less of a barrier to professional women such as Bachelet, due to the easy access to cheap domestic help such as a nana or maid.[17] While a very young and beautiful candidate might have struggled to be taken seriously in Chile, a professional mother in her 50s was a figure that many Chilean voters could identify with. Just as childcare is less of an issue for wealthy women in Latin America, so age is less of a barrier for women in Africa. Sirleaf's age conferred upon her a respect and authority that a younger woman might not have enjoyed, while also reassuring voters both of her experience and of her sincerity in wishing to serve a single term (a valued trait in an emerging democracy).

We can therefore conclude that the age double bind depends on the cultural context. In some countries, seniority and maternity may both be disadvantageous, leaving a narrow window of opportunity for women to pursue a political career. In others, maternity may not be seen as a barrier, while age might be seen as an asset. Sensitivity to cultural norms will need to be incorporated into any future comparative studies of women executive candidates.

Experience or Change

We noted in the introductory chapter that "change" may be the default position for women candidates. Women may enjoy certain advantages as perceived agents of renewal, although the "change" frame also carries with it the risk of being seen as inexperienced and under-qualified. The women candidates studied in this book, for the most part, centered their campaigns on *either* change *or* experience, but not both. Clinton attempted (unsuccessfully) to combine these assets by claiming that she was the candidate with "the experience to bring change."[18] However, by emphasizing her experience (as counseled by the gender and politics literature), she ceded the turf of change to Obama. Fernández also emphasized her experience, but was unable to represent change, despite being a woman candidate. Both these women were seen as representing a continuation of the policies that their husbands had pursued while president. Several other candidates chose to run on a platform of change, and in so doing, became framed as lacking the experience required to hold executive office. Sáez, Royal, and Palin all failed to persuade voters of their credentials as experienced politicians.

There is some cause for hope, however. Clark, Merkel, Sirleaf, and Bachelet all managed to overcome this double bind. Clark's considerable parliamentary experience, combined with the presence of Jenny Shipley as prime minister in the 1999 race, meant that the change/experience double bind was not applicable to the New Zealand case study. Bachelet was able to model herself as a candidate of change without a corresponding devaluation of her experience. Merkel and Sirleaf were also able to combine these two themes together. Their considerable experience and preparedness for office enabled them to embody change without sacrificing viability. It would seem that a woman candidate needs to emphasize her experience immediately, in order to establish her credentials for office. Once a woman's experience has been widely acknowledged, she can then afford to incorporate promises of change into her campaign. The benefits of change should be sought wherever possible, but only when a candidate's experience is already sufficiently established. The ability to combine these two assets does not yet appear to be available to all candidates, and the benefits of change depend on public satisfaction with the previous regime. The bind may disappear as more qualified women come forwards, resulting in a greater acceptance of women's experience and reduced potential for being viewed as a symbol of change simply by being a woman.

Connected or Independent

The "connected or independent" double bind is in some ways linked to the problem of being a "wife of." Those women who had political partners were viewed as dependent on their male partners for their political credentials, even when these women had their own autonomous political careers. The most interesting finding here is that, while connection to a powerful man has traditionally been a route into power for women,[19] the reverse now appears to be the case. Association with a powerful man may undermine a woman's credibility, and the majority of women studied in this book have achieved success and prominence while maintaining independence from other political figures. Merkel did enjoy the benefit of being a protégé of former Chancellor Helmut Kohl, but this connection was purely political and was not tarnished with the more negative associations of having "slept one's way to the top." Sáez, Palin, Clark, Sirleaf, and Bachelet all rose to prominence without any help from a male partner or benefactor, and it is likely that more and more women candidates in the future will ascend into power through political rather than personal ladders.

The remaining concern is the double standard whereby women are punished for having a political partner, while men do not incur a similar cost. As many people meet their partners through work, women should not suffer a loss of professional credibility for forming a relationship with someone else working in a similar domain. It should also be noted that Clinton, Royal, and Fernández had all been in relationships with their partners for at least 25 years, formed out of an early shared interest in politics and with political careers that developed in parallel with their partners, rather than through a relationship of dependence. This reality often evaded commentators, who downplayed the significance of the woman's career relative to that of her partner.

Silence or Shame

Only one candidate (Bachelet) succeeded in speaking out against sexist media coverage. Some of the frames discussed here, such as the perceived incompatibility of motherhood with political office, were kept off the agenda by Bachelet's willingness to denounce such reporting as sexist. Other candidates attempted to speak out about sexist portrayals in the media, but with more limited success. Palin's campaign denounced sexist media coverage and tried to protect the candidate, although they did not succeed in preventing gendered coverage and also reinforced the notion of Palin as a weak candidate. Royal frequently asked reporters "Would you ask a man that question?", but this approach only antagonized reporters and further damaged her relationship with the media. Clinton also had a poor relationship with the media, although she rarely drew direct attention to gendered media coverage. When Sáez did complain about sexist treatment by the media, this may have provoked a backlash against her by reporters. The double bind, therefore, held true for these candidates—either they endured sexist coverage in silence, or they faced the wrath of journalists if they spoke out. As a result, women voters often took the initiative on behalf of women candidates, creating support websites to highlight sexist media coverage.[20]

The "Mommy Problem"

The "Mommy Problem" combined two distinct phenomena. First, if ideological and issue stereotyping placed women to the left of men, this would favor right-wing candidates at the same time that it would hurt left-wing candidates, by bringing women from the right closer to the median voter while women from the left would be seen as too left-wing. Second, this stereotype might combine with stereotypes about women as mothers to damage women's electoral prospects. It was hypothesized that women on the right might be more successful than women on the left.

The "Mommy Problem" did manifest itself in various ways across the different elections, although it was less present than we might have expected. This was partly due to the limited applicability of ideological stereotyping outside the United States. Royal appears to have suffered from a "Mommy Problem," both through being a left-wing candidate who was too strongly associated with "feminine" issues (such as social policy), and from being too strongly associated with motherhood. Meanwhile, Merkel appears to have benefited from the same phenomenon, by being seen as strong on the masculine issues "owned" by the right, such as the economy and defense, while being seen as less hard-line than her male counterparts. Merkel was also unencumbered by issues of maternity; as Wiliarty argues, she transformed her lack of children into a role as the "mother" of the German nation.

For other candidates, the "Mommy Problem" hypothesis does not work as well. The ideological and issue stereotyping did not have the same impact in Latin America or Liberia. Clinton and Clark both ran "masculinized" campaigns which confounded expectations of left-wing women. Palin was a candidate on the right but did not benefit from ideological stereotyping once her right-wing views became known.

On the other hand, the question of motherhood was often raised in the different elections. While Royal and Palin faced questions about childcare, Clark and Merkel were criticized for their lack of children and hence, their inability to comprehend the needs of most women. Bachelet courted controversy for being a single mother with three children by two different fathers. Children rarely feature in the campaigns of male candidates other than as photogenic props, whereas women struggle to escape the motherhood double bind. Fernández was the exception here; her child was entirely absent from news coverage. As long as it is assumed that it is a woman's role to care for children, even when the father is present, these questions are likely to remain.

While the double binds predicted in the literature were not all present for every candidate, it is clear that women around the world face similar, distinctly gendered challenges when contesting executive elections. The summary of our findings is presented in Table 11.3.

EXTERNAL FACTORS

Jalalzai identified a number of factors which may facilitate the election of women leaders.[21] We argue that surprisingly few of these factors were evident in the case studies explored here, suggesting that women increasingly may be coming to power without the need for these enabling factors.

Easier to Be a Prime Minister than a President

This book only considered two case studies of women seeking prime ministerial rather than presidential office, so we cannot make broadly generalizable conclusions on the basis of such a small sample. In both

Table 11.3 Double Binds across the Different Case Studies

	Double Binds					
	Masculine/ Feminine	**Young/ Old**	**Experience/ Change**	**Connected/ Independent**	**Silence/ Shame**	**Mommy Problem**
Irene Sáez	Yes–too feminine	Maybe too young?	Yes–not enough experience	No	Yes	No
Ségolène Royal	Yes–too feminine	No	Yes–change but not experience	Yes–connected	Yes	Yes–problem
Hillary Rodham Clinton	Yes–too masculine	Yes–too old	Yes–experience but not change	Yes–connected	Yes	No
Sarah Palin	Yes–too feminine	Yes–too young (children)	Inexperienced	No	Yes	Just motherhood
Helen Clark	Yes–too masculine	No	No	No	No	"No kids = lesbian"
Angela Merkel	Yes–too masculine	No	No–associated with both	Not much	No	Yes–mostly beneficial
Ellen Johnson Sirleaf	No–combined both	No–seniority an advantage	No–associated with both	No	No	n/a
Michelle Bachelet	Femininity/ credibility rather than masculine/ feminine	No	No–change without experience problems	No	No–she spoke out about sexism	Only kids–children outside marriage
Cristina Fernández	Yes–feminine appearance but traits too masculine	No	Yes–experience but not change	Yes–connected	No	No

presidential and parliamentary elections, there was a clear emphasis on the individual candidate for executive office, with Merkel and Clark both receiving considerable attention as the leader of their party and potential future leader of the nation. Clark and Merkel do appear to have been less vulnerable to the gendered stereotypes, framing, and double binds explored in this book than some other candidates, but we would be cautious in drawing firm conclusions. Further research is clearly needed in the future before a definite answer to this question can be offered.

Family Ties

As noted above, family ties did not play a significant part in the success of the candidates explored in this book. Most candidates had no family ties, and those who did were not dependent on those ties as they had their own autonomous political careers. Where family ties were present, they were more likely to be a liability than an asset.

Crisis and Upheaval

The presence of a political crisis was hypothesized to facilitate women's entry into politics, for two reasons. First, the discrediting of male politicians might open a pathway for women that would otherwise be closed. Second, a situation of crisis might turn gender stereotypes to women's advantage, as the stereotypical feminine attributes of honesty, integrity, reconciliation, and renewal might be favorable under such circumstances. In our studies, we found that a political crisis had worked in Merkel's favor, and was a contributing factor in her ascent to leadership. Sirleaf and Bachelet both presented themselves as candidates who could heal the wounds of previous regimes and move the country forwards. For the remaining case studies, however, crisis was largely absent. Further, where crisis did occur, it did not always favor women in the ways hypothesized by the literature. Negative stereotypes about women might cast doubt on their strength and ability to lead in a situation of crisis, as was the case for Sáez. Times of military or economic difficulty would also renew the emphasis on these policy areas on the electoral agenda, shifting away from issues more favorably associated with women towards those typically associated with men. In the United States, Clinton's gender obliged her to vote in favor of the war in Iraq in order to avoid being seen as too weak to make tough and aggressive military choices. However, this cost her support amongst liberal voters and deflected attention away from her strong record on the more feminized areas of health care and women's rights. The consequences of crisis scenarios are therefore more

Table 11.4   External Factors across the Different Case Studies

	System (President/ Parliament)	Family Ties	Crisis	Left/Right Party
Irene Sáez	President	None	Yes– disadvantage	Center
Ségolène Royal	President	Male partner	No	Left
Hillary Rodham Clinton	President	Husband former president	No	Left
Sarah Palin	President	None	No	Right
Helen Clark	Parliament	None	No	Left
Angela Merkel	Parliament	None	Yes	Right
Ellen Johnson Sirleaf	President	None	No	n/a
Michelle Bachelet	President	None	No	Left
Cristina Fernández	President	Husband former president	No	Left

complex than has previously been considered in the literature, and the benefits in some situations are countered by negative consequences in other scenarios. While we consider it important to include this variable in future studies, we would caution against assumptions that crisis will benefit women candidates.

Overall, it appears that external factors do not play a clear-cut role in women's prospects of election. While at least some forms of gender discrimination appear to be universal, external factors appear to be somewhat contingent on individual circumstances. It does appear that women may benefit from running in parliamentary rather than presidential systems, while the benefits of family ties and crisis scenarios are rather more dubious. Our findings are summarized in Table 11.4.

A REVISED COMPARATIVE FRAMEWORK

The discussion above has both confirmed the expectations of the literature on gender and elections, and demonstrated its limitations when applied to executive elections across different countries. While we support many of the hypotheses proposed by the existing literature, we propose some modifications to the framework used in this book. On the basis of our findings, we suggest that a better framework for future research might be as follows:

Gender Stereotypes

Trait stereotypes continue to be of importance in executive elections, especially when attempts to counter these stereotypes drive a woman candidate towards a femininity/ masculinity double bind. Issue and ideological stereotypes may be less applicable due to international variations, the increased opportunity to discover candidates' positions, and the dominance of certain issues on the agenda of executive elections. While some of these stereotypes may have limited utility for the study of comparative executive elections, we would suggest continuing to monitor them, as they provide a useful indication of the changing role of gender in elections to executive office.

Media Framing

The emphasis on appearance and horse-race coverage, as well as the use of women's first name, all remain core aspects of the way journalists frame women's campaigns differently than men's. The presentation of women as historic firsts is also of interest, although it may be useful to consider its benefits as well as costs. Increased emphasis on women's emotions remains of interest, although women candidates appear to have anticipated this frame and sought to manage their public displays of emotion. The "wife of" frame is not universally applicable, but continues to be of concern where it is applied.

In addition, we suggest the addition of a new frame to the study of women executive candidates, which we label the "dominatrix" frame. The widespread sexualization of women, combined with the emphasis on women candidates' appearance, has resulted in the use of sexual language to depict some women candidates. Particularly notable among this language was the notion of powerful women beating men into submission. The "dominatrix" frame, which draws on negative stereotypes about aggressive women and emasculated men, was present in a number of case studies. Clark was referred to as a "political dominatrix." In Argentina, the image of male politicians sat underneath a stage, staring at the heeled shoe of Fernández as she stood above them, reinforced the notion of sexual subordination. Clinton was referred to as a "castrator" with a "testicle lockbox."[22] The dominatrix frame was also used for Thatcher, who was cast as an object of desire and power, capable of whipping her ministers into submission.[23] Until the idea of powerful women becomes normalized, the portrayal of women leaders as dominant (and domineering) is likely to continue.

Double Binds

The masculinity/femininity double bind remains central to any study of gender in executive elections, and should be its unifying theme.

Other double binds are also relevant, such as those of experience/change and silence/shame. The age double-bind is of interest but is also contingent on national cultures and attitudes towards ageing and childcare. An adapted version of this bind that is more sensitive to these cultural differences would be a useful inclusion for future studies. The connected/independent bind may be of greater relevance to some case studies that were not included in this book, alongside any future women whose political trajectories have involved a partnership with a male politician. The new bind introduced in this book, labeled the "Mommy Problem," might usefully be considered as two separate issues which have a cumulative effect when present in tandem with each other. The combined effect of ideology and issue stereotyping may have particular impacts at the executive level, although there was only limited evidence in this book to confirm this hypothesis. The "motherhood" double bind may be a more useful variant of the "too young/too old" dichotomy. A "motherhood" double bind would extend beyond the "womb/brain" bind defined by Jamieson,[24] as it would capture the particular problems for women who choose *not* to have children and yet seek to represent parents across the country.

It is clear that there are ripe opportunities for further research in this area, and we hope that more women will put themselves forward as executive candidates. The framework offered here must necessarily be a dynamic model which is capable of adapting to change. As more countries feature women candidates, a greater range of cultures and backgrounds will need to be integrated into future studies. Evolving societal norms, especially when combined with a greater acceptance of women in powerful positions, may also render some aspects of the framework redundant while introducing new questions.

CONCLUSION: HOW CAN WOMEN WIN?

The first rule to be identified by this book is that there are no golden rules that guarantee success. Pathways to victory have come in a variety of formats, and a formula that might have been successful in one context might have failed in another.

Despite this caveat, certain features do appear to crop up among successful candidates. The first is that a woman candidate needs to have sufficient experience. While men may be able to fast-track their way to the top, women are more likely to have their experience scrutinized and diminished, and a woman without sufficient experience is unlikely to be credible. Once experience has been firmly established, a woman might then be able to benefit from framing herself as a candidate of change. Experience in a variety of political portfolios, and especially in traditionally masculine areas such as foreign affairs, might also help women to overcome issue stereotypes.

The second observation is that women may benefit from a first career in a scientific or technical background. Merkel is a physical chemist; Bachelet is a medical doctor; Sirleaf is a Harvard-trained economist; Thatcher was a chemist. These backgrounds may allay stereotypical portrayals of women as less intelligent, rational, and capable than men. Although Clinton's campaign was not successful, her legal background may have contributed to perceptions of her as smart and competent. Proving herself in a male-dominated domain might also enhance a woman candidate's credibility when seeking to lead in the masculine world of politics.

Overcoming the dual hurdles of experience and competence—two areas in which women's qualities tend to be undervalued, as they continue to be measured in masculine terms—are necessary first steps in order to establish credibility and avoid gendered stereotypes. Once a woman candidate has gained sufficient authority in the eyes of voters, the remaining hurdle is that of likeability. In the absence of proven experience and competence, a feminized persona may play to gender stereotypes and be a liability. However, having proven her "equality" with male competitors, a woman might then be able to benefit from her "difference" as a woman candidate. In particular, women candidates need to strike a delicate balance between being tough and meeting societal expectations of warmth and femininity. Merkel, Sirleaf, and Bachelet all struck a slightly different balance, proving that there is no single magic formula. Clinton and Clark may have benefited from a somewhat warmer image.

The suggestions made above all account for the fact that women executive candidates are forced to play a gendered game in which the rules are tilted against their favor. Masculine traits, issues, and career trajectories continue to be valorized over their feminine counterparts. Women are obliged to perform masculinity without sacrificing too much femininity. Women candidates tend to be judged to a higher standard than men. We are aware of these double standards, and do not condone them. However, all the women studied in this book succeeded in cracking the highest glass ceiling, and the majority of them broke through. A cracked glass ceiling may still be a barrier, but it is no longer an invisible one, and each subsequent woman candidate helps challenge the norms that hold the ceiling in place. Hopefully, it is only a matter of time until the ceiling comes down once and for all, leaving men and women with a fair and equal chance of holding the highest office in the land.

NOTES

1. Farida Jalalzai, "Women Rule: Shattering the Executive Glass Ceiling," *Politics & Gender* 4, no. 2 (2008): 205–232.

2. My thanks to Jennifer Piscopo for this insight.

3. Deborah Alexander and Kristi Anderson, "Gender as a Factor in the Attribution of Leadership Traits," *Political Research Quarterly* 46, no. 3 (1993): 527–545; Leonie Huddy and Nayda Terkildsen, "Gender Stereotypes and the Perception of Male and Female Candidates," *American Journal of Political Science* 37, no. 1 (1993): 119–147. Alexander and Anderson, "Gender as a Factor"; Huddy and Terkildsen, "Perception of Male and Female Candidates"; Jeffrey Koch, "Do Citizens Apply Gender Stereotypes to Infer Candidates' Ideological Orientations?," *Journal of Politics* 62, no. 2 (2000): 414–429; Jeffrey Koch, "Gender Stereotypes and Citizens' Impressions of House Candidates' Ideological Orientations," *American Journal of Political Science* 46, no. 2 (2002): 453–462.

4. Lisa Hill, "The Political Gender Gap: Australia, Britain, and the United States," *Policy and Society* 22, no. 1 (2003): 69–96; Ronald Inglehart and Pippa Norris, "The Developmental Theory of the Gender Gap: Women's and Men's Voting Behaviour in Global Perspective," *The International Political Science Review* 21, no. 4 (2000): 441–463; Ronald Inglehart and Pippa Norris, *Rising Tide: Gender Equality and Cultural Change* (Cambridge: Cambridge University Press, 2003).

5. It is hard to say whether the elimination of the gender gap was a result of gender solidarity by women voters in favor of a woman candidate, or whether the gender gap in Chile is eroding in line with other nations.

6. Sebastián Valenzuela and Teresa Correa, "Pres Coverage and Public Opinion on Women Candidates: The Case of Chile's Michelle Bachelet," *International Communication Gazette* 71, no. 3 (2009): 202–223. My thanks to Gwynn Thomas for this insight.

7. Caroline Heldman, "Cultural Barriers to a Female President in the United States," in Lori Cox Han and Caroline Heldman, eds., *Rethinking Madam President: Are we Ready for a Woman in the White House?* (Boulder: Lynne Rienner, 2007), p. 28.

8. Regina Lawrence and Melody Rose, *Hillary Clinton's Race for the White House: Gender Politics & the Media on the Campaign Trail* (Boulder, CO: Lynne Rienner Publishers, 2009), p. 165.

9. Kathleen Hall Jamieson, *Beyond the Double Bind: Women and Leadership* (Oxford: Oxford University Press, 1995).

10. Lawrence and Rose, *Hillary Clinton's Race*, pp. 130–134.

11. Ibid., p. 87.

12. Anne Chemin, "Retraites, Santé, Handicap . . . les Principales Réponses de la Candidate," *Le Monde*, February 21, 2007.

13. Lawrence and Rose, *Hillary Clinton's Race*, pp. 47–50.

14. Ibid., p. 231.

15. Caroline Heldman, Susan J. Carroll, and Stephanie Olson, "She brought only a skirt: print media coverage of Elizabeth Dole's bid for the Republican presidential nomination," *Political Communication* 22, no. 3 (2005): 315–335; Farida Jalalzai, "Women Candidates and the Media: 1992–2000 Elections," *Politics and Policy* 34, no. 3 (2006): 606–633; Kim Fridkin Khan, "Does Gender Make a Difference? An Experimental Examination of Sex Stereotypes and Press Patterns in State-wide Campaigns," *American Journal of Political Science* 38 (1994): 162–195;

Kim Fridkin Khan, *The Political Consequences of Being a Woman: How Stereotypes Influence the Conduct and Consequences of Political Campaigns* (New York: Columbia University Press, 1996); Miki Caul Kittilson and Kim Fridkin, "Gender, Candidate Portrayals, and Election Campaigns: a Comparative Perspective," *Politics & Gender* 4, no. 3 (2008): 385; Pippa Norris, ed., *Women, Media, and Politics* (Oxford: Oxford University Press, 1997); Kevin Smith, "When All's Fair: Signs of Parity in Media Coverage of Female Candidates," *Political Communication* 14 (1997): 71–82.

16. www.rushlimbaugh.com, accessed December 17, 2007.

17. My thanks to Gwynn Thomas for these insights.

18. Lawrence and Rose, *Hillary Clinton's Race*, p. 135.

19. Jalalzai, *Women Rule*.

20. www.1milliondefemmessenervent.org (A French website condemning sexist treatment of Royal; accessed March 2007.); www.feministing.com (One of many sites in the United States that collected examples of sexist treatment of Clinton; accessed January 24, 2010.); http://palinsexismwatch.blogspot.com/ (This is an example of a U.S. website monitoring sexist treatment of Palin; accessed January 24, 2010.).

21. Jalalzai, *Women Rule*.

22. Lawrence and Rose, *Hillary Clinton's Race*, p. 200.

23. Wendy Webster, *Not a Man to Match Her: The Marketing of a Prime Minister* (London: The Women's Press, 1990).

24. Jamieson, *Beyond the Double Bind*.

Appendix

TV CONTENT ANALYSIS CODESHEET: PALIN

Variable Description	*Code*
Name of Media	_____
Date of Broadcast (month/day)	_____
Time of Broadcast (TV only–note AM or PM)	_____
Sex of Anchor/Reporter (1 = male, 2 = female, 3 = mixed)	_____
Sex of Guest(s) (1 = male, 2 = female, 3 = mixed)	_____

Type of Newscast

1 = News Story 2 = News Analysis 3 = Other, Specify   _____

*Amount and Prominence of Coverage

Number of Paragraphs about Palin   _____

*Tone of Coverage

Tone of Lead-In about Palin (1 = positive, 2 = negative,   _____
3 = mix, 4 = neutral)
Tone of News Story (1 = positive, 2 = negative, 3 = mix,   _____
4 = neutral)
Number of Personal Criticisms about Palin   _____
Number of Substantive Criticisms about Palin (related to   _____
governance, campaign, etc.)
Number of Paragraphs having more than one of the same   _____
personal criticisms
Number of Paragraphs having more than one of the same   _____
substantive criticisms

*Viability Coverage

Number of "Horse-race" Mentions   _____

"Horse-race" Content (7 = likely winner, 6 = likely winner, _____
but losing ground, 5 = competitive, but gaining ground,
4 = competitive, 3 = competitive, but losing ground,
2 = non-competitive, but gaining ground, 1 = noncompetitive,
sure loser, 0 = no mention of horse-race)
Campaign Resources (1 = positive, 2 = negative, 3 = mixed, _____
4 = neutral, 0 = not about campaign resources)
Qualifications (1 = mention of prior elective office, _____
2 = mention of prior appointive office, 3 = mention of other
qualifications, 4 = mention lack of qualifications,
0 = no mention)

Gender Coverage
Marital Status (1 = married, 2 = never married, _____
3 = divorced, 4 = widow, 0 = no mention)
Number of Mentions about Candidate's Spouse _____
Are children of candidate mentioned? (1 = yes, 0 = no) _____
Number of Mentions about Candidate's Appearance _____
Number of Mentions about Candidate's Gender _____
(first woman, etc.)

Issue Coverage
# of Mentions (#)
Tone of Coverage (T) (1 = positive, 2 = negative, 3 = mixed, 4 = neutral,
0 = no tone)

Issue	#	T	Issue	#	T
Defense Issues			Religion		
Economy			Veterans		
Bailout			Welfare/Poverty		
Nuclear Arms Control			Budget		
Taxes			Civil Rights/Women's Rights		
Treaties			Energy/Oil		
Foreign Affairs			Environment/"Green" Policies		
Welfare			Farm		
Education			Gay Marriage		
Health Care/Pres. Drugs			Immigration		
Childcare			Crime		

Parental Leave			Social Security		
Employment/Jobs			Iraq War		
Family/Small-town Values			Terrorism		
Abortion			Creationism/Evolution		
Government Spending			Violence Against Women		
Gay rights			Women in Politics		
Business			Congress		
Childcare			Culture of Life		
Special Interests/ Interest Grps.			White House/President Bush		
Media Elite/Liberal Media			Washington "Fat Cats"		
Sanctity of Trad. Marriage			Double Standards for Men & Women		
Gun Control			Family/Work Balance		
Human Rights			Trade		

Trait Coverage
# of Mentions

Positive	# of M	Negative	# of M
Honest		Dishonest	
Authentic		Untrustworthy	
Trustworthy		Inexperienced	
Experienced		Immoral	
Moral		Unintelligent	
Intelligent		Unknowledgeable	
Knowledgeable		Flip-flopper	

Independent		Weak Leader	
Strong Leader		Appearance Trait: "Beautiful" "Pretty" "Sexy"	
Funny		Sprightly	
Family-oriented		Washington Insider	
Religious		Reckless	
Charismatic		Victim	
Maverick/Rebel		Whiner	
Reformer		Nagger	
Tough/Strong		Shrill	
Fighter		Emotional	
Populist		Lack of Judgment	
Honorable		Uncapable	
Dignity		Bitchy	
Change Agent		Washington "Fat Cats"	
Capable		Family/Work Balance	
Determined		Political Expediency	
Patriotic		Overly Ambitious	
Viable		Opinionated	
Articulate		Sassy	
Assertive		Inarticulate	
Tenacity		Boring	
Washington Outsider		Incompetent	

Maternal		Desperate	
Ambitious			
Religious			
Other + Traits		Other – Traits	

Ideology of Palin   # of Mentions
1 = extremely liberal, 2 = liberal, 3 = moderate,   Content_____
4 = conservative, 5 = extremely conservative,
0 = No discussion of ideology

Bibliography

Alexander, Deborah, and Kristi Andersen. "Gender as a Factor in the Attribution of Leadership Traits." *Political Research Quarterly* 46, no. 3 (1993): 527–545.

Bystrom, Dianne G. "Advertising, Web Sites, and Media Coverage." In *Gender and Elections: Shaping the Future of American Politics*, edited by Susan J. Carroll and Richard L. Fox. Cambridge: Cambridge University Press, 2006.

Bystrom, Dianne G., Marcy C. Banwart, Lynda Lee Kaid, and Terry A. Robertson. *Gender and Candidate Communication: VideoStyle, WebStyle, NewsStyle.* London: Routledge, 2004.

Carroll, Susan J. "Reflections on Gender and Hillary Clinton's Presidential Campaign: The Good, the Bad, and the Misogynic." *Politics & Gender* 5. no. 1 (2009): 1–20.

Carroll, Susan J., and Richard L. Fox. eds. *Gender and Elections: Shaping the Future of American Politics.* Cambridge: Cambridge University Press, 2006.

Devitt, James. "Framing Gender on the Campaign Trail: Women's Executive Leadership and the Press." Report to the Women's Leadership Fund, 1999.

Dolan, Kathleen. *Voting for Women: How the Public Evaluates Women Candidates.* Boulder: Westview Press, 2004.

——— "Do Women Candidates Play to Gender Stereotypes? Do Men Candidates Play to Women? Candidate Sex and Issues Priorities on Campaign Websites." *Political Research Quarterly* 58, no. 1 (2005): 31–44.

Duerst-Lahti, Georgia. "Reconceiving Theories of Power: Consequences of Masculinism in the Executive Branch." In *The Other Elites: Women, Politics, and Power in the Executive Branch*, edited by Mary Anne Borrelli and Janet M. Martin. Boulder. CO: Lynne Reinner, 1997.

——— "Presidential Elections: Gendered Space and the Case of 2004." In *Gender and Elections: Shaping the Future of American Politics*, edited by Susan J. Carroll and Richard L. Fox. Cambridge: Cambridge University Press, 2006.

——— "Masculinity on the Campaign Trail." In *Rethinking Madam President: Are We Ready for a Woman in the White House?* edited by Lori Cox Han and Caroline Heldman, 87–112. Boulder: Lynne Rienner, 2007.

Falk, Erika. *Women for President: Media Bias in Eight Campaigns*. Chicago: University of Illinois Press, 2008.

Heldman, Caroline, Susan J. Carroll, and Stephanie Olson. "She brought only a skirt: print media coverage of Elizabeth Dole's bid for the Republican presidential nomination." *Political Communication* 22, no. 3 (2005): 315–335.

Huddy, Leonie, and Nayda Terkildsen. "Gender Stereotypes and the Perception of Male and Female Candidates." *American Journal of Political Science* 37, no. 1 (1993a): 119–147.

——— "The Consequences of Gender Stereotypes for Women Candidates at Different Levels and Types of Office." *Political Research Quarterly* 46, no. 3 (1993b): 503–525.

Jalalzai, Farida. "Women Candidates and the Media: 1992–2000 Elections." *Politics and Policy* 34, no. 3 (2006): 606–633.

——— "Women Rule: Shattering the Executive Glass Ceiling." *Politics & Gender* 4, no. 2 (2008): 205–232.

Jamieson, Kathleen Hall. *Beyond the Double Bind: Women and Leadership*. Oxford: Oxford University Press, 1995.

Kahn, Kim Fridkin. "Does Being Male Help? An Investigation of the Effects of Candidate Gender and Campaign Coverage on Evaluations of U.S. Senate Candidates." *Journal of Politics* 54, vol. 2 (1992): 497–517.

——— "Gender Differences in Campaign Messages: the Political Advertisements of Men and Women Candidates for U.S. Senate." *Political Research Quarterly* 46, no. 3 (1993): 481–502.

——— "Does Gender Make a Difference? An Experimental Examination of Sex Stereotypes, and Press Patterns in Statewide Campaigns." *American Journal of Political Science* 38 (1994): 162–195.

——— *The Political Consequences of Being a Woman: How Stereotypes Influence the Conduct and Consequences of Political Campaigns*. New York: Columbia University Press, 1996.

Kittilson, Miki Caul and Kim Fridkin. "Gender, Candidate Portrayals, and Election Campaigns: a Comparative Perspective." *Politics & Gender* 4, no. 3 (2008): 385.

Koch, Jeffrey. "Do Citizens Apply Gender Stereotypes to Infer Candidates' Ideological Orientations?" *Journal of Politics* 62, no. 2 (2000): 414–429.

——— "Gender Stereotypes and Citizens' Impressions of House Candidates' Ideological Orientations." *American Journal of Political Science* 46, no. 2 (2002): 453–462.

Lawrence, Regina, and Melody Rose. *Hillary Clinton's Race for the White House: Gender Politics & the Media on the Campaign Trail*. Boulder. CO: Lynne Rienner Publishers, 2009.

Norris, Pippa, ed. *Women. Media, and Politics*. Oxford: Oxford University Press, 1997.

Sczesny, Sabine, Janine Bosak, Daniel Neff, and Birgit Schyns. "Gender Stereotypes and the Attribution of Leadership Traits: a Cross-Cultural Comparison." *Sex Roles* 51, no. 11/12 (2004): 633.

Smith, Kevin. "When All's Fair: Signs of Parity in Media Coverage of Female Candidates." *Political Communication* 14 (1997): 71–82.

Index

About the Authors

MELINDA ADAMS is an assistant professor in the Department of Political Science at James Madison University. She has published in *Politics & Gender*, the *International Feminist Journal of Politics*, and the *Journal of Women, Politics & Policy*.

DIANNE BYSTROM is the director of the Carrie Chapman Catt Center for Women and Politics at Iowa State University. A frequent commentator about political and women's issues for state, national, and international media, Dr. Bystrom is a co-author, co-editor, and contributor to 14 books, including *Gender and Candidate Communication*.

JILL CARLE is a graduate student in the School of Politics and Global Studies at Arizona State University.

KIM L. FRIDKIN is a professor in the School of Politics and Global Studies at Arizona State University. She has contributed articles to the *American Political Science Review*, *American Journal of Political Science*, and the *Journal of Politics*. She is the co-author of *No-Holds Barred: Negative Campaigning in U.S. Senate Campaigns* (2004), co-author of *The Spectacle of U.S. Senate Campaigns* (1999), and the author of *The Political Consequences of Being a Woman* (1996).

SUSAN FRANCESCHET is Associate Professor of Political Science at the University of Calgary (Canada). She is the author of *Women and Politics in Chile* (2005), as well as several articles on gender and politics in Latin America published in *Politics & Gender*, the *Latin American Research Review*, and *Comparative Political Studies*.

MAGDA HINOJOSA is an assistant professor in the Department of Political Science at Arizona State University. Dr. Hinojosa has published in *Politics & Gender* and is working on a monograph on women's political representation and candidate selection in Latin America. She was awarded a Ford Foundation Postdoctoral Fellowship in 2007–2008.

RAINBOW MURRAY is a Lecturer (Assistant Professor) in the Department of Politics at Queen Mary, University of London. Her research focuses on gender, representation, and elections. She is the author of *Parties, Gender Quotas and Candidate Selection in France* (2010) and has published in journals such as *Party Politics*, *Politics & Gender*, and *Parliamentary Affairs*. She convenes the Women and Politics specialist group of the Political Studies Association, and is the founder and convener of the international research network on Women in French Politics.

JENNIFER M. PISCOPO will receive her Ph.D. in Political Science from the University of California, San Diego in February 2011. She is a noted expert on the study of gender quotas and women's representation in Latin America. Her work has appeared in the journal *Politics & Gender* and her dissertation won the 2009 Carrie Chapman Catt Prize for Research on Women & Politics.

GWYNN THOMAS is an assistant professor in the Department of Global Gender Studies at the University at Buffalo, SUNY. Dr. Thomas, a recipient of the Elsa Chaney Award from the Gender and Feminist Studies Section of the *Latin American Studies Association*, has a forthcoming book tentatively titled, *The Political Is Personal: Contesting Political Legitimacy through Familial Beliefs in Chile*.

NATASJA TREIBERG is a Ph.D. Candidate in the Department of Political Science at the University of Alberta. Her research focuses on the intersection of gender, popular culture, and international relations. In her dissertation, she examines the role country music played in reinforcing support for the War on Terror. She has also co-authored several papers with Linda Trimble on the representation of female politicians in the media.

LINDA TRIMBLE is a professor in the Political Science Department at the University of Alberta. Her research focuses on women and political representation and the political role of the media, and her recent books include *Mediating Canadian Politics* (2010, co-edited with Shannon Sampert) and *Representing Women in Parliament* (2006, co-edited with Marian Sawer and Manon Tremblay).

SARAH ELISE WILIARTY earned her Ph.D. in political science from the University of California, Berkeley. She is currently Assistant Professor of Government at Wesleyan University, Connecticut. Her research interests include political parties, women and politics, and Christian Democracy. She has published articles in *German Politics* and *Politics & Gender*. She co-edited the book *The Transformation of Postwar Germany: Democracy, Prosperity and Nationhood* (1999). Her academic awards include a German Chancellor's Fellowship from the Alexander von Humboldt Foundation, a Small Research Grant from the American Political Science Association, and a Rotary Club Fellowship.

GINA SERIGNESE WOODALL is a lecturer in the School of Politics and Global Studies at Arizona State University. She has co-authored several publications in books and journals such as the *Journal of Politics*.